T0184018

Communications
in Computer and Information Science 1309

Commenced Publication in 2007
Founding and Former Series Editors:
Simone Diniz Junqueira Barbosa, Phoebe Chen, Alfredo Cuzzocrea,
Xiaoyong Du, Orhun Kara, Ting Liu, Krishna M. Sivalingam,
Dominik Ślęzak, Takashi Washio, Xiaokang Yang, and Junsong Yuan

Editorial Board Members

Joaquim Filipe ⓘ
   Polytechnic Institute of Setúbal, Setúbal, Portugal
Ashish Ghosh
   Indian Statistical Institute, Kolkata, India
Igor Kotenko ⓘ
   *St. Petersburg Institute for Informatics and Automation of the Russian
   Academy of Sciences, St. Petersburg, Russia*
Raquel Oliveira Prates ⓘ
   Federal University of Minas Gerais (UFMG), Belo Horizonte, Brazil
Lizhu Zhou
   Tsinghua University, Beijing, China

More information about this series at http://www.springer.com/series/7899

Rafael Valencia-García ·
Gema Alcaraz-Marmol ·
Javier Del Cioppo-Morstadt ·
Néstor Vera-Lucio · Martha Bucaram-Leverone (Eds.)

Technologies and Innovation

6th International Conference, CITI 2020
Guayaquil, Ecuador, November 30 – December 3, 2020
Proceedings

 Springer

Editors
Rafael Valencia-García
Universidad de Murcia
Espinardo, Murcia, Spain

Gema Alcaraz-Marmol
Universidad de Castilla la Mancha
Toledo, Toledo, Spain

Javier Del Cioppo-Morstadt
Universidad Agraria del Ecuador
Guayaquil, Ecuador

Néstor Vera-Lucio
Universidad Agraria del Ecuador
Guayaquil, Ecuador

Martha Bucaram-Leverone
Universidad Agraria del Ecuador
Guayaquil, Ecuador

ISSN 1865-0929 ISSN 1865-0937 (electronic)
Communications in Computer and Information Science
ISBN 978-3-030-62014-1 ISBN 978-3-030-62015-8 (eBook)
https://doi.org/10.1007/978-3-030-62015-8

© Springer Nature Switzerland AG 2020
This work is subject to copyright. All rights are reserved by the Publisher, whether the whole or part of the material is concerned, specifically the rights of translation, reprinting, reuse of illustrations, recitation, broadcasting, reproduction on microfilms or in any other physical way, and transmission or information storage and retrieval, electronic adaptation, computer software, or by similar or dissimilar methodology now known or hereafter developed.
The use of general descriptive names, registered names, trademarks, service marks, etc. in this publication does not imply, even in the absence of a specific statement, that such names are exempt from the relevant protective laws and regulations and therefore free for general use.
The publisher, the authors and the editors are safe to assume that the advice and information in this book are believed to be true and accurate at the date of publication. Neither the publisher nor the authors or the editors give a warranty, expressed or implied, with respect to the material contained herein or for any errors or omissions that may have been made. The publisher remains neutral with regard to jurisdictional claims in published maps and institutional affiliations.

This Springer imprint is published by the registered company Springer Nature Switzerland AG
The registered company address is: Gewerbestrasse 11, 6330 Cham, Switzerland

Preface

The 6th International Conference on Technologies and Innovation (CITI 2020) was held during November 30 – December 3, 2020, in Guayaquil, Ecuador. The CITI conference series aims to become an international framework and meeting point for professionals who are mainly devoted to research, development, innovation, and university teaching, within the field of Computer Science and Technology, applied to any important field of innovation. CITI 2020 was organized as a knowledge-exchange conference consisting of several contributions about current innovative technology. These proposals deal with the most important aspects and future prospects from an academic, innovative, and scientific perspective. The goal of the conference was to understand the feasibility of investigating advanced and innovative methods and techniques and their application in different domains in the field of Computer Science and Information Systems, which represents innovation in current society.

We would like to express our gratitude to all the authors who submitted papers to CITI 2020, and our congratulations to those whose papers were accepted. There were 41 submissions this year. Each submission was reviewed by at least three Program Committee (PC) members. Only the papers with an average score of ≥ 1.0 were considered for final inclusion, and almost all accepted papers had positive reviews. Finally, the PC decided to accept 16 full papers.

We would also like to thank the PC members, who agreed to review the manuscripts in a timely manner and provided valuable feedback to the authors.

December 2020

Rafael Valencia-García
Gema Alcaraz-Marmol
Javier Del Cioppo-Morstadt
Néstor Vera-Lucio
Martha Bucaram-Leverone

Organization

Honor Committee

Martha Bucaram Leverone   Universidad Agraria del Ecuador, Ecuador
Javier Del Cioppo-Morstadt   Universidad Agraria del Ecuador, Ecuador
Emma Jácome Murillo   Universidad Agraria del Ecuador, Ecuador
Teresa Samaniego Cobo   Universidad Agraria del Ecuador, Ecuador

Organizing Committee

Rafael Valencia-García   Universidad de Murcia, Spain
Gema Alcaraz-Mármol   Universidad de Castilla-La Mancha, Spain
Martha Bucaram Leverone   Universidad Agraria del Ecuador, Ecuador
Javier Del Cioppo-Morstadt   Universidad Agraria del Ecuador, Ecuador
Néstor Vera Lucio   Universidad Agraria del Ecuador, Ecuador

Program Committee

Jacobo Bucaram Ortiz   Universidad Agraria del Ecuador, Ecuador
Martha Bucaram Leverone   Universidad Agraria del Ecuador, Ecuador
Rina Bucaram Leverone   Universidad Agraria del Ecuador, Ecuador
Rafael Valencia-García   Universidad de Murcia, Spain
Ricardo Colomo-Palacios   Østfold University College, Norway
Ghassan Beydoun   University of Technology Sydney, Australia
Antonio A. López-Lorca   The University of Melbourne, Australia
José Antonio
  Miñarro-Giménez   Universidad de Murcia, Spain
Catalina Martínez-Costa   Universidad de Murcia, Spain
Chunguo Wu   Jilin University, China
Siti Hajar Othman   Universiti Teknologi Malaysia, Malaysia
Anatoly Gladun   V. M. Glushkov Institute of Cybernetics, National
  Academy of Sciences of Ukraine, Ukraine
Aarón Ayllón-Benítez   Université de Bordeaux, France
Giner Alor-Hernández   Instituto Tecnológico de Orizaba, Mexico
José Luis Ochoa   Universidad de Sonora, Mexico
Ana Muñoz   Universidad de Los Andes, Venezuela
Miguel Ángel
  Rodríguez-García   Universidad Rey Juan Carlos, Spain
Lucía Serrano-Luján   Universidad Rey Juan Carlos, Spain
Eugenio Martínez-Cámara   Universidad de Granada, Spain
Gema Alcaraz-Mármol   Universidad de Castilla-La Mancha, Spain
Gustavo Zurita   Universidad de Chile, Chile

Francisco M. Fernandez-Periche	Universidad Antonio Nariño, Colombia
Ali Pazahr	Islamic Azad University Ahvaz Branch, Iran
Diego Gabriel Rossit	Universidad Nacional del Sur and CONICET, Argentina
Victor Rafael Bravo Bravo	Universidad de los Andes, Venezuela
Alvaro David Torrez Baptista	Universidade Federal do ABC, Brazil
Mónica Marrero	Delft University of Technology, The Netherlands
Ricardo Coelho Silva	Federal University of Ceará, Brazil
Alejandro Rodríguez-González	Universidad Politécnica de Madrid, Spain
Carlos Cruz-Corona	Universidad de Granada, Spain
Dagoberto Catellanos-Nieves	Universidad de la Laguna, Spain
Juan Miguel Gómez-Berbís	Universidad Carlos III de Madrid, Spain
Jesualdo Tomás Fernández-Breis	Universidad de Murcia, Spain
Francisco García-Sánchez	Universidad de Murcia, Spain
Antonio Ruiz-Martínez	Universidad de Murcia, Spain
Manuel Quesada-Martínez	Universidad Miguel Hernández, Spain
Maria Pilar Salas-Zárate	Tecnológico Nacional de México and ITS de Teziutlán, Mexico
Mario Andrés Paredes-Valverde	Tecnológico Nacional de México and ITS de Teziutlán, Mexico
Luis Omar Colombo-Mendoza	Tecnológico Nacional de México and ITS de Teziutlán, Mexico
José Medina-Moreira	Universidad Agraria del Ecuador, Ecuador
Thomas Moser	St. Pölten University of Applied Sciences, Austria
Lisbeth Rodriguez Mazahua	Instituto Tecnologico de Orizaba, Mexico
Jose Luis Sanchez Cervantes	Instituto Tecnologico de Orizaba, Mexico
Cristian Aaron Rodriguez Enriquez	Instituto Tecnologico de Orizaba, Mexico
Humberto Marin Vega	Instituto Tecnologico de Orizaba, Mexico
Salud M. Jiménez Zafra	Universidad de Jaén, Spain
M. Abirami	Thiagarajar College of Engineering, India
Gandhi Hernandez	Universidad Tecnológica Metropolitana, Mexico
Manuel Sánchez-Rubio	Universidad Internacional de La Rioja, Spain
Mario Barcelo-Valenzuela	Universidad de Sonora, Mexico
Alonso Perez-Soltero	Universidad de Sonora, Mexico
Gerardo Sanchez-Schmitz	Universidad de Sonora, Mexico
José Luis Hernández Hernández	Universidad Autónoma de Guerrero, Mexico
Mario Hernández Hernández	Universidad Autónoma de Guerrero, Mexico

Severino Feliciano Morales	Universidad Autónoma de Guerrero, Mexico
Guido Sciavicco	University of Ferrara, Italy
José Aguilar	Universidad de los Andes, Venezuela
Ángel García Pedrero	Universidad Politécnica de Madrid, Spain
Miguel Vargas-Lombardo	Universidad Tecnologica de Panama, Panama
Denis Cedeño Moreno	Universidad Tecnologica de Panama, Panama
Viviana Yarel Rosales Morales	Instituto Tecnologico de Orizaba, Mexico
José Javier Samper-Zapater	Universidad de Valencia, Spain
Raquel Vasquez Ramirez	Instituto Tecnologico de Orizaba, Mexico
Claudia Victoria Isaza Narvaez	Universidad de Antioquia, Colombia
Janio Jadán Guerrero	Universidad Tecnológica Indoamérica, Ecuador
José Antonio García-Díaz	Universidad de Murcia, Spain
Yordani Cruz Segura	Universidad de las Ciencias Informáticas, Cuba
Gilberto Fernando Castro-Aguilar	Universidad Catolica de Santiago de Guayaquil, Ecuador
Freddy Mauricio Tapia León	Universidad de las Fuerzas Armadas, Ecuador
Nemury Silega Martínez	Universidad de las Ciencias Informáticas, Cuba
Astrid Duque Ramos	Universidad de Antioquia, Colombia
Santiago Cristobal Perez	Cerecon, Universidad Tecnológica Nacional, Argentina
Nelson Becerra Correa	Universidad Distrital Francisco José de Caldas, Colombia
Alireza Khackpour	Østfold University College, Norway

Local Organizing Committee

Katty Lagos Ortiz (General Coordinator)	Universidad Agraria del Ecuador, Ecuador
Andrea Sinche Guzmán	Universidad Agraria del Ecuador, Ecuador
Mario Cárdenas Rodríguez	Universidad Agraria del Ecuador, Ecuador
Elke Yerovi Ricaurte	Universidad Agraria del Ecuador, Ecuador
Mitchell Vásquez Bermúdez	Universidad Agraria del Ecuador, Ecuador

Sponsoring Institutions

http://www.uagraria.edu.ec/

Contents

Mobile and Collaborative Technologies

Semantic Technologies and Machine Learning

Ontological Analysis of Outcomes of Non-formal and Informal Learning for Agro-Advisory System AdvisOnt

Serhii M. Pryima[1], Oksana V. Strokan[1(✉)], Julia V. Rogushina[2], Anatoly Ya. Gladun[3], Dmitro V. Lubko[1], and Vira M. Malkina[1]

[1] Dmytro Motornyi Tavria State Agrotechnological University, 18 B.Khmelnytsky Ave, Melitopol 72312, Zaporizhzhia obl., Ukraine
{pryima.serhii,oksana.strokan,dmytro.lubko,
vira.malkina}@tsatu.edu.ua

[2] Institute of Software Systems of National Academy of Sciences of Ukraine, Kiev, Ukraine
ladamandraka2010@gmail.com

[3] International Research and Training Center of Information Technologies and Systems of National Academy of Sciences of Ukraine and Ministry of Education and Science of Ukraine, Kiev, Ukraine
glanat@yahoo.com

Abstract. Agricultural advisory systems are widely used now for fast dissemination of agricultural knowledge and information, introduction of modern scientific research and technologies in production, mobility and constant advanced training of agricultural specialists. Their implementation becomes an important factor in competitiveness of rural economy. We consider advisory systems used by various countries and regions, their specifics and aims, and knowledge bases that can be used as bedrock for agro-advisory applications – the European Multilingual Classifier of Skills, Competences, Qualifications and Occupations ESCO ontology, ontologies of learning resources (on example of MOOCs), user profile ontologies. Analyses of the intelligent Web-oriented informational technologies shows an expedience of advisory development based on the Semantic Web standards of knowledge representation and processing. An important factor of advisory efficiency deals with semantic documentation and validation of non-formal and informal learning outcomes typical for agriculture. We propose semantic advisory system AdvisOnt based on ontological representation of knowledge about competencies, vacancies, training courses, user profiles, employers and companies. AdvisOnt services match available vacancies and applicant profiles to recommend employment or further learning of wanting competences by analysis of their formal, non-formal and informal learning outcomes.

Keywords: Agro-advisory · ESCO · Ontology · Semantic Web · AdvisOnt

© Springer Nature Switzerland AG 2020
R. Valencia-García et al. (Eds.): CITI 2020, CCIS 1309, pp. 3–17, 2020.
https://doi.org/10.1007/978-3-030-62015-8_1

1 Introduction

Information technologies and their use in consulting become now the characteristic features of the innovative development of agricultural production and increasing the competitiveness of agricultural enterprises. Development of the agricultural sector causes the dissemination of modern knowledge among agricultural manufacturers, relevant and efficient training and information support of their employees. Support for sustainable development of agriculture and implementation of new technologies in this field are emphasized in the United Nations General Assembly resolution "Transforming our world: the 2030 Agenda for Sustainable Development" (September 25, 2015) [1].

In particular, one of the goals is defined as "End hunger, achieve food security and improved nutrition and promote sustainable agriculture". This goal requires growth of agricultural productivity and incomes of small food manufacturers, including family farms etc. by ensuring guaranteed and equal access not only to land but to other productive resources and services of agricultural knowledge.

The success of the agricultural sector largely depends on its effective implementation of modern technologies, the use of market tendencies, as well as relevant organizational changes. The agricultural advisory system is intended to perform these tasks by improvement of the welfare of the rural population and the development of rural areas through raising their knowledge level and improving the practical skills.

The agricultural advisory system is intended to perform these tasks by improvement of the welfare of the rural population and the development of rural areas through raising their knowledge level and improving the practical skills [2]. The main purpose of agricultural advisory activities is to promote the improvement of the welfare of the rural population and the development of rural areas through raising the level of knowledge and improving the practical skills of the rural population and agricultural producers.

As practice shows, the sustainable development of agro-industrial production in the most developed countries is impossible without the rapid spread of agricultural knowledge and information, the adoption of modern production technologies, increasing of mobility and continuous training of agricultural specialists [3–5].

Development of information technologies (IT) in all spheres of human life defines the feasibility of their use in the implementation of advisory activities and determines the development of new e-tools aimed at support of various advisory services oriented on the specifics of agricultural practices. Development of interactive intelligent software for consulting increases the functionality of such services.

Electronic advisory systems used now in practice of advisory activities, solve a wide range of problems: counseling; distance learning; information dissemination and exchange; access to multimedia information resources, etc.

However, state-of-the-art of some aspects of the use of IT in the advisory activities is not sufficient for their current needs.

Agricultural market is developing dynamically in recent years in many countries around the world. There for, one of the issues facing farmers is to provide this industry with appropriate staff with modern competencies and skills [6]. These qualifications, competencies and skills are often informal and can be described in various terms. The use of informal characteristics requires the application of semantic matching of such descriptions. Information support of agricultural manufactures assistance needs in services based on the use of data processing at the knowledge level. Such serviced are aimed at formalizing, analyzing and processing the semantics of information resources. This approach significantly increases the efficiency of advisory services, improves their quality and ultimately saves means for agricultural producers.

The main objective of this research work is to develop the set of the agricultural advisory services that are able to analyze the results of non-formal and informal learning and provide their identification and documentation of on semantic level.

The structure of the article is as follows. In Sect. 2 we consider the specifics and main features of agricultural advisory systems and analyze the achievements of scientific research in this field. Section 3 existing knowledge bases used for advisory systems, ESCO (the European Multilingual Classifier of Skills, Competences, Qualifications and Occupations) is analysed. Section 4 consider informational technologies enabled for semantization of advisory systems and methods of their use for competence analysis with validation of non-formal and informal learning outcomes. Section 5 describes the architecture, main functions and user interface of ontology-based advisory system AdvisOnt that demonstrates facilities of proposed approach.

2 Agricultural Advisory Systems

Advisory systems originated in 19th century in England during the Industrial Revolution, when the competition forced the entrepreneur to improve management methods. Thus, the first practical attempts to spread new knowledge were made at Cambridge University in 1867-1868. Then the first professional advisers and advisory services appeared. More than 54 countries (USA, Canada, Germany, Holland, Great Britain, etc.) established advisory services supported by their governments in the first half of the 20th century after the Great Depression, and about 130 countries – after the Second World War due to the post-war acceleration of development. The next period of advisory development began at the end of the 20th century, when the countries of the former Soviet Union and Eastern Europe began to move to market conditions with taking into account the national cultural traditions.

In the European Union, the importance of the agricultural advisory system is reflected both in the legal acts of the member countries of this organization and in the legal acts of the European Union. Regulation (EU) № 73/2009 of the Council establishing common rules for direct support schemes for farmers under the common agricultural policy and establishing certain support schemes for farmers, amending Regulation (EC) 1290/2005, (EU) 247/2006, (EU) 378/2007. The aim of these documents is to assist farmers in standardization of modern, high-quality agriculture and to use the comprehensive consulting.

The advisory activities are divided at the following directions: training, information support, demonstrations and counseling. The trainings are based on fundamentally new approaches to the learning of the adult rural population with the use of active methods. Demonstrations help in adaptation of new knowledge (innovations) to specific socio-economic conditions in order to their further disseminate and use in educational programs.

The effective functioning of any advisory service is impossible without the use of modern IT that support new forms of rapid dissemination of information based on modern computer networks and communications. The fundamental role of the IT in advisory activities is the use of modern computer tools and telecommunications for the accumulation, sharing and dissemination of information.

Specialized Web-oriented software with elements of artificial intelligence can improve their applications and enrich them by new functionalities. Advisory activities based on Web services allow to use heterogeneous information resources of the agricultural sector and optimize information processes, to provide high-quality service changes in the process of information exchange and create favorable conditions for further cooperation, research and communication, to guarantee the economic efficiency of consulting due to the immediacy of service provision [7].

An important example of experience in developing a system of agricultural consulting is e-Extension [3]. The basis of this electronic consulting system is to provide objective scientific, technical and educational information and prompt responses to producers and the public. e-Extension achieves these results with the help of the creation of an interactive national USA database of high-quality information and a mechanism for its dissemination. All e-Extension users have open access to the advisory information they need and can learn by various educational programs at any time.

Theoretical and practical foundations of IT and artificial intelligence use in agricultural consulting activities are considers by many researchers [5]. Scientific concepts dealt with advisory e-services concerned above are directed on consultative information granting and generation of recommendations for administrative decisions. But all these systems don't analyze the competencies represented by agricultural labor market and therefore are not able to build personal educational trajectories for applicants according to their personal professional profiles (in consideration of the results of non-formal and informal learning) and available vacancies.

The analysis of the advisory system state of the world showed the need to implement services based on semantic technologies. It is advisable to use relevant ontologies to represent the learning outcomes specifics for agricultural domain.

The novelty of the work is the application of ontological analysis to support advisory services in the agricultural sector, designed for semantic identification and documentation of the results of non-formal and informal learning. The functioning of the services is based on the ontological representation of knowledge about objects of the advisory field (competencies, vacancies, training courses, user profiles, employers, companies) and in comparing semantic models in solving tasks of assessing the competence of specialists, selection of relevant training courses, consulting help services, which expands the functionality of advisory systems.

3   Means of Qualifications Classification

We proposed to use the ESCO (the European Multilingual Classifier of Skills, Competences, Qualifications and Occupations) ontology [8] to represent the specifics of the non-formal and informal learning outcomes in agriculture. Main elements of ESCO are professions, skills and qualifications. ESCO can be used as a dictionary, describing, identifying and classifying professional occupations, skills, and qualifications relevant for the EU labor market and education and training. It is available in online portal and is free of charge. Now ESCO contains descriptions of 2,942 occupations and 13,485 skills linked to these occupations, translated into 27 languages.

ESCO combines the labor market and the education market, on the one hand, it helps education providers better understand the needs of the labor market and adapt curricula to the conditions, and on the other, it helps employers understand the learning outcomes of job seekers [9].

Europe-wide recruitment databases (like EURES) can match people with jobs in all EU countries, even when CVs and vacancy notices are in different languages. Each profession represented in the ESCO has a professional profile, which contains explanations of the occupation in the form of a description, notes on the scope and definition and the list of the knowledge, skills and abilities that experts considered appropriate for this profession on a European scale.

This classification extends the SKOS ontology by usage of specific data model, which expresses sets of types, predicates and their meaning.

Within the ESCO data model, each term is a separate element related to the concept. All ESCO concepts such as professions or qualifications have at least one unique term for each of the EU language. ESCO groups terms with a similar meaning and records only the best representations of the content, but some concepts may refer to several terms (synonymous, abbreviations, etc.) regularly used by job seekers, employers, or educational service providers to refer to concepts described in the preferred term classification. ESCO also captures hidden terms (commonly used in the job market to refer to a profession terms that also considered obsolete or erroneous) for indexing, search, and text search purposes.

ESCO is published as Linked Open Data, and developers can use it in various formats (SKOS-RDF, CSV) in software that provide services such as job search, career guidance and self-assessment. It provides a local API and Web Services API so that applications and Web services can request information from the classifier in real time.

The practice of the ESCO classifier use demonstrates its effectiveness in a number of international projects and initiatives. One example of the ESCO implementation is the European Employment Services (EURES) [10]. The aim of the EURES network is to provide information to employers and employees on job search across Europe in order to facilitate the movement of workers within the European Union (EU) and the European Economic Area, and thus the development of the European employment market. EURES focuses on reducing structural barriers in the labor market, combining training and employment processes at EU level, and unemployment control. EURES uses the Web online information as sources of job vacancies across Europe.

4 Semantic Technologies Used for Validation of Outcomes of Non-formal and Informal Learning

4.1 Semantic Web and Ontologies

Agricultural advisory systems operate with such complex information objects (IOs) as user profiles, qualifications, vacancies, learning courses etc. Their matching requires the use of formalized and standardized knowledge about structure of such IOs and their attributes. Use of ontologies provides the basis for the sufficient expressiveness and reuse of knowledge. Now ontological analysis is supported by various languages and tools for knowledge processing developed by Semantic Web [11] project that is directed on transformation of the Web into the global knowledge base.

Semantic Web contains three main components: ontologies [12, 13] for interoperable representation of domain knowledge that reflect different aspects of the real world, Web-services for processing and transformation of information and knowledge; software agents that can use Web-services according to interests and goals of their users.

Now ontologies are widely used in distributed informational systems for shared and reused representation of domain-specific rules, facts and concepts. Fundamental concepts of domain correspond to classes of ontology, and domain facts can be defined as a member of ontological class that has fixed values of attributes. Possible attributes of class members, their meaning and their types are defined directly by ontological formal model as properties of instances enable to assert general facts and relations. Classes can be connected by hierarchical relation "class-subclass". The sets of concepts and relations are defined either by domain specifics or by the task of information system that uses this ontology, but the same domain can be represented by different ontologies.

Agricultural advisory system has to process various IOs ("qualification", "vacancy", "learning outcome" etc.) with complex structure that can be defined formally by relevant ontological classes and properties of instances of such classes. Direct matching of individuals of different classes is not expedient. But if we know that values of different properties are represented by the sets of elements from the same type (for example, "competencies") than we can compare these sets and analyse their intersection.

For example, individuals of classes "learning course" and "Applicant" have identical properties "address" but similarity by it's value is not important for advisory goals. Meanwhile, individuals of classes "learning course" and "Applicant" have properties "proposed qualification" and "needs in", respectively. Names and semantics of these properties differ but they have properties of the same type (this information is formally fixed by ontological model). Therefore, we can match directly the values of these parameters for class individuals (for example, if we search for appropriate learning resources for some user after analysis of existing vacancies). According to problem specifics the most usable class type is "Competence". But domain competencies have very complex structure that causes it's formalization by ontological representation for competence management.

We propose to use ontological Reference Model of Qualification Framework (RMQF) that contains semantic properties and relations of IOs related to various learning outcomes (formal, informal or non-formal). Use of RMQF provides matching of IO from different classes by set of associated competencies with use of their hierarchy [9, 14]. RMQFis represented by OWL Light language and can be processed by ontology editor Protégé.

Other ontologies used for adaptation of agricultural advisory services for personified needs of user can be exported in RDF format from semantic Wiki-resources relevant to domain or region specifics or to personified user view [15].

The above analysis indicates the feasibility of development of agro–advisory system with use of the following Semantic Web development as software agents capable to work autonomously and rationally into open environment and cooperate with other agents for user purposes by use of Web–services; semantic Web-services to support analysis, formalization and matching of vacancies, learning resources and resumes at the semantic level; ontologies to interoperable and formal representation of domain knowledge dealt with professions, competencies skills and qualifications specific for agriculture domain.

4.2 Ontology-Based User Profiles

Ontological technologies are widely applied for user modeling in various adaptive systems oriented on the Web [16–18].

The problem of translation between different user models is a great challenge of modern intelligent ISs. User profiles contain information about needs, goals, plans and tasks of user, demographic characteristics (age, gender, native language etc. and more complex cultural and social features such as qualification and education level), user's location, environment, access devices etc. They are widely used in e-learning, recommender and retrieval systems providing personified representation of user knowledge and interests as a subset of elementary components of domain knowledge learning domain (categories, topics, learning outcomes). Integration of different models of user profiles is based on ontologies – centralised reference high-level ontology or matching (manual or automated) of independent ontologies [6].

Now a lot of adaptive ISs use open user models that provide various means of control such as contents view, visualization and modifying. Users can analyze model of their knowledge according to their understanding of domain concepts. Development of ontologies that describe user profiles becomes a promising research direction in the Web-oriented user modeling.

4.3 Open Learning Resources and Their Use in Advisory Services

Today many available by the Web open informational resources are used for non-formal and informal education and provide various skills and competences.

Massive Open Online Courses (MOOCs) [19] are free online courses available for anyone. They provide an affordable and flexible way to learn new skills, advance career and deliver quality educational experiences. MOOCs propose users to study the learning content on a self-paced way and to communicate for help with a large community of other learners through discussions forums [20]. The pioneers are Coursera, edX, and Udacity, MIT Open Courseware, Udacity, Khan Academy, FutureLearn, Canvas Network, MyEducationKey. In Ukraine typically provided by higher education institutions are Prometheus, EdEra, Courses for agrotechnology etc. Learning outcomes of MOOCs are certificated but these certificates differ from legal accreditation.

Recommended systems help users in choice optimal courses that cover the needs of the competence of the specialty, position, certain requirements, instructions [21]. Competency ontology allows to evaluate courses (including mass online MOOCs) on their compliance with certain competencies desired by the user or appropriate for some position. In order to recommend appropriate courses to users, the intelligent consulting system needs in ontological model of the user (personal user profile, user ontology) to compare it with the semantic model of MOOCs courses. Based on the results of comparison and application of the competence ontology, recommended system allow the user to select the etc.

Use of recommender systems based on Semantic Web knowledge representation about MOOCs can help learners in retrieval of relevant courses and in objective evaluation of their knowledge and skills represented by learner profile [22]. Algorithm of matching is described in details in [19].

5   Semantic Agro-Advisory System AdvisOnt

For successful and effective functioning of the advisory system we develop an agro-advisory support services that ensure semantic identification and documentation of non-formal and informal learning results. This enrichment of advisory allows to satisfy the needs of participants in obtaining the necessary vacancies and acquisition of competencies. The general architecture of AdvisOnt contains the following components (Fig. 1): applicant – person who needs in some work in agricultural domain and has a set of relevant competencies and skills; employer – person or organization who needs in employees

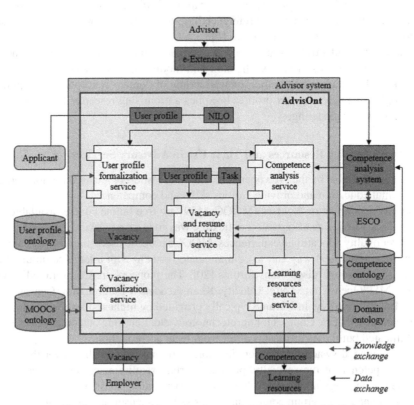

Fig. 1. General architecture of agro-advisory system AdvisOnt

for execution of some task or work on some position; providers of learning services – organizations that propose various (formal, non-formal and informal) learning means for expansion of personal competencies; advisor – expert specialized in agricultural domain of fixer region that can use domain knowledge for refinement of mutual interests of employers and applicants and provides advising services if applicant qualification needs in additional learning according to employer demands.

We distinguish the following parameters: user profile – non-formalized representation of main features values of user proposed by applicant; formalized user profile – formalized representation (according to selected ontological structure) of main features values of user with pre-defined data types such as demography, skills, qualification, background, cognitive style, restrictions, etc. expressed by the non-empty finite set of competencies; NILO (non-formal and informal learning outcomes) – non-formalised set of additional competences and skills of user that need in formalization and adaptation with user profile model; formalized NILO – formalised set of additional competences and skills of user expressed by the non-empty finite set of competencies; task – non-formalized representation of employer needs for work execution that can be covered by one or more vacancies; vacancy – non-formalized representation of employer needs and demands to employees; formalized vacancy – formalized representation of employer needs (according to selected onto-logical structure) and demands to employees expressed by the finite set of competencies.

This general architecture of agro-advisory system AdvisOnt defines the main relations and data flows between AdvisOnt services (Table 1) and external informational resources. In this work we don't consider in details the functions and software realization of these services that are usual for agro-advisory systems but analyse their modification

Table 1. AdvisOnt services

	Service	Functionality	Input	Output
1.	*user profile formalization service*	transforms basic information about user into representation with fixed structure and data types	User profile, NILO	Formalized user profile, formalized NILO
2.	*vacancy formalization service*	transforms information about the needs of the employer and the requirements for employees into representation with fixed structure and data types	Vacancy	Formalized vacancy, the set of competences

(continued)

Table 1. (*continued*)

	Service	Functionality	Input	Output
3.	*competency analysis service*	matches properties of finite sets of competencies for information objects from various classes in consideration of competence hierarchy	Formalized user profile, formalized NILO	The set of competences
4.	*vacancy and resume matching service*	matches the needs of the employer and the capabilities of the employee represented by the finite sets of competences	The set of competences, formalized user profiles, formalized vacancies	The set of formalized vacancies
5.	*educational resources search service*	provides semantic matching of educational resources with formalized user profile and capabilities of the employee represented by the finite sets of competences (agricultural advisory domain ontologies are used as a knowledge sources in this matching).	The set of competences, formalized user profiles, formalized vacancies, formalized NILO	The set of educational resources

provided by validation of outcomes of non-formal and informal learning (by formalized NILO processing).

AdvisOnt services are oriented on use of external knowledge represented by ontologies provided by various pertinent independent sources. This set of ontologies can be changed according to task without changes of AdvisOnt architecture (Table 2).

In this work we use definitions of agro-advisory services based on Service-oriented architecture (SOA) [5] paradigm terms and its semantic extension defined by OWL-S ontology. Functionality of AdvisOnt system is defined by the set of services: service for vacancy formalization; service for user profile formalization; service for learning course formalization; service for learning course retrieval; service for matching of vacancies and resumes.

Table 2. Use of external ontologies by AdvisOnt services

	Service	Input knowledge
1.	*user profile formalization service*	User profile ontology
2.	*vacancy formalization service*	ESCO, competence ontology, agroadvisory domain ontology
3.	*competency analysis service*	ESCO, competence ontology, agroadvisory domain ontology
4.	*vacancy and resume matching service*	Domain ontologies, linguistik knowledge bases
5.	*educational resources search service*	MOOC ontology

Data types of input and output of these services are defined with the help of external ontologies: ontology of user profiles, ESCO and ontology of agricultural domain. These ontologies define the structure of analyzed data and contain information about types of their attributes, restrictions and conditions of their use. An important feature of SOA-based system is it's interoperability – we can select other external ontologies instead of these ones for other subject domain or for other view on system tasks and goals without changing of services. For example, service "Vacancy formalization" is defined by: functionality (representation of information about employer task in terms of competence management); input (vacancy – text; ESCO ontology - OWL; domain ontology – OWL); ouput (the formalized vacancy - agricultural advisory system vacancy (by ESCO ontology)); the set of vacancy competencies (atomic competence (from Competence ontology); the set of vacancy qualifications: list of text items (from ESCO ontology)); model (transformation of semi-structured natural language text into the lists of text data from the sets predefined final sets).

AdvisOnt is based on domain ontology "Agro-advisory" created with use of ontology editor Protégé [23] represented by RDF. Then we integrate this ontology into the RDF repository that provides universal and flexible method of decomposition of knowledge into small parts – triplets with account of their semantics. This approach allows to specify the structure of the source description and to operate statements based on predicates. "Agro-advisory" ontology is stored by use of the database of semantic graphs GraphDB. This large-scale semantic repository includes a repository of triplets, a conclusion mechanism and a SPARQL query handler. GraphDB can be considered as RDF-graph database (triplet storage). GraphDB can perform scaled semantic inference that allows users to create new semantic facts from existing ones.

AdvisOnt uses external information resources and knowledge bases: ESCO as a source of structured representation of domain competencies and qualifications which classes stored in the Turtle-file [8, 24]. User model ontology that defines the structure of applicant model; Domain ontologies that contain facts and rules about agricultural tasks specifics; E-extension system that provides formalization of vacancies, resumes and RNINs according to expert knowledge and soft skills; Open learning services such as MOOC proposed as part of a regular online study program or oriented on informal learning.

AdvisOnt obtains information from RDF-storage through SPARQL query language requests. SPARQL receives application requirements in the form of a query and returns this information in the form of a set of links or as an RDF graph. Use of connectors speeds up the work with the storage. GraphDB connectors provide fast search (simple and faceted) that typically implemented by external component or service such as Lucene. When this connector receives the text in it's field it executes search for defined labels and returns reference to the class corresponds to the specified query. The query consists of prefixes to access a specific part of the ontology, namely the connectors, without touching the main part. Thus is more secure, because the application haven't direct access to the ontology.

One of the benefits of using GraphDB connectors is automatic updating of data from GraphDB repositories. Connectors provide entity-level synchronization, where an entity is defined as something with unique identifier (URI) and with the set of properties and property values. Connectors support of the property chains (sequence of triples where the object of each triple is the subject of the next triple).

AdvisOnt users interact with information from the RDF repository by the Web server that processes requests to the repository and analyses the request results. This server developed with use of PHP and PHP Laravel framework that speeds up the development process: PHP Laravel framework provides increased security and readiness to install plug-ins and libraries and has such features as RESTful-routing, caching, user management and authentication.

User interface of AdvisOnt is developed on base of React framework that allows to create large web applications with data that changes over time without page reloading. The React framework has the following advantages: speed, simplicity, scalability. The React concept on the user interface consists of separate self-sufficient components that are quite simple to maintain and extend. User interface is realized as functional panel and working window. An example in Fig. 2 shows a working form for search of agro-specialists by parameters of formalized vacancy: the name of the profession, age,

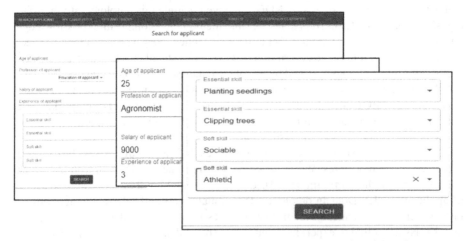

Fig. 2. Agricultural advisory system user request form to search for a job seeker

salary, basic and additional skills. Names of search conditions are defined by appropriate ontology.

Search results gives out the list of applicants relevant to the values of specified parameters. Information about competencies of applicants is extracted from their formalized resumes. Such formalization is provided by appropriate agricultural advisory service of AdvisOnt and consists in matching of non-formal descriptions of user skills and knowledge with elements of competence ontology.

Now AdvisOnt is realized as prototype and is available by the Web http://www.tsatu. edu.ua/kn/advisont-agricultural-advisory-system/.

6 Conclusions

Sustainable development of agro-industrial production is impossible without the rapid spread of agricultural knowledge and information, mobility and continuous training of agricultural specialists providing by advisory systems. Development of services based on the semantic data processing provides intelligent support and professional assistance to the participants of the rural sphere.

An important problem of advisory systems deals with non-formal representation of information about main subjects (employers, companies, advisors, learning organizations etc.) and objects (vacancies, competencies, training courses, user profiles) of agricultural manufacturing that complicates the it automates processing and correct matching by appropriate software. We propose to use external ontological knowledge bases as a source of information about structure and possible values of these elements. We consider the subproblem of advisory task caused by need in automated means for identification and validation of informal and non-formal learning outcomes available for comparison with existing classifications of competences. Methods of such complex objects matching based on atomic competence approach and ontological representation of knowledge are proposed.

Advisory system AdvisOnt releases proposed approach based on the ontological representation of advisory knowledge and their processing on semantic level. AdvisOnt consist of the set of services that provide semantic identification and documenting of non-formal and informal learning outcomes, formalization and matching of semantic models of advisory objects. AdvisOnt user can receive recommendations about employment assistance and training courses provided relevant competences.

In this paper we describe the general structure of the AdvisOnt agro-advisory system and it's links with external knowledge bases and intelligent applications. ESCO ontology is used by AdvisOnt as a base of reference model of skills, competencies, qualifications and professions. Service-oriented architecture ensures possibilities for expansion of its functionality and integration with other advisory and learning software based on the Semantic Web standards.

Further progress of AdvisOnt we connect with more deep semantic integration with agricultural and organizational ontologies for improvement of recommendations personification and dynamics. It depends of the prospects of the Semantic Web standards and their implementation by external software providers.

An important feature of AdvisOnt is a possibility of it's further usage for other external ontologies with knowledge about domain competencies and educational resources without changing of general structure of system. Therefore we plan to integrate AdvisOnt with various national and international knowledge bases for more deep semantic matching of vacancies and user profiles.

Anoser aspect of AdvisOnt use deals with export of user profiles for their processing in other intelligent applications – semantic search, recommendation systems, e-learning etc. Such export of knowledge is supported by user profile ontology for semantic structuring of information and facilitates adaptation of these application for individual user needs.

Acknowledgement. The work is performed within the research of Dmytro Motornyi Tavria State Agrotechnological University «Theoretical justification and development of the information system of semantic identification, documenting and result processing of non-formal and informal learning» on request of the Ministry of Education and Science of Ukraine, registration number 0119U000272.

References

1. Resolution Adopted by the General Assembly on 25 September 2015. https://www.un.org/en/development/desa/population/migration/generalassembly/docs/globalcompact/A_RES_70_1_E.pdf
2. On the Agricultural Advisory Activity: Law of Ukraine (Закон України Про сільськогосподарську дорадчу діяльність) 17.06.2004. № 1807-IV. Information of the Verkhovna Rada. № 38. c. 470. (2004). https://zakon.rada.gov.ua/laws/show/1807-15
3. Anderson, J.R.: Agricultural Advisory Services. Background Paper for the World Development Report 2008 (2008)
4. http://abi.gtk.szie.hu/system/files/upload/course_material/5._agricultural-advisor-services_wdr_2008.pdf
5. Campbell, B., Thornton, P., Christensen, S., Sunga, I., Solomon, D.: Agricultural Advisory Services at a Global Scale (2018). https://ccafs.cgiar.org/blog/agricultural-advisory-services-global-scale#.XsU49kQzbIU
6. Lagos-Ortiz, K., Medina-Moreira, J., Morán-Castro, C., Campuzano, C., Valencia-García, R.: An ontology-based decision support system for insect pest control in crops. In: Valencia-García, R., Alcaraz-Mármol, G., Del Cioppo-Morstadt, J., Vera-Lucio, N., Bucaram-Leverone, M. (eds.) CITI 2018. CCIS, vol. 883, pp. 3–14. Springer, Cham (2018). https://doi.org/10.1007/978-3-030-00940-3_1
7. Mykhailova, L.: Scientific and methodological foundations of human resourcing in agribusiness (Науково-методологічні засади кадрового забезпечення агропромислового виробництва). Econ. Sci. **2**(5), 195–201 (2013). http://nbuv.gov.ua/UJRN/znptdau_2013_2(5)__28. (Scientific Papers of Tavria State Agrotechnological University)
8. Kalna-Dubinyuk, T., Kudinova, I.: E-extension system development in Ukraine (Развитие электронной системы E-EXTENSION в Украине). Eur. Cooperation **10**(17), 39–47 (2016)
9. ESCO (the European Multilingual Classifier of Skills, Competences, Qualifications and Occupations). https://ec.europa.eu/esco/portal/home. Accessed 20 Oct 2019

10. Rogushina, J., Pryima, S.: The use of ontologies and semantic web to provide for the transparency of qualifications frameworks. East.-Eur. J. Enterp. Technol. **1**(2, 85), 25–31 (2017). http://journals.uran.ua/eejet/article/view/92815

11. EURES. http://ec.europa.eu/eures. Accessed 05 Jan 2020

12. Berners-Lee, T., Hendler, J., Lassila, O.: The semantic web. Sci. Am. **284**(5), 34–43 (2001)

13. Gruber, T.R.: The Role of Common Ontology in Achieving Sharable, Reusable Knowledge Bases. https://www.cin.ufpe.br/~mtcfa/files/10.1.1.35.1743.pdf

14. Pryima, S., Rogushina, J., Strokan', O.: Use of semantic technologies in the process of recognizing the outcomes of non-formal and informal learning. In: CEUR Workshop Proceedings, vol. 2139, pp. 226–235 (2018). http://ceur-ws.org/Vol-2139/226-235.pdf

15. Rogushina, J., Pryima, S.: Use of competence ontological model for matching of qualifications. Chem. Bul. J. Sci. Educ. **26**(2), 216–228 (2017). http://khimiya.org/show_issue.php?y=2017&vol=26&issue=2&i_id=66

16. Rogushina, J.: Semantic wiki resources and their use for the construction of personalized ontologies (Семантические wiki-ресурсы и их использование для построения персонифицированных онтологий). In: CEUR Workshop Proceedings, vol. 1631, pp. 188–195 (2016). http://ceur-ws.org/Vol-1631/188-195.pdf

17. Lundqvist, K.O., Baker, K.D., Williams, S.A.: An Ontological Approach to Competency Management

18. Pryima, S., Rogushina, J.: Development of methods for support of qualification frameworks transparency based on semantic technologies. Inf. Technol. Learn. Tools **59**(3), 201–210 (2017). http://journal.iitta.gov.ua/index.php/itlt/article/view/1655/1201

19. Sosnovsky, S., Dicheva, D.: Ontological technologies for user modelling. Int. J. Metadata Semant. Ontol. **5**(1), 32–71 (2010)

20. Massive Open Online Courses (MOOCs). www.mooc.org. Accessed 12 May 2020

21. Gladun, A., Khala, K., Sammour, G., Al-Zoubi, A., Schreurs, J.: MOOCs in universities: Intelligent model for delivering online learning content. In: Proceedings of IEEE 7th International Conference on Intelligent Computing and Information Systems, ICICIS-2015, pp. 168–173 (2015)

22. García-Sánchez, F., García-Díaz, J.A., Gómez-Berbís, J.M., Valencia-García, R.: Ontology-based advertisement recommendation in social networks. In: De La Prieta, F., Omatu, S., Fernández-Caballero, A. (eds.) DCAI 2018. AISC, vol. 800, pp. 36–44. Springer, Cham (2019). https://doi.org/10.1007/978-3-319-94649-8_5

23. Gladun, A., Khala, K., Sammour, G., Al-Zoubi, A., Schreurs, J.: Semantic web and ontologies for personalisation of learning in MOOCs. In: Proceedings of IEEE 7th International Conference on Intelligent Computing and Information Systems, ICICIS-2015, pp. 185–190 (2015)

24. Noy, N.F., Sintek, M., Decker, S., Crubezy, M., Fergerson, R.W., Musen, M.A.: Creating semantic web contents with protege-2000. IEEE Intell. Syst. **16**(2), 60–71 (2001)

25. Rogushina, J., Pryima, S.: Ontological approach to qualifications matching on base of competences: Model and methods. Naukovyi Visnyk Natsionalnoho Hirnychoho Universytetu **6**, 162–168 (2017). http://www.nvngu.in.ua/jdownloads/pdf/2017/06/06_2017_Rogushina.pdf

CropPestO: An Ontology Model for Identifying and Managing Plant Pests and Diseases

Miguel Ángel Rodríguez-García[1] and Francisco García-Sánchez[2](✉)

[1] Department of Computer Sciences, Universidad Rey Juan Carlos, Madrid, Spain
miguel.rodriguez@urjc.es
[2] Dept. Informática y Sistemas, Universidad de Murcia, 30071 Murcia, Spain
frgarcia@um.es

Abstract. Organic agriculture practices have the potential to improve soil fertility and biodiversity while ensuring a more sustainable development. However, given that no chemicals can be used in crop cultivation, fighting against harmful plant pests and diseases becomes an even greater challenge. According to the organic agriculture principles, prevention and avoidance constitute the first line of defense against pests and diseases. There are many guides, manuals and codes of practice available relating to all aspects of organic agriculture scattered throughout the Web. The challenge is providing farmers with the information that they need to confront potential risks, improve yields and reduce insect damage. Semantic technologies can be useful assisting in the process of data gathering, integration and exploitation to provide insightful recommendations. Ontologies constitute the necessary bedrock for Semantic Web-based applications to work properly. In this work, we describe the process to build an ontology to model the plant pests and diseases application domain. This ontology is expected to allow the development of a knowledge base to enable a decision support system for farmers interested in applying organic agriculture practices.

Keywords: Ontology · Ontology development · Semantic Web · Organic agriculture · Pest control

1 Introduction

According to the Food and Agriculture Organization (FAO) of the United Nations, "*the main source of food for the population of the world is agriculture*" [1]. Horticulture is the part of agriculture that deals with plants and plant cultivation for human use. Fruits and vegetables constitute the basis for a healthy diet [2]. However, a major danger for agriculture, and hence for food provisioning, is that of plant pests and diseases [3]. Climate change, among other factors, is fostering the emergence of new, more severe diseases [4]. Farmers are bound to rely on Integrated Pest Management (IPM) to control insect pests in agricultural production by combining the use of biological, cultural and chemical practices. Yet, the amount of information available about the different conditions that can negatively affect each individual crop is overwhelming

© Springer Nature Switzerland AG 2020
R. Valencia-García et al. (Eds.): CITI 2020, CCIS 1309, pp. 18–29, 2020.
https://doi.org/10.1007/978-3-030-62015-8_2

and is usually dispersed throughout a number of different heterogeneous data sources. Moreover, farmers should be aware of new diseases outbreaks and their control measures.

Over the last few years, Semantic Web technologies have proved to be effective for information integration in a number of different application domains [5–7]. Ontologies constitute the backbone of the Semantic Web [8]. Recently, semantic technologies have also extensively leveraged for different purposes in the agricultural domain [9]. In particular, a number of research teams worldwide are exploring the benefits semantics empowered approaches to pest identification and control [10–12]. Likewise, other applications of Information and Communication Technologies (ICT) in the agricultural domain have also focused on pest recognition and management recommendation [13–15].

For a semantic strategy to be used in the pest control field, an ontological model for representing the key concepts and their relationships in this domain is required. A number of different ontologies and less formal representation models with which to characterize agricultural systems and the environment [16–18]. In this work, we describe the construction of an ontology for modeling the plant pests and diseases domain. This ontology has been built in order to support the development of tools to assist farmers in recognizing the pests and diseases affecting their crops, and suggesting the appropriate control measures, which is currently a work-in-progress. In building this lightweight, domain ontology, we tried to adhere to ontology best practices [19].

The rest of this paper is organized as follows. Some recognized agricultural ontologies and structured vocabularies are explored in Sect. 2, with the focus on those specifically designed for crop pests and diseases modeling. Then, the process undertaken to construct the Crop Pest and Diseases Ontology (CropPestO) is detailed in Sect. 3. A preliminary validation analysis of the resulting ontology and its compliance with the expected scope is described in Sect. 4. Finally, conclusions and future work are put forward in Sect. 5.

2 Related Works

In the last few years, different knowledge representation techniques have been used in the agricultural domain, either in the form of ontologies [20] or knowledge graphs [21] for different purposes. Next, some well-known ontologies and structured vocabularies in this domain are enumerated and more specific crop-pest knowledge models are scrutinized.

A reference resource when dealing with vocabularies and ontologies to represent and annotate agronomic data is AgroPortal [16], a platform to host these vocabularies and ontologies constituting a vast ontology repository for the agronomy domain. Among the ontologies available in the repository it is possible to find those built by reference consortiums in the field such as Planteome (http://planteome.org/) or CGIAR (http://cgiar.org/). Planteome currently maintains four ontologies, namely, the Plant Ontology, the Plaint Trait Ontology, the Plant Experimental Conditions Ontology and the Plant Stress Ontology. The Plant Ontology includes concepts related to plant anatomy and morphology, and stages of development for all plants. Some researchers have combined the Plant Ontology with vocabularies imported from other ontologies such as the Gene Ontology (GO) or the Phenotypic Quality Ontology (PATO) to extend the Infectious Disease Ontology (IDO) to the plants domain, resulting in the IDOPlant ontology [18]

On the other hand, CGIAR is working on the development of the Agronomy Ontology (AgrO) [22]. This ontology aims at defining a model to semantically integrate data from different disciplines such as crop, livestock, among others. Yet, the most widely used resource of those available in the AgroPortal repository is AGROVOC [23], a controlled vocabulary published by FAO and available in 29 languages that covers elements related to food, nutrition, agriculture, environment, plant cultivation techniques, etc. This concept scheme has been used to build the CropPestO ontology described here.

At a closer scope, it is possible to find ontologies specifically built and dedicated for modeling plant diseases or pests that attack crops. In [24], the authors design and implement a crop-pest ontology that includes an organism taxonomy to classify different types of pests such as pathogens and nematodes. The ontology also contains the concepts '*Pest Management*' and '*Pesticides*' to describe biological strategies and chemical substances that can be used to control pests. In the same context, the Plant-Pathogen Interactions Ontology (PPIO) is described in [17] and expresses plant phenotypic responses when pathogens interact with plants. Unlike the previous work, in PPIO the pathogens have been included in the organism taxonomy instead of creating an exclusive Plant concept, and the ontology defines the concept '*Trait*' which has been imported from Plant Trait Ontology. PPIO utilizes this concept to describe parts and phenotypes of plants. Besides, in [25] the PPIO ontology is used as a core together with NCBI, PubChem and ChEBI to define the "Pests in Crops and their Treatments" Ontology (PCT-O).

Finally, some semantically-enriched expert systems have been built that assist in plant diseases identification and management. In [25], the PCT-O ontology is leveraged to build a recommendation system that suggests the treatment for a given pest. In [26] the authors introduce an ontology-based approach to identify plant diseases from existing symptoms on plant and test it on rice crops by developing a rice disease ontology. AgriEnt, a knowledge-based decision support system that assists farmers in insect pest diagnosis and management, is presented in [10]. AgriEnt relies on the AgriEnt-Ontology, which captures expert's knowledge about crop insect pests' management and empowers a rule-based inference engine providing diagnoses. In this work we describe CropPestO, an ontology covering crops (plants and plant products), related pests and diseases, their associated symptoms, and suggested control methods. As opposed to previous works, we put the focus on organic agriculture, and consequently the construction of this new domain ontology is fully justified. Moreover, given that we plan to populate the ontology through an automatic process from Spanish reference guides for IPM in different crops, the ontology has been labelled in Spanish (besides English).

3   CropPestO: Crop Pests and Diseases Ontology

In this section, the process to create the CropPestO ontology is detailed. The steps considered are based on the 'Ontology Development 101' [27], which among the large number of methodologies [28], was the best suited for our needs. The process involves the following steps: (1) determine the domain and scope of the ontology, (2) consider reusing existing ontologies, (3) enumerate important terms in the ontology, (4) define the classes and class hierarchy, (5) define the properties of classes—slots, (6) define the facets of the slots, and (7) create instances.

3.1 Ontology Domain and Scope

To determine the ontology domain and its scope, we need to answer the following questions:

1. *What is the domain that the ontology will cover?* The ontology will cover the domain of detection, treatment and prevention of pests and diseases in crops through organic farming.

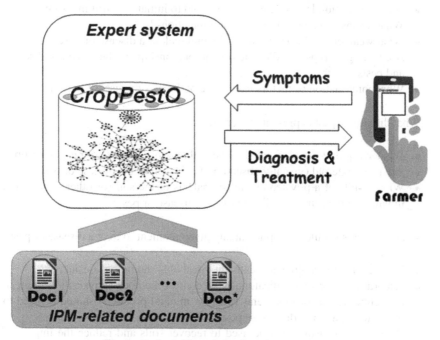

Fig. 1. Projected knowledge-based expert system

2. *For what we are going to use the ontology?* The ontology will constitute the basis to build a knowledge base as exhaustive as possible about the incidence of pests and diseases in different types of crops and their treatment and prevention following recognized and accepted practices in organic agriculture. This knowledge base will be exploited in an expert system (see Fig. 1) for the detection of pests and the recommendation of treatments and preventive measures in accordance with the policies, rules and regulations governing organic farming [29].

3. *For what types of questions the information in the ontology should provide answers?* The main questions the ontology should help answering (i.e., competency questions) are as follows:

Q1: What measures should be applied to prevent the outbreak of a disease or pest?

- What are the good practices of organic farming for the crop's management?

- What measures can be applied in organic farming to minimize the development of diseases and pests?
- What control and monitoring mechanisms should be used to identify the outbreak of a disease or pest?

Q2: What evidence does an outbreak of a disease or pest suggest in a crop?

- What are the factors that predict the outbreak of a disease or pest?
- What population levels determine the need to initiate control measures?
- What means can be used to monitor populations?
- What weather conditions promote the outbreak of a disease or pest?
- Are there geographic and / or temporal relationships in the spread of diseases and pests?
- What combination of factors lead to the outbreak of a disease or pest?

Q3: What disease or pest is present in a crop?

- What symptoms are associated to the outbreak of a disease or pest in a crop?
- Are there external (visually observable) evidence of the disease or pest?
- What results of a physico-chemical analysis of the soil (or other control and monitoring measures) are linked to each disease or pest?

Q4: What measures should be applied at any given moment to treat a disease or pest?

- What economic/ecological treatment thresholds should be considered?
- According to current indicators, what control methods (physical, biological, biotechnological) or treatments (plant or mineral products) should be used to limit the impact of a disease or pest?
- What other measures can be used to recover soils and reduce the impact of diseases or pests?
- What evidence suggest the stabilization at desired levels of a disease or pest?

4. *Who will use and maintain the ontology?* Researchers with experience in knowledge representation will build the ontology. The users will be farmers who are looking for recommendations about control methods and preventive practices to combat and reduce the impact of pests and diseases on crops.

3.2 Ontology Reuse

As pointed out in Sect. 2, there are many ontology models and structured vocabularies related to the agronomy domain. Besides those mentioned in Sect. 2 it is possible to highlight FAO's supported "Global Agricultural Concept Scheme" (GACS, https://agr isemantics.org/#GACShome/), a Linked Open Data concept scheme created by mapping frequently-used concepts at the intersection of three major agricultural thesauri: the AGROVOC Thesaurus, the CAB Thesaurus (CABT), and NAL Thesaurus (NALT).

For the purposes of our work, we made extensive use of the terms included in AGROVOC, as a standardized vocabulary, to organize the knowledge related to organisms, plants and their products.

3.3 Terms

The list of terms that can be extracted from the battery of questions set out in Sect. 3.1 is as follows: Plant, Plant Product, Yield, Crop, Soil, Organic Farming, Pathogen, Pest, Disease, Symptom, Plant Part, Weather, Pest Control, Mechanical Control, Biological Control, Chemical Control, Preventive Cultural Practices, Acceptable Pest Levels.

3.4 Classes and Class Hierarchy

To develop CropPestO, a strategy that combines both the top-down and bottom-up approaches was used. The original taxonomy was built by considering the terms pointed out in the previous section, and then it was further completed by adding more specific concepts. An excerpt of the class hierarchy is depicted in Table 1.

Table 1. Classes and superclasses list.

— Plant Products	— Pests	— Control methods
• Legume	• Bacteria	• Chemical control
• Fresh fruits	• Fungus	• Mechanical control
• Cereals	• Mollicutes	• Cultural practices
• Oilseeds	• Nematodes	• Biological control
	• Viroid	
— Plantae	— Symptoms	
• Plants		

3.5 Properties

In OWL 2 (Web Ontology Language, https://www.w3.org/TR/owl2-overview/), two kinds of properties can be defined, namely, data properties (i.e., class attributes) and object properties (i.e., relations). Table 2 collects the most representative properties linked to some of the identified classes.

3.6 Properties Characteristics

In OWL2, both data properties and object properties can be associated to facets, which restrict their values and cardinalities. Value constraints are used to limit the range of a property when it is linked to a data range or a class specification. In contrast, cardinality constraints are used to specify the number of values a property can take. Next, the most outstanding restrictions in CropPestO are detailed.

Table 2. Featured classes properties.

Class	Relationship
Plantae	produces (*range*: Plant Products)
Plant Products	hasPest (*range*: Pests)
Symptoms	isInfluencedBy (*range*: Pests)
Control methods	controls (*range*: Pests)
Pests	isPestOf (*range*: Plant Products)
	influences (*range*: Symptoms)
	isControlledBy (*range*: Control methods)

For instance, a specific pest can require different types of control methods (i.e., chemical control, technology control, cultural practices, biological control, or other methods). As a result, the relation `controls` defines a cardinality of 1 to n (1:Many). On the other hand, each instance of plantae produces one and only one type of crop; consequently, the relation `produces` defines a cardinality of 1 to 1 (1:1).

3.7 Instances

Finally, we list the instances of the classes defined above. In Table 3, some of the instances created along with their assigned classes are shown. A semi-supervised tool has been implemented that gathers relevant entities from AGROVOC and populates with them the ontology by instantiating the corresponding classes. The input of the tool is a previously collected list with crops. The tool iterates over this list exploring crop by crop, trying to find a match in the AGROVOC taxonomy. If a term is found in AGROVOC matching the crop name, then an instance is created in the ontology and broader concepts in the AGROVOC taxonomy are also incorporated into the ontology until the 'Plantae' concept is reached. For example, let us assume that the system is inputted the crop 'Arroz' (rice). It searches AGROVOC for that term and, once found, it asserts a new instance in the ontology. Then, it recursively traverses through the AGROVOC hierarchy inserting rice broader concepts, such as 'Cereales' and 'Productos de origen vegetal', into the knowledge base until it reaches the 'Plant Products' concept.

On the other hand, we take advantage of certain relations defined in AGROVOC such as `hasPest` and `isProducedBy` to identify new types of pests and plants. First, the property `hasPest` is utilized in AGROVOC to express when an organism causes harm in another organism. Second, the relation `isProducedBy` is defined to link crops to their plants. Hence, in the ontology instantiation process, we have used those properties to enrich the taxonomy of the CropPestO ontology. When an instance of crop from AGROVOC is inserted in the ontology, those properties are checked, and if the AGROVOC concept has some of these relations, then the tool systematically extracts the related entities, creates new instances in the ontology, and finally, it links them by using those relations. Following the example provided above, when the crop 'Arroz' is inserted as an instance in the ontology, the tool systematically inserts (i) 'Oryza

Table 3. List of initial instances.

Class	Instances
Plantae	Sour cherry, Common apricot tree, Pistacia vera, Citrus limon, Citrus reticulata, ...
Plant Products	Grapes, Barley, Rice, Plums, Apples, Oranges, ...
Symptoms	Reddish_bark, Black_underside, Yellowish_flower, Discoloration_leaves, Groove_plant, Tumour_trunk, ...
Control methods	Chemical control (taphina spp), Technological control (aceria oleae), Biological measures (panonychus citry), Physical measures (catareus aspersus), ...
Pests	Taphrina spp, Aceria oleae, Phytophthora spp ...
Bacteria	Agrobacterium tumefaciens, Agrobacterium rhizogenes, Rhizobium vitis, ...
Viroids	Citrus bent leaf viroid (cblvd), Hop latent vorid (hlvd), Eggplant latent viroid (elvd), ...

sativa' as instance of the plant concept, and 'Nilaparvata lugens' as instance of the pest concept; they both obtained from the AGROVOC relations isProducedBy and hasPest, respectively. Similarly, the tool will link those instances by utilizing the object properties with such names in the ontology schema.

To finish populating the ontology and to periodically augment the knowledge base, we intend to use a natural language processing tool to gather data from specialized, unstructured documents and instantiate the ontology with the generated triples.

4 Discussion

We built the ontology in OWL 2 by using the Protégé ontology editor (https://protege.sta ndford.edu). Figure 2 depicts an excerpt of the ontology including the high-level classes. The ontology is available at http://agrisemantics.inf.um.es/ontologies/CropPestO.owl

In order to verify the ontology correctness (i.e., that it provides the necessary elements to cope with the foreseen scope), the obtained ontology schema has been checked against the competency questions described in Sect. 3.1. In Table 4 the correspondences between competency questions and the associated ontology elements are shown. Each association in the table provides a twofold proof. On the one hand, the accuracy of the content defined in the conceptual model (content validity) and, on the other hand, the applicability of the conceptual model for its designed purpose (application validity). In particular, all the classes and properties represented in the ontology appear at the right column of Table 4, which means that they all are necessary to achieve the desired outcome (i.e., content validity). Likewise, there are elements in the ontology that assist in answering all the competency questions conceived (i.e., application validity). For instance, once the ontology has been fully populated, one might find out what disease or pest is present in a crop (i.e., competency question Q3) by exploring the visible Symptoms on the plant, which are directly connected to the Pests in the ontology.

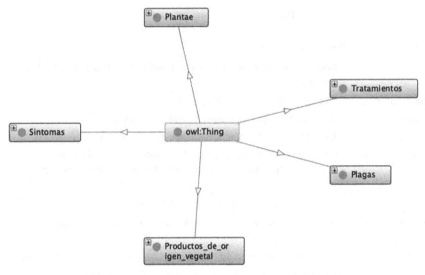

Fig. 2. Excerpt of the CropPestO ontology (in Spanish)

Table 4. Ontology model vs. competency questions.

Competency question	Ontology element
Q1	Pests, Symptoms, Control Methods, controls, isControlledBy, influences, isInfluencedBy
Q2	Plantae, Plant Products, Pests, Symptoms, influences, isInfluencedBy, hasPest, isPestOf
Q3	Pests, Plantae, Plant Product, Sypmtoms, hasPest, isPestOf
Q4	Control Methods, Pests, controls, isControlledBy

5   Conclusions and Future Work

Plant pests and diseases cause yield losses. Apart from the obvious financial losses, it endangers the worldwide food supply. Chemical pest control methods present a series of serious drawbacks and risks, the most important one being the harmful effect to both the environment and people [30]. Organic agriculture provides a more sustainable alternative, avoiding the use of chemical fertilizers and pesticides. Information about organic agriculture-compliant practices is scattered across the Web and it should be integrated and put at the farmers' disposal. The technologies around the Semantic Web have proven effective for information extraction, integration and recommendation [31]. Ontologies provide the formal basis for semantic applications to be effective.

While there are a number of ontologies in the agronomy domain and, more specifically, in the crop pests and diseases field, no one fits the requirements of an organic agriculture-based pest control recommender system. Consequently, in this work we describe the process followed to build CropPestO, an ontology model to semantically describe plants, plant products, related pests and diseases, their associated symptoms, and suggested control methods. The scope of the ontology has been defined in the form of four high-level competency questions that it should help answering. Those questions, associated with the identification and later treatment of plant diseases, guided the selection of the classes and properties that form part of the ontology.

A number of different research lines are open for future work. First, the ontology can be further improved by aligning it with other available resources. For example, symptoms can be described by using phenotypic ontologies that facilitate the semantic definition of plant damages caused by pests. Also, information about chemical control methods can be completed by using chemical databases. Second, a more in-depth validation of the ontology should be performed. In [32] the authors propose a framework to evaluate agricultural ontologies. Third, the pest control domain is an evolving, ever changing field, and so we plan to develop a semi-supervised ontology evolution tool. The ontology can then be constantly enriched and updated by considering the state-of-the-art knowledge. This tool will also assist in maintaining the ontology up to date with the changes in the reference vocabularies used (i.e., AGROVOC). Forth, manually instantiating the ontology would require the assistance of experts in the field, and it would be very time consuming. Instead, we seek to build an ontology population tool that can gather relevant data from available unstructured sources to instantiate the ontology. Lastly, once the knowledge base is complete, the next step would be to develop a semantically-enhanced pest management decision support system that, given some evidence (e.g., observable pathologies in plants, images or other indicators), provides an accurate diagnosis and suggests effective, organic-compliant control methods.

Acknowledgements. This work has been partially supported by the Seneca Foundation-the Regional Agency for Science and Technology of Murcia (Spain)-through project 20963/PI/18, the Spanish National Research Agency (AEI) and the European Regional Development Fund (FEDER/ERDF) through projects KBS4FIA (TIN2016-76323-R) and LaTe4PSP (PID2019-107652RB-I00), Research Talent Attraction Program by the Comunidad de Madrid with grants references 2017-T2/TIC-5664, and Young Researchers R+D Project. Ref. M2173 – SGTRS (co-funded by Rey Juan Carlos University).

References

1. Food and Agriculture Organization: How the world is fed. In: Agriculture, food and water (2003)
2. Drescher, L.S., Thiele, S., Mensink, G.B.M.: A new index to measure healthy food diversity better reflects a healthy diet than traditional measures. J. Nutr. **137**, 647–651 (2007). https://doi.org/10.1093/jn/137.3.647
3. Fletcher, J., et al.: Emerging infectious plant diseases. In: Scheld, W.M., Grayson, M.L., Hughes, J.M. (eds.) Emerging Infections, pp. 337–366. ASM Press, Washington DC (2010)
4. Velásquez, A.C., Castroverde, C.D.M., Yang He, S.: Plant-pathogen warfare under changing climate conditions. Current Biol. **28**, R619–R634 (2018). https://doi.org/10.1016/j.cub.2018.03.054

5. García-Sánchez, F., García-Díaz, J.A., Gómez-Berbís, J.M., Valencia-García, R.: Financial knowledge instantiation from semi-structured, heterogeneous data sources. In: Silhavy, R. (ed.) CSOC2018 2018. AISC, vol. 764, pp. 103–110. Springer, Cham (2019). https://doi.org/10.1007/978-3-319-91189-2_11

6. Prudhomme, C., Homburg, T., Ponciano, J.-J., Boochs, F., Cruz, C., Roxin, A.-M.: Interpretation and automatic integration of geospatial data into the Semantic Web. Computing **102**(2), 365–391 (2019). https://doi.org/10.1007/s00607-019-00701-y

7. Bernabé-Díaz, J.A., Legaz-García, M. del C., García, J.M., Fernández-Breis, J.T.: Efficient, semantics-rich transformation and integration of large datasets. Expert Syst. Appl. **133**, 198–214 (2019). https://doi.org/10.1016/j.eswa.2019.05.010

8. Studer, R., Benjamins, R., Fensel, D.: Knowledge engineering: Principles and methods. Data Knowl. Eng. **25**, 161–197 (1998). https://doi.org/10.1016/S0169-023X(97)00056-6

9. Drury, B., Fernandes, R., Moura, M.-F., Andrade Lopes, A.: A Survey of Semantic Web Technology for Agriculture. Information Processing in Agriculture. 1–15 (2019). https://doi.org/10.1016/J.INPA.2019.02.001

10. Lagos-Ortiz, K., Salas-Zárate, M. del P., Paredes-Valverde, M.A., García-Díaz, J.A., Valencia-García, R.: AgriEnt: A knowledge-based web platform for managing insect pests of field crops. Appl. Sci. **10**, 1040 (2020). https://doi.org/10.3390/app10031040

11. Xiaoxue, L., Xuesong, B., Longhe, W., Bingyuan, R., Shuhan, L., Lin, L.: Review and trend analysis of knowledge graphs for crop pest and diseases. IEEE Access. **7**, 62251–62264 (2019). https://doi.org/10.1109/ACCESS.2019.2915987

12. Garcerán-Sáez, J., García-Sánchez, F.: SePeRe: Semantically-enhanced system for pest recognition. In: Valencia-García, R., Alcaraz-Mármol, G., Cioppo-Morstadt, Jd, Vera-Lucio, N., Bucaram-Leverone, M. (eds.) CITAMA2019 2019. AISC, vol. 901, pp. 3–11. Springer, Cham (2019). https://doi.org/10.1007/978-3-030-10728-4_1

13. Hernández-Castillo, C., Guedea-Noriega, H.H., Rodríguez-García, M.Á., García-Sánchez, F.: Pest recognition using natural language processing. In: Valencia-García, R., Alcaraz-Mármol, G., Del Cioppo-Morstadt, J., Vera-Lucio, N., Bucaram-Leverone, M. (eds.) CITI 2019. CCIS, vol. 1124, pp. 3–16. Springer, Cham (2019). https://doi.org/10.1007/978-3-030-34989-9_1

14. Labaña, F.M., Ruiz, A., García-Sánchez, F.: PestDetect: Pest recognition using convolutional neural network. In: Valencia-García, R., Alcaraz-Mármol, G., Cioppo-Morstadt, Jd, Vera-Lucio, N., Bucaram-Leverone, M. (eds.) CITAMA2019 2019. AISC, vol. 901, pp. 99–108. Springer, Cham (2019). https://doi.org/10.1007/978-3-030-10728-4_11

15. Martinelli, F., Scalenghe, R., Davino, S., Panno, S., Scuderi, G., Ruisi, P., Villa, P., Stroppiana, D., Boschetti, M., Goulart, L.R.: Advanced methods of plant disease detection. A review. Agron. Sustain. Dev. **35**, 1–25 (2015). https://doi.org/10.1007/s13593-014-0246-1ï

16. Jonquet, C., Toulet, A., Arnaud, E., Aubin, S., Dzalé Yeumo, E., Emonet, V., Graybeal, J., Laporte, M.-A., Musen, M.A., Pesce, V., Larmande, P.: AgroPortal: A vocabulary and ontology repository for agronomy. Comput. Electron. Agric. **144**, 126–143 (2018). https://doi.org/10.1016/j.compag.2017.10.012

17. Rodríguez Iglesias, A., Egaña Aranguren, M., Rodríguez González, A., Wilkinson, M.D.: Plant-pathogen interactions ontology (PPIO). In: Rojas, I., Ortuño Guzman, F.M. (eds.) International Work-Conference on Bioinformatics and Biomedical Engineering, IWBBIO 2013, Granada, Spain, March 18–20, 2013, Proceedings, pp. 695–702. Copicentro Editorial, Granada, Spain (2013)

18. Walls, R., Smith, B., Elser, J., Goldfain, A., Stevenson, D.W., Jaiswal, P.: A plant disease extension of the Infectious Disease Ontology. In: Cornet, R., Stevens, R. (eds.) Proceedings of the 3rd International Conference on Biomedical Ontology (ICBO 2012), KR-MED Series, pp. 1–5. CEUR-WS.org, Graz, Austria (2012)

19. Ontology Best Practices - OSF Wiki. https://wiki.opensemanticframework.org/index.php/Ontology_Best_Practices, last accessed 03/28/2020

20. Dalvi, P., Mandave, V., Gothkhindi, M., Patil, A., Kadam, S., Pawar, S.S.: Overview of agriculture domain ontologies. Int. J. Recent Adv. Eng. Technol. **4**, 5–9 (2016)
21. Xiaoxue, L., Xuesong, B., Longhe, W., Bingyuan, R., Shuhan, L., Lin, L.: Review and trend analysis of knowledge graphs for crop pest and diseases. IEEE Access. **7**, 62251–62264 (2019). https://doi.org/10.1109/ACCESS.2019.2915987
22. Devare, M., Aubert, C., Laporte, M.-A., Valette, L., Arnaud, E., Buttigieg, P.L.: Data-driven agricultural research for development a need for data harmonization via semantics. In: Jaiswal, P., Hoehndorf, R., Arighi, C.N., and Meier, A. (eds.) Proceedings of the Joint International Conference on Biological Ontology and BioCreative, CEUR Workshop Proceedings 1747. CEUR-WS.org, Corvallis, Oregon, United States (2016). https://doi.org/10.1186/2041-1480-4-43
23. Caracciolo, C., Stellato, A., Morshed, A., Johannsen, G., Rajbhandari, S., Jaques, Y., Keizer, J.: The AGROVOC linked dataset. Semant. Web **4**, 341–348 (2013). https://doi.org/10.3233/SW-130106
24. Beck, H.W., Kim, S., Hagan, D.: A Crop-pest ontology for extension publications. In: 2005 EFITA/WCCA Joint Congress on IT in Agriculture, pp. 1169–1176, Vila Real, Portugal (2005)
25. Lacasta, J., Lopez-Pellicer, F.J., Espejo-García, B., Nogueras-Iso, J., Zarazaga-Soria, F.J.: Agricultural recommendation system for crop protection. Comput. Electron. Agric. **152**, 82–89 (2018). https://doi.org/10.1016/j.compag.2018.06.049
26. Jearanaiwongkul, W., Anutariya, C., Andres, F.: An ontology-based approach to plant disease identification system. In: Proceedings of the 10th International Conference on Advances in Information Technology - IAIT 2018, pp. 1–8. ACM Press, New York (2018). https://doi.org/10.1145/3291280.3291786
27. Noy, N.F., McGuinness, D.L.: Ontology Development 101: A Guide to Creating Your First Ontology (2001)
28. Cristani, M., Cuel, R.: A survey on ontology creation methodologies. In: Sheth, A.P., Lytras, M.D. (eds.) Semantic Web-Based Information Systems: State-of-the-Art Applications, pp. 98–122. IGI Global (2007). https://doi.org/10.4018/978-1-59904-426-2.ch004
29. Organic farming|European Commission. https://ec.europa.eu/info/food-farming-fisheries/farming/organic-farming/. Accessed 28 Mar 2020
30. Nicolopoulou-Stamati, P., Maipas, S., Kotampasi, C., Stamatis, P., Hens, L.: Chemical pesticides and human health: The urgent need for a new concept in agriculture. Front. Public Health. **4** (2016). https://doi.org/10.3389/fpubh.2016.00148
31. García-Sánchez, F., Colomo-Palacios, R., Valencia-García, R.: A social-semantic recommender system for advertisements. Inf. Process. Manage. **57**, 102153 (2020). https://doi.org/10.1016/J.IPM.2019.102153
32. Goldstein, A., Fink, L., Ravid, G.: A Framework for Evaluating Agricultural Ontologies (2019). https://arxiv.org/abs/1906.10450

Automatic Misogyny Detection with Linguistic and Morphological Features in Spanish

Mar Cánovas-García⬤, José Antonio García-Díaz$^{(\boxtimes)}$⬤,
and Rafael Valencia-García⬤

Facultad de Informática, Universidad de Murcia,
Campus de Espinardo, 30100 Murcia, Spain
{mariamar.canovasg,joseantonio.garcia8,valencia}@um.es

Abstract. Social media allows many people to keep in touch and get updated of their surroundings, but these positive features do not bury the fact that another large portion of the users employ this tool with the intention of harassing people under anonymity. Due to the amount of content created on these platforms, spotting hate comments individually becomes an impossible task, and automatic hate speech detectors take place on those tasks. Furthermore, identifying hate speech towards women is specially complex due to the cultural background and the subtlety that characterizes it, which makes it interesting to consider it as a phenomenon by itself, differentiating it from traditional hate speech. Our contribution to automatic misogyny identification entails the creation of a machine-learning model based on linguistic and morphological features, applied to the training set of corpus developed at the Automatic Misogyny Evaluation task which contains 3307 tweets written in Spanish. We evaluate our proposal with different machine-learning classifiers achieving the best accuracy of 77% applying Support Vector Machines.

Keywords: Misogyny detection · Text classification · Natural Language Processing

1 Introduction

Apart from the obvious positive improvements social media has provided on information diffusion and divulgation, it is in fact not exempt from users who use it to harass others effortlessly. The Internet has become into a hostile environment for certain groups because certain people have found a place to gain a huge amount of power over people lives behind anonymity [14]. In fact, a survey driven by the PEW Research Center stated that roughly 40% of Americans have experienced online harassment [7]. Among those, trait-based harassment is one of the most experienced forms of harassment. For example, the 21% of women between 18 and 29 years old usually encounter sexualized forms of harassment, like receiving explicit images that were not asked for.

© Springer Nature Switzerland AG 2020
R. Valencia-García et al. (Eds.): CITI 2020, CCIS 1309, pp. 30–42, 2020.
https://doi.org/10.1007/978-3-030-62015-8_3

Misogyny is the term to refer to social environments where *"women will tend to face hostility of various kinds because they are women in a man's world who are held to be failing to live up to men's standards"* [16]. Discrediting and silencing women voices are one of many consequences online misogyny result on. In [13], it is described the phenomenon where vulgar messages completely change the subject of the conversation, demeaning the original author and therefor despising the relevancy of the mentioned issue, which is a practice only found in posts where the author is publicly female.

As gender-based harassment entails taking into consideration specific aspects related to social and cultural stigma, it is interesting to set the misogyny identification aside from common hate speech attitudes [21]. In other words, finding aggressive content is not enough to identify misogynistic content. In the spirit of building safe spaces on the Internet and due to the technological challenge posed by the automatic arrest of misogyny, various workshops of Natural Language Processing (NLP) have proposed tasks for the identification of hate messages in social networks [5,9].

Our contribution regarding automatic misogyny detection consists in the development and evaluation of linguistic and morphological features with machine-learning models for the misogyny detection. We evaluate our proposal with the training subset of AMI task from IberEval 2018 [9], composed by 3307 tweets written in Spanish.

The reminder of the paper is organised as follows: Sect. 2 involves the state of the art of misogyny detection and different technologies related to our proposal. Section 3 describes the materials and methods applied in our proposal. Section 4 explains the linguistic, statistical and technical approach taken on the experiments performed. Finally, Sect. 5 summarises the conclusions of the paper and defines future research directions.

2   Related Work

In this paper we perform the evaluation of different models for misogyny detection on tweets written in Spanish. Therefore, this section analyses related works concerning already existing tools oriented to misogyny identification (see Sect. 2.1) and a description of feature engineering approaches to represent text documents as feature vector (see Sect. 2.2)

2.1   Automatic Misogyny Identification

Due to its social impact and relevance, the identification of misogyny has become a popular task at Natural Language Processing workshops. The IberEval 2018 workshop[1] was organised by the Spanish Society of Natural Language Processing (SEPLN) and proposed a specific task for misogyny identification called AMI (Automatic Misogyny Identification). In IberEval 2018, organizers released

---

[1] https://sites.google.com/view/ibereval-2018/home.

two corpora, one of them in English and the other one in Spanish. Independently of the language, the participants of the task could submit their models to compare their results in two classification challenges: (1) a simple misogyny classification (binary); and (2) a fine-grained misogyny identification (multi-class) of specific misogynous traits, namely stereotype, dominance, derailing, sexual harassment, and discredit. The participants of AMI 2018 task used different approaches including n-grams, word embeddings, and linguistic features, and they also used different machine learning classifiers, such as Support Vector Machines or deep-learning models. The overview of both of the AMI 2018 subtasks can be consulted at [9]. The *Associazione Italiana di Linguistica Computazionale* proposed a similar task in the EvalIta workshop [8] offering Italian and English corpus. In [11], the authors compile a corpus regarding misogyny divided into three sets: (1) violence towards relevant women, (2) messages classified from different Spanish-spoken countries, and (3) general traits related to misogyny. During their research, they evaluate different feature sets, including sentence word embeddings and linguistic features as well as different machine learning models.

Apart from the previously mentioned tasks, most of the research regarding misogyny identification found in the bibliography is oriented to English. In this sense, Lynn et al. [15] compiled slang words from Urban Dictionary[2] to compare the performance of deep-learning techniques to conventional machine learning techniques. Their results showed that deep-learning techniques, such as bidirectional long short-term memory recurrent neural networks (Bi-LSTM) and bidirectional gated recurrent unit recurrent neural networks (Bi-GRU) outperformed traditional machine learning techniques. In their conclusions, they highlight the drawback of the lack of interpretability of deep learning results. In the same line, Tanvi Banerjee et al. [4] developed a machine learning classifier that identifies gender-based violence topics within a text according to its pragmatic function that distinguishes among beliefs, queries, figurative language or fact reporting. During their research, they manually compiled and labelled a corpus with the help of three independent annotations per tweet message. One of these pragmatic functions, figurative language, is one of the most challenging ones regarding natural language [23].

2.2 Feature Engineering

In order for a machine to process natural language, texts has to be transformed to feature vectors. Feature engineering refers to the selection and extraction of different characteristics of a message which purpose is to represent it for classifying tasks. The most popular ones can be categorised as (1) statistical or (2) linguistic.

On the one hand, statistical features represent documents as vectors of words from a dictionary. The baseline model to this day is the Bag of Words (BoW) model, which compiles all the words present on a corpus to generate a

---

[2] https://www.urbandictionary.com/.

dictionary as a vector with the frequencies of each specific word in the current text. Despite its simplicity, BoW is still commonly used in document classification tasks. However, as the BoW handles individual words, it does not capture complex linguistic phenomena, and the size of the corpus and the vocabulary plays a very important role on the performance of the model, because as the size increases, the vector gets more sparse being time and memory consuming. To solve these problems, there have been approaches like (1) the incorporation of joint-words (bigrams, trigrams) to include the context where some word appears within the text, (2) the usage of sequences of characters instead of words [1], and (3) more complex approaches for measuring the frequency of each term like the term-frequency inverse document-frequency (TF-IDF) which dismisses the relevance of a word if it appears frequently in the rest of the documents in the corpus [31].

On the other hand, linguistic features refer to these features that measure the frequency of appearance of certain linguistic phenomena, for example, the number of uppercase words, expressive lengthening or the number of words belonging to a certain Part of Speech (PoS) category. These features are context dependant, so it is not trivial to translate them to another language [27]. There are already existing tools that allow the extraction of linguistic features from natural language. In this sense, Linguistic Inquiry and Word Count (LIWC) [28] is the de facto tool for text analysis that counts words within pre-established psychological categories and capture content-words (nouns, verbs or adjectives), and style-words (prepositions, articles, conjunctions or auxiliary verbs). LIWC has been applied in several tasks about suicide [18], cyber-bullying [26], and satire detection [24]. LIWC has different versions for numerous languages and Spanish is one of them. Similar to LIWC, UMUTextStats is a novel linguistic extraction tool capable of extracting linguistic features focused on Spanish [10]. The main difference with LIWC is that UMUTextStats considers a wide variety of linguistic features related to Spanish, such as grammatical gender or fine-grained detail of part-of-speech categories.

In addition to linguistic and statistical features we can also consider contextual features. Those features represent information about the context and the environment in which the communication took place. Examples of contextual features can be the author of the post, the moment where it was written or published or even the location. Contextual features can be very helpful in domains where shared knowledge between sender and receiver is relevant for the classification of a text, like in sarcasm detection [3].

3   Materials and Methods

The Spanish dataset used for this experiment is the provided as training in the AMI task at the IberEval 2018 workshop. This dataset is almost a balanced corpus where the documents were classified as "positive" (1658 tweets) and "negative" (1649 tweets) whether they have misogynous traits or not. Due to the lack of availability of the labelled testing dataset, we performed our evaluation applying a 10-fold cross validation to the training set to calculate the mean accuracy.

The obtained features can be classified into:

- **Format and structural features**. These features refer to the way the message is structured. In our model they are located in the first ten positions of the vector, being some of them the length of the document, the number of words, the percentage of words in uppercase, or presence of hashtags and hyperlinks. These features are extracted by using mostly regular expressions, which allow to look for patterns within a text and spot how many of them there are [29].
- **Keyword presence**. It is important to detect if the message contains words from dictionaries regarding insults or misogynous slang. In this case, it is particularly relevant to differentiate between feminine and masculine insults, because this could be a very discerning feature to distinguish misogyny among other forms of hate speech.
- **Morphology and syntactical features**. We extract from each tweet morphological and syntactical features such as the verb tense and mode of each verb, or we count the percentage of feminine adjectives. Spanish makes an intensive use of inflection, which can be observed in some grammatical elements that inflects according to the gender of noun they refer to. This linguistic phenomena, known as gender agreement, can be hinted by guess the gender of the target of a utterance. Moreover, verbal tense can be used to determine the intentions of a writer, determining if they are expressing beliefs or spotting facts. We make use of FreeLing tool [19] to obtain these features. Once the content of the message has been analyzed, for each word a token that identifies its nature is generated, and by the application of regular expressions we can determine to which feature it corresponds.

All of these features result in a vector 60 positions long that will summarize the characteristics of each tweet as the input of the classification methods.

Here we can see examples of vectorized messages, two of them classified as misogynous and another two classified as non misogynous, with some of the resulting stats from the model vector that represents its content. In the Evaluation section, we will explain why these indicators are specially correlated to the classification process.

The first one would be a demeaning tweet using the imperative and capital letters to tell a women to shut up, calling her insulting words like "perra". It is a direct reply, so we can also see there is a mention to that person the message is directed to:

"@Hxrry_again CÁLLATE PERRA"

- Misogynous: 1
- Length: 26
- Words: 3
- Mentions: 1
- Capital Words: 2

- % Capital Words: 0.66
- Words Per Sentence: 3
- Sentences: 1
- Punctuation: 1
- Fem. insults: 1

- Imperative verbs: 1
- 2nd pers. verbs: 1
- Singular verbs: 1

The second misogynous tweet is a condescending "joke" using the similarity between the Spanish words *"votar"* and *"botar"*, which mean *"vote"* and *"bounce"*. This message comes to saying the only thing women should *"vote"*/*"bounce"* would be their breast when doing exercise. This is an example of a tweet that, even though is not an insult to a specific person, is extremely misogynous:

"Lo único que debe votar una mujer son sus tetas cuando hacen deporte. #GravedadAnteTodo"

- Misogynous: 1
- Length: 87
- Words: 14
- Hashtags: 1

- Words Per Sentence: 14
- Sentence: 2
- Punctuation: 1
- Infinitive verbs: 1

- Present verbs: 3
- 3rd person verbs: 3
- Singular verbs: 1
- Plural verbs: 2

For the third example, we analyse a tweet that, despite using insulting words (*"puta"*), is related to a very different topic and has nothing to do with woman issues, so is classified as non misogynous. This is, as in the first example, an answer directed to a concrete person.

"@johnny21es Algun@ no tiene ni puta idea de fútbol, desengáñate. Decir cientos de nombres y tonterías al tuntún y que cuatro inocentes se las crean es ser un charlatán, no saber de fútbol."

- Misogynous: 0
- Length: 188
- Words: 33
- Mentions: 1
- Words Per Sentence: 33
- Sentences: 3
- Punctuation: 5

- Masc. adjectives: 1
- Singular adjectives: 1
- Common names: 9
- Fem. names: 3
- Masc. names: 5
- Singular names: 5
- Plural names: 4

- Imperative verbs: 1
- Infinitive verbs: 3
- Present verbs: 3
- 2nd person verbs: 1
- 3rd person verbs: 3
- Singular verbs: 3
- Plural verbs: 1

Lastly, we analyze yet another non misogynous tweet containing insulting words but on another unrelated topic, in this case, films.

"@TurokJr Si, eso es lo "terrorífico" del cine de horror, pero cuál es la gracia de las malditas tonterías, para eso veo una puta comedia"

- Misogynous: 0
- Length: 138
- Words: 26
- Mentions: 1
- Words Per Sentence: 26
- Sentences: 1
- Punctuation: 3
- % Singular words: 0.51

- Fem. adjectives: 1
- Plural adjectives: 1
- Common names: 7
- Fem. names: 4
- Masc. names: 3
- Singular names: 6
- Plural names: 1
- Demonstrative Pron.: 2

- Singular Pron.: 3
- Indicative verbs: 3
- Present verbs: 3
- 1st person verbs: 1
- 3rd person verbs: 2
- Singular verbs: 3

Following the study in [25], the algorithms used to carry the studies and comparisons are the listed below:

- **Naïve Bayes.** This classifier is based on probabilities with a statistical learning method, which tries to learn a probabilistic theory to use it in decision making when there is uncertainty. At categorization, the classifier calculates the probability of a vector belonging to a certain class using Bayes theorem [17].
- **Random Forest.** The algorithm Random Forest has its foundations on decision trees, where each node of the tree refers to an feature evaluated positively or negatively, and each leaf represents the assigned class, resulting if the document is classified or not as expected. It is known that the phenomenon of overfitting tends to appear in this kind of classification methods [12]. Overfitting describes the problem of a solution being too tight to the training data, so this is why this algorithm usually is executed several times, generating several decision trees known as Random Forest.
- **Support Vector Machines.** This algorithm represents the position on a geometric space constructed with the characteristics that compose the input model and tries to find the plane that divides more precisely the positive and negative samples with as much margin between them as possible. This results on a robust classification to the problem of *overfitting* and allows the model to escalate into bigger dimensions.

As the labelled test dataset of the AMI 2018 task was not available, we compare our results with two baseline models: (1) a Bag of Word (generating a model based on presence of words or not [32]) combined with N-Grams models (congregating a n number of words as a single token, looking for its presence or absence alike the Bag of Words [6]), and (2) Sentiment Lexicons (dictionary based classification that hints the sentiment of a message as positive or negative [30]). It is worth noting that the reliability of the second baseline could be improved with the addition of specific misogyny lexicons. The addition of domain specific lexicons has proven to be effective in sentiment classification, such as the work presented in [22]. However, we decided to avoid custom lexicons in order to compare our proposal with a basic hate-speech detector.

All the experiments were executed using Python with Scikit-learn [20]. Each model was trained following a 10-fold cross validation approach. The performance of each machine learning classifier was evaluated comparing their accuracy (see Eq. 1).

$$Accuracy = TP + TN/(TP + TN + FP + FN) \qquad (1)$$

4   Evaluation

First, we use the Bag of Words (BoW) model with unigrams, bigrams, and trigrams applying the Naïve Bayes classifier to obtain a baseline to which contrast our remaining experiments. The results of this baseline model are shown in Table 1, where we can observe that the best accuracy is obtained by the bigram model with a 67.2% of accuracy.

Table 1. Baseline model with Bag Of Words and Naïve Bayes applying unigrams, bigrams, trigrams

Features	Accuracy
BoW Unigrams	0.637
BoW Bigrams	0.672
BoW Trigrams	0.636

As we previously mentioned, we use FreeLing [19] to extract the linguistic features, resulting in a classification in positive and negative messages. In our experiment, we consider that negative messages are those which are misogynous, as a regular Hate Speech detector would do. The results of this experiment are presented in Table 2.

Table 2. Treating AMI as sentiment analysis

Features	Accuracy
Sentiment Analysis	0.583

As depicted in Table 2, the outcome of the classification is not much higher than the 58%, so we can once again confirm that misogyny is not only related to insulting or aggressive language, but are in fact more complex and deep and requires to treat it aside from regular Hate Speech.

Over our model we apply Naïve Bayes (NB), Random Forest (RF) and Support Vector Machine (SVM) algorithms. Results of the experiments are depicted in Table 3. In comparison with the obtained with BoW, the achieved results are lower with NB and similar to the bigram and trigram models with RF and SVM. In particular, the SVM performance reaches the accuracy obtained by Maria Anzovino methodology in [2], designer of the IberEval AMI task and hence designer of the corpus we are currently using, with a 69% accuracy.

Table 3. Evaluation of our model with the AMI 2018 dataset applying Naive Bayes (NB), Random-Forest (RF), and Support-Vector Machines (SVM)

Classifier	Accuracy
NB	0.557
RF	0.672
SVM	0.693

Consequently to these results, as the difference between the baseline model with the our proposal is small, we explore the combination of both models. For that, we concatenate both vector generated by both models, having then more variables where the classifiers can deliberate. Furthermore, we also tried the N-Gram variants of the BoW model. The results can be seen in Table 4.

As shown in the results, the combination of the vectors does not contribute to the improvement of the accuracy, but it also does it less time efficient.

Table 4. Combination of baseline model with BoW and linguistic and morphological features

			Accuracy
Model	SVM		0.69
	RF		0.67
BOW	SVM	UNIGRAM	0.77
		BIGRAM	0.76
	RF	UNIGRAM	0.75
		BIGRAM	0.73
BOW + MODEL	SVM	UNIGRAM	0.67
		BIGRAM	0.66
	RF	UNIGRAM	0.75
		BIGRAM	0.74

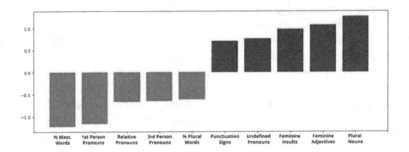

Fig. 1. Top 10 correlated features

We selected the top 10 more correlated attributes of our model, depicted in Fig. 1, aiming for the understand which features contributes most in the achieved model. We can observe that the percentage of masculine words is a good indicator that the content of the message is not related to women, neither in a positive or negative approach, and as we can see is key to discard misogyny. Also, the presence of 1st and 3rd person pronouns indicate us the absence of 2nd noun pronouns, so a intimidating direct redaction style can be discarded by that, as well as relative pronouns, used in common language but not in threats or similar texts. Having all of these features present in a message allows us to discard its complementary: feminine nouns and directly written 2nd person messages commonly referred to a single individual. Likewise, encountering feminine insults and adjectives are a very clear way to distinguish that the target of a utterance is a women, referring to her in a descriptive and threatening way, as well as the excessive punctuation use.

With this shortening, the results obtained by the classification algorithms remained the same, but implying a less time consuming processing. Despite the results do not perform like a robust classifier would do, the accuracy obtained by our best execution overcome the accuracy obtained by Anzovino's work [2] by an 8%.

5   Conclusions and Future Work

Automatic Misogyny Identification has gained relevance thanks to congresses like IberEval2018 [9], EvalIta2018 [8] or HatEval2019 [5]. The evaluation of linguistic features has proven to improve the accuracy of the classification made by María Anzovino [2], creator of the corpus and IberEval2018 and EvalIta2018 AMI tasks, from 69% to 77%.

In sight of the results, it is evident that at classifying misogynous tweets, linguistic and morphological features are not enough to make a robust classifier. Furthermore, results obtained by BoW models and its N-Gram variants are not that far from the highest accuracy obtained in our experiments, so it leads into thinking that the presence of certain keywords are a distinctive factor at categorization.

On the other side, the fact that there are radically different categories all of them considered as misogynous (for example, discrediting messages and sexual harassment related messages) makes the joining of all of them counterproductive when looking for a common pattern that identifies them. Because of the corpus was not totally classified in those sub-categories, being some of them only around 20 messages, makes it especially difficult to identify the tendencies of the messages in that category. This is why, having not many precedent investigations related to this topic and being the corpus relatively small in comparison with the amount of data classifiers usually train with, among other details like it is not fully sub-categorized, the results are improvable.

As the future work goes, there are many possibilities available in order to improve the investigation on this area. The more straight forward improvement would be seeking for other types of classification algorithms that work better with the kind of model we are generating and adjusting the vector to its needs. An interesting approach are Neural Networks, that have been used lately in many classifiers. Another option would be adapting the model in order to focus on the sub-classification task, or adding the probability of belonging to a certain sub-class to our already existing model as a feature. Due to all of the improvements mentioned rely on the quality of the corpus, a good starting point would be enlarging or sub-classifying the already existing corpus, or compiling a new one from scratch. Also, a feature that could be included in corpus related to misogyny detection is knowing the gender of the users involved in the conversation, which could be extracted from the user information of the Twitter account. It could also be interesting for further investigation analysing tweets under the same women related hashtag, and determine which ones have been written to support the movement and those who are against it.

Summarizing, the study of the misogyny and its identification still has a long way to go, since it has hardly been taken into consideration for the latest years, and can be very useful as a filter or tool for penalization in places where you do not want to allow toxic environments, such as different social networks, forums, video games, or any similar community.

Acknowledgments. This work has been supported by the Spanish National Research Agency (AEI) and the European Regional Development Fund (FEDER/ERDF) through projects KBS4FIA (TIN2016-76323-R) and LaTe4PSP (PID2019-107652RB-I00). In addition, José Antonio García-Díaz has been supported by Banco Santander and University of Murcia through the Doctorado industrial programme.

References

1. Aiyar, S., Shetty, N.P.: N-Gram assisted Youtube spam comment detection. Procedia Comput. Sci. **132**, 174–182 (2018)
2. Anzovino, M.: Misogyny Detection on Social Media: A Methodological Approach. Master's Thesis, Department of Informatics, Systems and Communication (2018)
3. Bamman, D., Smith, N.A.: Contextualized sarcasm detection on Twitter. In: Proceedings of the Ninth International Conference on Web and Social Media, ICWSM. pp. 574–577. Springer (2015). http://www.aaai.org/ocs/index.php/ICWSM/ICWSM15/paper/view/10538
4. Banerjee, T., Yazdavar, A.H., Hampton, A., Purohit, H., Shalin, V.L., Sheth, A.P.: Identifying pragmatic functions in social media indicative of gender-based violence beliefs. Manuscript Submitted for Publication ([nd])
5. Bauwelinck, N., Jacobs, G., Hoste, V., Lefever, E.: LT3 at SemEval-2019 task 5: multilingual detection of hate speech against immigrants and women in Twitter (hatEval). In: 13th International Workshop on Semantic Evaluation (SemEval-2019), Collocated with NAACL 2019, pp. 436–440. Association for Computational Linguistics (ACL) (2019)
6. Brown, P.F., Della Pietra, V.J., Desouza, P.V., Lai, J.C., Mercer, R.L.: Class-based N-gram models of natural language. Comput. Linguist. **18**(4), 467–480 (1992)
7. Duggan, M.: Online Harassment 2017. Technical Report, Pew Research Center (2017)
8. Fersini, E., Nozza, D., Rosso, P.: Overview of the EVALITA 2018 task on automatic misogyny identification (AMI). EVALITA Evaluation of NLP and Speech Tools for Italian, vol. 12, p. 59 (2018)
9. Fersini, E., Rosso, P., Anzovino, M.: Overview of the task on automatic misogyny identification at IberEval 2018. IberEval@ SEPLN 2150, pp. 214–228 (2018)
10. García-Díaz, J.A., Cánovas-García, M., Valencia-García, R.: Ontology-driven aspect-based sentiment analysis classification: an infodemiological case study regarding infectious diseases in Latin America. Future Gener. Comput. Syst. **112**, 614–657 (2020). https://doi.org/10.1016/j.future.2020.06.019

11. García-Díaz, J.A., Cánovas-García, M., Colomo-Palacios, R., Valencia-García, R.: Detecting misogyny in Spanish tweets: an approach based on linguistics features and word embeddings. Future Gener. Comput. Syst. **114**, 506–518 (2021). https://doi.org/10.1016/j.future.2020.08.032. http://www.sciencedirect.com/science/article/pii/S0167739X20301928

12. Ho, T.K.: Random decision forests. In: Proceedings of 3rd International Conference on Document Analysis and Recognition, vol. 1, pp. 278–282. IEEE (1995)

13. Jane, E.A.: "Back to the kitchen, cunt": speaking the unspeakable about online misogyny. Continuum **28**(4), 558–570 (2014)

14. Levmore, S., Nussbaum, M.C.: The Offensive Internet: Speech, Privacy, and Reputation. Harvard University Press, Cambridge (2010)

15. Lynn, T., Endo, P.T., Rosati, P., Silva, I., Santos, G.L., Ging, D.: A comparison of machine learning approaches for detecting misogynistic speech in urban dictionary. In: 2019 International Conference on Cyber Situational Awareness, Data Analytics And Assessment (Cyber SA), pp. 1–8. IEEE (2019)

16. Manne, K.: Down Girl: The Logic of Misogyny. Oxford University Press, Oxford (2017)

17. Maron, M.E.: Automatic indexing: an experimental inquiry. J. ACM (JACM) **8**(3), 404–417 (1961)

18. O'dea, B., Larsen, M.E., Batterham, P.J., Calear, A.L., Christensen, H.: A linguistic analysis of suicide-related Twitter posts. Crisis: J. Crisis Interv. Suicide Prev. **38**(5), 319 (2017)

19. Padró, L., Stanilovsky, E.: FreeLing 3.0: towards wider multilinguality. In: LREC2012 (2012)

20. Pedregosa, F., et al.: Scikit-learn: machine learning in Python. J. Mach. Learn. Res. **12**, 2825–2830 (2011)

21. Richardson-Self, L.: Woman-hating: on misogyny, sexism, and hate speech. Hypatia **33**(2), 256–272 (2018)

22. Ruiz-Martínez, J.M., Valencia-García, R., García-Sánchez, F., et al.: Semantic-based sentiment analysis in financial news. In: Proceedings of the 1st International Workshop on Finance and Economics on the Semantic Web, pp. 38–51 (2012)

23. Salas-Zárate, M.P., Alor-Hernández, G., Sánchez-Cervantes, J.L., Paredes-Valverde, M.A., García-Alcaraz, J.L., Valencia-García, R.: Review of English literature on figurative language applied to social networks. Knowl. Inf. Syst. **62**(6), 2105–2137 (2020). https://doi.org/10.1007/s10115-019-01425-3

24. del Pilar Salas-Zárate, M., Paredes-Valverde, M.A., Rodriguez-García, M.Á., Valencia-García, R., Alor-Hernández, G.: Automatic detection of satire in twitter: a psycholinguistic-based approach. Knowl. Based Syst. **128**, 20–33 (2017). https://doi.org/10.1016/j.knosys.2017.04.009

25. Sebastiani, F.: Machine learning in automated text categorization. ACM Comput. Surv. **34**, 1–47 (2002). Consiglio nazionale delle ricerche

26. Singh, V.K., Ghosh, S., Jose, C.: Toward multimodal cyberbullying detection. In: Proceedings of the 2017 CHI Conference Extended Abstracts on Human Factors in Computing Systems, pp. 2090–2099 (2017)

27. Sylak-Glassman, J., Kirov, C., Yarowsky, D., Que, R.: A language-independent feature schema for inflectional morphology. In: Proceedings of the 53rd Annual Meeting of the Association for Computational Linguistics and the 7th International Joint Conference on Natural Language Processing, vol. 2: Short Papers, pp. 674–680 (2015)

28. Tausczik, Y.R., Pennebaker, J.W.: The psychological meaning of words: LIWC and computerized text analysis methods. J. Lang. Soc. Psychol. **29**(1), 24–54 (2010)

29. Thompson, K.: Programming techniques: regular expression search algorithm. Commun. ACM **11**(6), 419–422 (1968)
30. Turney, P.D.: Thumbs up or thumbs down? Semantic orientation applied to unsupervised classification of reviews, pp. 417–424. arXiv preprint cs/0212032 (2002)
31. Yun-tao, Z., Ling, G., Yong-cheng, W.: An improved TF-IDF approach for text classification. J. Zhejiang Univ.-Sci. A **6**(1), 49–55 (2005). https://doi.org/10.1007/BF02842477
32. Zhang, Y., Jin, R., Zhou, Z.H.: Understanding bag-of-words model: a statistical framework. Int. J. Mach. Learn. Cybern. **1**(1–4), 43–52 (2010)

Knowledge Extraction from Twitter Towards Infectious Diseases in Spanish

Óscar Apolinario-Arzube[1], José Antonio García-Díaz[2],
Harry Luna-Aveiga[1], José Medina-Moreira[3],
and Rafael Valencia-García[2(✉)]

[1] Facultad de Ciencias Matemáticas y Físicas, Universidad de Guayaquil,
Cdla. Universitaria Salvador Allende, Guayaquil 090514, Ecuador
{oscar.apolinarioa,harry.lunaa}@ug.edu.ec
[2] Facultad de Informática, Universidad de Murcia,
Campus de Espinardo, 30100 Murcia, Spain
{joseantonio.garcia8,valencia}@um.es
[3] Facultad de Ciencias Agrarias, Universidad Agraria del Ecuador,
Av. 25 de Julio, Guayaquil, Ecuador
jmedina@uagraria.edu.ec

Abstract. Infodemiology consists in the extraction and analysis of data compiled on the Internet regarding public health. Among other applications, Infodemiology can be used to analyse trends on social networks in order to determine the prevalence of outbreaks of infectious diseases in certain regions. This valuable data provides better understanding of the spread of infectious diseases as well as a vision about social perception of citizens towards the strategies carried out by public healthcare institutions. In this work, we apply Natural Language Processing techniques to determine the impact of outbreaks of infectious diseases such as Zika, Dengue or Chikungunya from a compiled dataset with tweets written in Spanish.

Keywords: Infodemiology · Information retrieval · Opinion mining · Sentiment analysis · Machine learning

1 Introduction

Almost all daily tasks have undergone some kind of revolution due to recent advances in telecommunication technologies. Nowadays, the way in which knowledge is acquired and shared has led to important advances in areas such as education, healthcare or world trade [44]. One of the milestones that caused this revolution was the rising of Web 2.0, which shifted the way in which information is spread on the Internet, giving to the users a main role in the creation of content [23]. However, the content on the Internet is usually published in natural language, which hinders the capability of exploit it automatically, but recent advances in machine learning algorithms along with new techniques concerning Natural Language Processing (NLP) are overcoming these difficulties.

© Springer Nature Switzerland AG 2020
R. Valencia-García et al. (Eds.): CITI 2020, CCIS 1309, pp. 43–57, 2020.
https://doi.org/10.1007/978-3-030-62015-8_4

In regard to the healthcare domain, the benefits of communication technologies has derived in a new research field known as infodemiology, which provides first hand information from the Internet in order to carry out epidemiological studies for the evaluation, prediction and mitigation of outbreaks of infectious diseases [16]. Infodemiology provides new data sources apart from traditional ones, such as mortality data, public surveys, laboratory data, or demographic data among others [38]. It is worth noting that the applications of infodemiology are not limited to the infectious diseases domain and other topics has been analysed from an infodemiology perspective, such as childhood vaccination [45], or supporting decision-making on health-related issues [9].

Infectious diseases, such as Zika or Dengue, have a high prevalence in tropical areas [37]. These diseases are commonly transmitted by arthropod vectors and have rapidly expanded becoming a serious health and economic threat [31]. Consequently, in this work we apply an infodemiological approach based on NLP techniques with a self-compiled corpus from tweets regarding the Zika, Dengue, and Chikungunya viruses in tweets written in Spanish. This corpus is analysed in-depth in order to discover what are the issues that concern citizens as well as we apply Sentiment Analysis (SA) techniques in order to analyse users opinions in a fine-grained detail.

The rest of the paper is structured as follows: Sect. 2 contains background information related to Infodemiology and NLP techniques such as SA. Section 3 describes the corpus based on descriptive statistics and geolocation data. Section 4 describes the representation techniques and supervised learning algorithms that will provide clarity of the research carried out, and, finally, Sect. 5 suggests some future lines regarding this research.

2 Background Information

This section contains focused information of the technologies involved in this work: (1) Infodemiology (see Sect. 2.1) and (2) Sentiment Analysis (see Sect. 2.2).

2.1 Infodemiology

Infodemiology is a novel field of study focused on improving public health by tracking data from the Internet and mobile phones [15]. One of the key-benefits of Infodemiology is that it allows to compile epidemiological data faster than traditional approaches as citizens write and share the experiences on social networks [8]. The first works that made reference to infodemiology were based on finding a correlation between user's search queries in search engines and messages in social networks. Some of the diseases analysed were the flu [14], the H1N1 [8], or the SARS [13]. The correlation between data on the Internet and the prevalence of infectious diseases suggests that public health events can be anticipated and confronted.

One of the challenges of infodemiology is that the information on the Internet sometimes lacks scientific rigour, or it is misleading, resulting in poor quality data. This is a risk in itself as can be seen in [22], in which the authors conducted an study regarding the prevention methods of the COVID-19 disease by analysing the information by using popular search engines. The authors found significant differences regarding certain recommendations, such as those related to the conditions in which to wear facial masks were recommended. Another example related to the quality of information on the Internet can be seen in [10], in which the authors searched for misleading health information regarding COVID-19 and they found poor quality rates of the information which is a severe risk to public health.

We can find in the bibliography works that deal specifically with Zika and Dengue. In [12], for example, the authors extracted information in real-time from Twitter regarding Dengue and Typhoid Fever in the Philippines. They found a strong positive correlation between the tweets and official surveillance data. In [7], the authors extracted information concerning Zika virus from several social networks, such as Facebook, Youtube, Instagram, or Twitter; and they categorised each piece of information as useful, not useful or misleading. Although an important amount of misleading and not useful information was found, the authors concluded that social media is a useful resource to find out about the Zika virus. Another work can be found at [2], in which the authors conducted an infodemiology-based study with a balanced corpus of infectious diseases compiled from Central America in which two machine-learning classifiers based on decision trees and Support Vector Machines (SVM) as well as different statistical methods regarding SA were compared.

2.2 Sentiment Analysis

NLP is a subfield of Artificial Intelligence (AI) in which several computational techniques are applied for the automatic analysis and representation of human language such as part-of-speech (PoS) tagging, machine translations, or chatbots [46]. Although the origins of NLP go back to the 50s, recent advances in computer science and telecommunications have led NLP to be on trend. One of the causes of this success is Machine Learning (ML), which provides computers with the capacity of inferring predictive models from discovering underlying patterns from data without being explicitly programmed for it. In this sense, computers gain the ability to learn through experience instead of the need of being explicitly programmed for solving specific tasks [5]. ML can be categorised into supervised learning [6] and unsupervised learning [27], according if for a set of input data we know the correct output data beforehand or not.

SA consists in the extraction of the subjective polarity of a text [35]. SA has several practical applications: healthcare [41], finances [40], election forecasting [39], or product's review and marketing [34,36] just to name a few. In a nutshell, the objective of SA is to find tuples with (1) the entity being under consideration, (2) the specific part of the entity being analysed (known as the aspect), (3) the time in which the opinion was expressed, (4) the person who holds the sentiment and the (5) the subjective polarity of the opinion expressed [29]. However, it is common to find in the bibliography works that simplifies this tuple according to the scope of the problem addressed.

It is possible to conduct SA with different approaches, being the most popular: (1) keyword localisation, (2) lexical affinity, and (3) statistical methods. The first approach, keyword localisation, consists in the identification of sentiment words, such as *happy, sad, scared, boring* or, in general, any word in which a general sentiment can be assigned. An example of this approach can be found in [30], in which the authors obtained the polarity of different aspects regarding asthma. Their approach consisted in the identification of keywords in the texts and calculate their sentiment by averaging the sentiment of the surrounding words by using sentiment lexicons, such as SentiWordNet [4]. However, methods based on keyword localisation are weak because they do not handle well some linguistic phenomena such as the ambiguity of the language or the usage of negations. In this sense, methods based on lexical affinity take into account the grammatical relationships between the words and not only the words by themselves [11,25]. Statistical methods, on the other hand, take advantage of ML techniques in order to obtain the sentiment from linguistic [19,43], statistical [28], and contextual features [1]. Statistical methods are usually based on supervised classification, such as the work described in [32], in which the polarity was extracted by applying different classifiers from a corpus that was previously annotated by volunteers.

Among the approaches for conducting SA, those based on statistical methods with deep-learning are actually the most popular [46]. In order to apply these approaches, the texts must be encoded as vectors so computers can handle natural language. A popular and simple approach to encode documents as vectors is the Bag of Words (BoW) model, which consists in the representation of a text as the frequencies of the words that belong to a certain domain. A work in which the BoW model is used for SA is described in [42], in which the authors compared three machine classifiers: Bayes Network (BayesNet), Maximum entropy (ME) and Sequential Minimal Optimisation (SMO) from SVM classifiers. To solve the high dimensionality of the feature vector obtained by BoW, the authors employed different feature selection strategies, such as Information Gain (IG) or the Rough Set Theory (RST).

Aspect-based Sentiment Analysis (ABSA) is a type of SA capable to identify the specific part of the entity on which the affect is felt (the aspect) [26]. ABSA is challenging because the identification of aspects may require to apply knowledge-based technologies, such as ontologies or knowledge graphs, in order to detect the relationship among the concepts. An example of ABSA related to the infectious disease domain can be found at [18], in which the authors used a domain ontology for aspect extraction including those aspects that appeared explicitly in the texts as well as other aspects that were directly related to those concepts. For example, they assumed that if a text contains words related to mosquito bites, the document is also related (but in a minor degree) to specific mosquito-borne diseases. When all explicit and implicit aspects were extracted, the authors calculated the percentage of positive, neutral and negative sentiments of each aspect with a weighted average of the sentiment assigned to each text and the degree in which this document is related to that aspect.

3 Corpus

Twitter has become a popular social network that links users worldwide for sharing information on many topics to share their experiences, feelings and thoughts. One of the biggest Twitters strengths to conduct infodemiological studies is its public nature, allowing the analysis of posts through a public API [20]. This fact, along with the improvements of text mining techniques and machine learning algorithms, has caused Twitter to become popular among the research community [17].

For this research we compiled tweets regarding the Zika, Dengue, and Chikungunya viruses. All the tweets were written in Spanish and compiled between 2017 and 2020. Tweets were compiled periodically and, apart from the text of the tweet we also extracted their location (when available), their number of retweets (how many times has been shared), and their number of likes (how many times other users have reacted positively to it). In addition, we compiled data from the authors of the tweets, including their number of followers, how many people they are following, and how often they publish new content. While the tweets were being compiled, they were manually labelled by a group of volunteers who rated each tweet in the following categories: *very positive, positive, neutral, negative, very-negative, do-not-know,* and *out-of-domain.*

Once the tweets were compiled and labelled, we applied unsupervised methods in order to extract the polarity and subjectivity of the tweets. It is worth noting that the manual classification of the tweets have priority since we only use this information to obtain a estimate of the corpus quality. On the one hand, to calculate the polarity, we average the sentiment words of the tweets with a sentiment lexicon that contained general words that expressed *positive, neutral,* and *negative* sentiments. On the other, to calculate subjectivity we used the `Naive Bayes Analyzer`, which is based on the Stanford NLTK [24].

The statistics of the compiled corpus and the distribution of the sentiments are shown in Table 1. It will be observed that the corpus is unbalanced with a predominance of neutral tweets, which represents a 32.4771% of the whole corpus. The union of the *negative* and *very-negative* labels represents the 28.1341% of the corpus whereas the union of *positive* and *very-positive* represents only the 16.9993%. Tweets have an average number of words of 14.3450. This number varies from 2 to 55 but mostly falls between 8 and 16 words. We can also observe that the majority of tweets are between 45 and 145 characters but some of them are shorter whereas only a few reached to the Twitter's max length of 280 characters. Words have an average length of 6.4143 in ranges from 3 to 11, being 7 the most common length. Finally, we can observe that tweets labelled as *positive* and *very-positive* have a slightly larger average length of 97.62555 over the *negative* and *very-negative* tweets with an average length of 86.42129 (Fig. 1).

In order to obtain what are the keywords and topics most popular of the corpus, we obtained a representation of their word-embeddings. Word embeddings is one of the most popular representation of document vocabulary because it is capable of capturing the semantic and syntactic similarity among the words in

Table 1. Corpus statistics

Sentiment	Number	Avg. words	Avg. length	Avg. word	Polarity (%)	Subjectivity (%)
very_positive	1424	15.6580	100.8904	6.5102	0.1422	2.2885
positive	5101	14.7270	96.6880	6.6655	0.0289	1.9210
neutral	12,466	14.5233	91.2163	6.3758	0.0929	2.1264
negative	7565	14.0317	86.0002	6.1999	0.0544	1.8879
very_negative	3234	14.2718	87.4063	6.1911	0.0550	1.7791
do_not_know	441	14.0072	86.0003	6.4875	1.5584	3.3115
out_of_domain	9577	14.0021	82.0352	6.5576	0.3319	3.4725
Total	39,808	14.3450	88.6995	6.4143	0.1498	2.3693

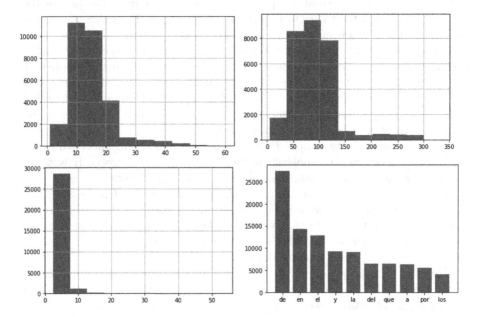

Fig. 1. Histograms representing (1) the number of words per tweet, (2) the length of the tweets, (3) the average length of words in the tweets, and the stop Word most used in the corpus.

a set of documents. The word-embeddings were calculated with Word2Vec [33], that is a technique to learn word embeddings using shallow neural networks. For this representation, we ignored words that appear less than 200 times. The word embeddings are shown in Fig. 2, where it can be observed that some related terms are clustered, such as *limpieza* (cleaning) and *fumigación* (fumigation); or the relationship between *aedes* and *mosquito* (mosquito) with *transmisión* (transmission). We can also observe that words that share meaning, such as *incremento* and *aumento* (increase), are clustered.

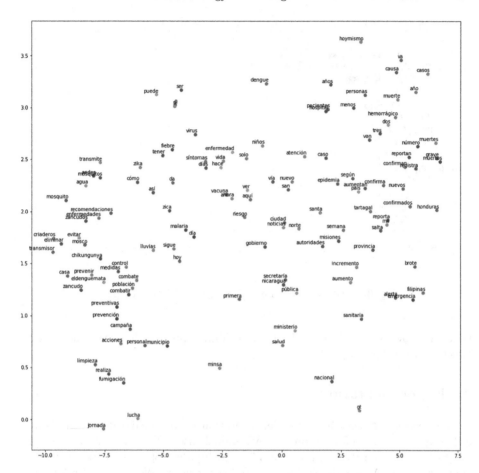

Fig. 2. Word-embeddings representation

Next, we extracted the named entities in order to determine if the tweets contain information regarding places, organisations or individuals. The ratio in which entity is found in the corpus is shown in Fig. 3, where we can observe that *PERSON*, which refers to people (including fictitious ones) and *Organisations* (ORG), which refers to companies or institutions, are the entities which appear more frequently followed by locations (GPE).

Finally, we extracted the geolocation of the tweets. On Twitter, users can decide what personal information they want to share. Regarding geolocation data, they can decide to share the exact location in which each tweet is published. However, as this option is disabled by default, it is hard to find tweets with its exact position in the map. In order to solve this drawback, we determined the geolocation of the tweets within a greater area by applying a reverse geocoding to the location of the author as it is common that users include in their profiles in which city or country they live. A heatmap with the distribution of compiled

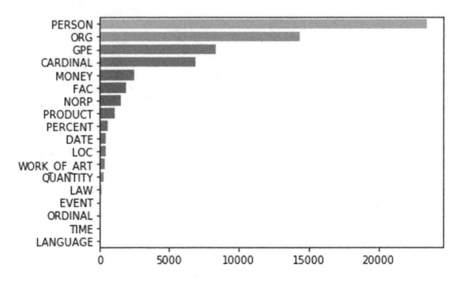

Fig. 3. Entities most commonly mentioned in the corpus.

tweets is shown in Fig. 4 in which intense colours represent the areas where more tweets were compiled.

4   Experimentation

In this section we describe the experimentation we have carried out, including a description of the information-retrieval models used. To carry out this experimentation, we used Python (version 3.5), the Jupiter Notebook workbench that comes with the Anaconda workbench, and scikit-learn. We also used relational databases to store the tweets, their contextual features and its geolocation.

The workflow for this experiment is depicted in Fig. 5. In a nutshell, the process starts with the Twitter API for the corpus compilation (see Sect. 3). Then, the corpus is divided into training and testing, and we carry out a feature extraction process in order to transform the documents into a meaningful representation that a machine can understand. Specifically, we applied the Bag of Words (BoW) model, which represents a document as a vector of a fixed-length vector which measures the frequency of certain words that belong to a pre-defined list. In its most simplest approach, BoW counts how many times each word of our dictionary appears in the document. Other approaches rely on TF-IDF (Term-Frequency Inverse Document Frequency) that downplays words that appear very frequently in the text [21]. In our proposal, we discarded low-appearance words in order to prevent odd words as well as words with high-appearance. Next, we evaluate the following machine learning classifiers: (1) Linear SVC (LSVC), (2) Logistic Regression (LR), (3) Multinomial Naive Bayes (MNB), and (4) Random Forest (RF). The comparison of these machine learning models is perform with the following metrics: accuracy (see Eq. 1), precision (see Eq. 2), recall (see Eq. 3)

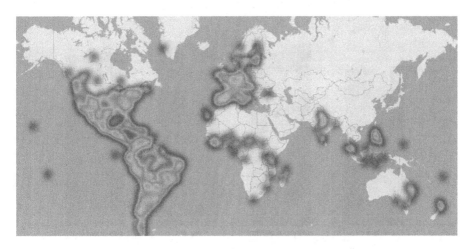

Fig. 4. Heatmap of the tweets of the corpus(Color figure online)

and F-measure (see Eq. 4). In order to compare our models, we will apply F1 score, that is the weighted average of the precision (how many selected instances are relevant) and recall (how many relevant instances are selected). Finally, the best machine learning model is used to label the validation dataset (Fig. 6).

$$Accuracy = TP + TN/(TP + TN + FP + FN), \tag{1}$$

$$Precision = TP/(TP + FP) \tag{2}$$

$$Recall = TP/(TP + FN) \tag{3}$$

$$F - Measure = 2 * (Precision * Recall)/(Precision + Recall) \tag{4}$$

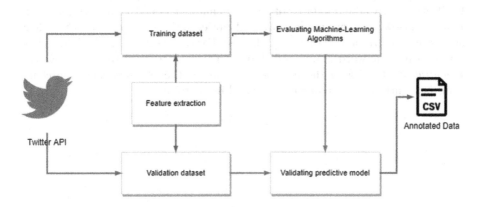

Fig. 5. Workflow architecture

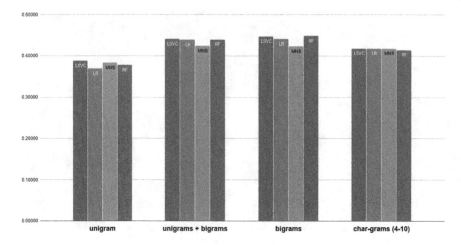

Fig. 6. Comparison of accuracy for unigrams, unigrams + bigrams, bigrams, and chargrams with the classifiers Linear SVC (LSVC), Logistic Regression (LR), Multinomial Naive Bayes (MNB) and Random Forest (RF)

The results of our experimentation are shown in Table 2. These results are based on a multi-class classification, composed in five-class: (1) very-positive, (2) positive, (3) neutral, (4) negative, and (5) very-negative.

With respect to the performance of the classifiers, we can observe that LR is the classifier that achieves the best accuracy when using unigrams alone or in combination with the bigrams. However, the accuracy of LR is slightly superior when bigrams are applied separately. In case of the char-grams, the results are similar to the ones obtained by the models based on BoW. In addition, we observe that the results achieved with RF achieves lower scores regarding precision which indicates that with this classifier very few of your positive predictions are true.

Since we performed a multi-class classification, we obtained the confusion matrix for the testing dataset of the best model based on word-gram and the best model based on char-gram (see Fig. 7). We can observe that the classifier classifies correctly a high number of tweets manually labelled as *negative, neutral,* or *positive*. However, both models have difficulties in the identification of the edge cases (*very-negative* and *very-positive* labels). For the tweets manually labelled as very-negative, the word-grams and char-grams considers that they are *negative* or *neutral*. In the case of the *very-positive* tweets, the classifier based on char-grams is slightly better than the one based in unigrams.

Table 2. Comparison of the precision (P), recall (R), F1 measure (F1) and accuracy (ACC) for unigrams, bigrams, unigrams and trigrams, and char-grams with the machine-learning classifiers: Linear SVC (LSVC), Logistic Regression (LR), Multinomial Naive Bayes (MNB), and Random Forest (RF)

Model	Classifier	P	R	F1	ACC
unigram	LSVC	0.2630	0.2614	0.2572	0.3880
	LR	0.2888	0.2710	0.2578	0.4413
	MNB	0.2740	0.2751	0.2550	**0.4476**
	RF	0.0837	0.2000	0.1180	0.4185
unigrams + bigrams	LSVC	0.2476	0.2481	0.2436	0.3696
	LR	0.2798	0.2650	0.2490	0.4394
	MNB	0.2639	0.2749	0.2579	**0.4419**
	RF	0.0837	0.2000	0.1180	0.4185
bigrams	LSVC	0.2481	0.2439	0.2385	0.3834
	LR	0.2708	0.2436	0.2232	**0.4246**
	MNB	0.2573	0.2535	0.2377	0.4241
	RF	0.0837	0.2000	0.1180	0.4185
char-grams (4–10)	LSVC	0.2669	0.2541	0.2516	0.3780
	LR	0.2943	0.2568	0.2337	0.4402
	MNB	0.2744	0.2603	0.2205	**0.4493**
	RF	0.1644	0.2015	0.1206	0.4149

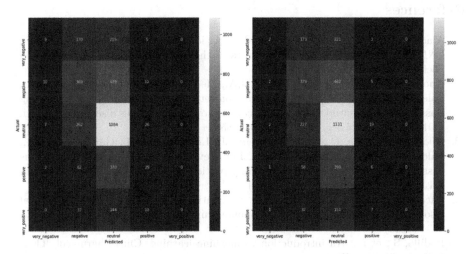

Fig. 7. Confusion matrix for the best models based on word-gram and char-gram respectively

5 Conclusions and Further Work

This paper describes an infodemiology study concerning infectious diseases, such as Zika, Dengue, and Chikungunya from tweets written in Spanish. In addition, this study evaluated the performance of several machine-learning algorithms to set a baseline regarding sentiment analysis in a five-class problem. This research is part of the project described in [3], that consists in the development of an intelligent platform for the monitoring of infectious diseases based on social networks and citizen participation. During the remaining time of the project, we will complete more scientific reports regarding intelligent data analysis guided by ontologies as well as we will evaluate the performance of deep-learning models based on word embeddings to conduct SA. Although the case studies designed to validate this platform were focused on infectious diseases such as Zika or Dengue, we are adapting this platform to recent outbreaks such as the COVID-19. In this sense, as the process of translating and identifying synonyms of an domain ontology is a time-consuming, we are studying techniques for the automatic translation of the terms.

Acknowledgements. This work has been supported by the Spanish National Research Agency (AEI) and the European Regional Development Fund (FEDER/ ERDF) through projects KBS4FIA (TIN2016-76323-R) and LaTe4PSP (PID2019-107652RB-I00). In addition, José Antonio García-Díaz has been supported by Banco Santander and University of Murcia through the Doctorado industrial programme.

References

1. Ajao, O., Bhowmik, D., Zargari, S.: Fake news identification on twitter with hybrid CNN and RNN models. In: Proceedings of the 9th International Conference on Social Media and Society, pp. 226–230 (2018)
2. Apolinardo-Arzube, O., García-Díaz, J.A., Medina-Moreira, J., Luna-Aveiga, H., Valencia-García, R.: Evaluating information-retrieval models and machine-learning classifiers for measuring the social perception towards infectious diseases. Appl. Sci. (2019). https://doi.org/10.3390/app9142858
3. Apolinario-Arzube, Ó., Medina-Moreira, J., Luna-Aveiga, H., García-Díaz, J.A., Valencia-García, R., Estrade-Cabrera, J.I.: Prevención de enfermedades infecciosas basada en el análisis inteligente en rrss y participación ciudadana. Procesamiento del Lenguaje Nat. **63**, 163–166 (2019)
4. Baccianella, S., Esuli, A., Sebastiani, F.: SentiWordNet 3.0: an enhanced lexical resource for sentiment analysis and opinion mining. In: LREC, vol. 10, pp. 2200–2204 (2010)
5. Badillo, S., et al.: An introduction to machine learning. Clin. Pharmacol. Ther. **107**(4), 871–885 (2020)
6. Baviera, T.: Técnicas para el análisis de sentimiento en twitter: aprendizaje automático supervisado y sentistrength. Rev. Dígitos **1**(3), 33–50 (2017)
7. Chandrasekaran, N., et al.: The utility of social media in providing information on Zika virus. Cureus **9**(10), e1792 (2017)
8. Chew, C., Eysenbach, G.: Pandemics in the age of Twitter: content analysis of tweets during the 2009 H1N1 outbreak. PLoS ONE **5**(11), e14118 (2010)

9. Cortés, V.D., Velásquez, J.D., Ibáñez, C.F.: Twitter for marijuana infodemiology. In: Proceedings of the International Conference on Web Intelligence, pp. 730–736 (2017)
10. Cuan-Baltazar, J.Y., Muñoz-Perez, M.J., Robledo-Vega, C., Pérez-Zepeda, M.F., Soto-Vega, E.: Misinformation of COVID-19 on the internet: infodemiology study. JMIR Public Health Surveill. 6(2), e18444 (2020). https://doi.org/10.2196/18444. http://publichealth.jmir.org/2020/2/e18444/
11. Dey, L., Haque, S.K.: Opinion mining from noisy text data. In: Proceedings of SIGIR 2008 Workshop on Analytics for Noisy Unstructured Text Data, AND 2008 (2008). https://doi.org/10.1145/1390749.1390763
12. Espina, K., Estuar, M.R.J.E.: Infodemiology for syndromic surveillance of dengue and typhoid fever in the Philippines. Procedia Comput. Sci. 121, 554–561 (2017). https://doi.org/10.1016/j.procs.2017.11.073. http://www.sciencedirect.com/science/article/pii/S1877050917322731
13. Eysenbach, G.: SARS and population health technology. J. Med. Internet Res. 5(2), e14 (2003)
14. Eysenbach, G.: Infodemiology: tracking flu-related searches on the web for syndromic surveillance. In: AMIA Annual Symposium Proceedings, vol. 2006, p. 244. American Medical Informatics Association (2006)
15. Eysenbach, G.: Medicine 2.0: social networking, collaboration, participation, apomediation, and openness. J. Med. Internet Res. 10(3), e22 (2008)
16. Eysenbach, G.: Infodemiology and infoveillance: framework for an emerging set of public health informatics methods to analyze search, communication and publication behavior on the internet. J. Med. Internet Res. 11(1), e11 (2009)
17. Fiesler, C., Proferes, N.: "Participant" perceptions of Twitter research ethics. Soc. Media+ Soc. 4(1) (2018). https://doi.org/10.1177/2056305118763366
18. García-Díaz, J.A., Cánovas-García, M., Valencia-García, R.: Ontology-driven aspect-based sentiment analysis classification: an infodemiological case study regarding infectious diseases in Latin America. Future Gener. Comput. Syst. Impress 112, 641–657 (2020)
19. García-Díaz, J.A., Cánovas-García, M., Colomo-Palacios, R., Valencia-García, R.: Detecting misogyny in Spanish tweets: an approach based on linguistics features and word embeddings. Future Gener. Comput. Syst. 114, 506–518 (2021). https://doi.org/10.1016/j.future.2020.08.032. http://www.sciencedirect.com/science/article/pii/S0167739X20301928
20. Gu, Y., Qian, Z.S., Chen, F.: From Twitter to detector: real-time traffic incident detection using social media data. Transp. Res. Part C: Emerg. Technol. 67, 321–342 (2016)
21. Havrlant, L., Kreinovich, V.: A simple probabilistic explanation of term frequency-inverse document frequency (TF-IDF) heuristic (and variations motivated by this explanation). Int. J. Gen. Syst. 46(1), 27–36 (2017)
22. Hernández-García, I., Giménez-Júlvez, T.: Assessment of health information about COVID-19 prevention on the internet: infodemiological study. JMIR Public Health Surveill. 6(2), e18717 (2020). https://doi.org/10.2196/18717. https://publichealth.jmir.org/2020/2/e18717
23. Hockx-Yu, H.: The Web as History (2018)
24. Jeevan Nagendra Kumar, Y., Mani Sai, B., Shailaja, V., Renuka, S., Panduri, B.: Python NLTK sentiment inspection using Naïve Bayes classifier. Int. J. Recent Technol. Eng. (2019). https://doi.org/10.35940/ijrte.B1328.0982S1119
25. Khan, A., Baharudin, B., Khan, K.: Sentiment classification using sentence-level lexical based. Trends Appl. Sci. Res. 6(10), 1141–1157 (2011)

26. Kim, S.M., Hovy, E.: Identifying and analyzing judgment opinions. In: HLT-NAACL 2006 - Human Language Technology Conference of the North American Chapter of the Association of Computational Linguistics, Proceedings of the Main Conference (2006). https://doi.org/10.3115/1220835.1220861

27. Larsson, G., Maire, M., Shakhnarovich, G.: Learning representations for automatic colorization. In: Leibe, B., Matas, J., Sebe, N., Welling, M. (eds.) ECCV 2016. LNCS, vol. 9908, pp. 577–593. Springer, Cham (2016). https://doi.org/10.1007/978-3-319-46493-0_35

28. Lim, W.L., Ho, C.C., Ting, C.-Y.: Tweet sentiment analysis using deep learning with nearby locations as features. In: Alfred, R., Lim, Y., Haviluddin, H., On, C.K. (eds.) Computational Science and Technology. LNEE, vol. 603, pp. 291–299. Springer, Singapore (2020). https://doi.org/10.1007/978-981-15-0058-9_28

29. Liu, B.: Sentiment analysis and opinion mining. Synth. Lect. Hum. Lang. Technol. **5**(1), 1–167 (2012)

30. Luna-Aveiga, H., et al.: Sentiment polarity detection in social networks: an approach for asthma disease management. In: Le, N.-T., Van Do, T., Nguyen, N.T., Thi, H.A.L. (eds.) ICCSAMA 2017. AISC, vol. 629, pp. 141–152. Springer, Cham (2018). https://doi.org/10.1007/978-3-319-61911-8_13

31. Mayer, S.V., Tesh, R.B., Vasilakis, N.: The emergence of arthropod-borne viral diseases: a global prospective on Dengue, Chikungunya and Zika fevers. Acta Tropica **166**, 155–163 (2017). https://doi.org/10.1016/j.actatropica.2016.11.020. http://www.sciencedirect.com/science/article/pii/S0001706X16306246

32. García-Díaz, J.A., et al.: Opinion mining for measuring the social perception of infectious diseases. an infodemiology approach. In: Valencia-García, R., Alcaraz-Mármol, G., Del Cioppo-Morstadt, J., Vera-Lucio, N., Bucaram-Leverone, M. (eds.) CITI 2018. CCIS, vol. 883, pp. 229–239. Springer, Cham (2018). https://doi.org/10.1007/978-3-030-00940-3_17

33. Mikolov, T., Chen, K., Corrado, G., Dean, J.: Efficient estimation of word representations in vector space (2013)

34. Mostafa, M.M.: More than words: social networks' text mining for consumer brand sentiments. Expert Syst. Appl. **40**(10), 4241–4251 (2013)

35. Pang, B., Lee, L., et al.: Opinion mining and sentiment analysis. Found. Trends® Inf. Retrieval **2**(1–2), 1–135 (2008)

36. Paredes-Valverde, M.A., Colomo-Palacios, R., Salas-Zárate, M.d.P., Valencia-García, R.: Sentiment analysis in Spanish for improvement of products and services: a deep learning approach. Sci. Program. **2017** (2017)

37. Patterson, J., Sammon, M., Garg, M.: Dengue, Zika and Chikungunya: emerging arboviruses in the new world. West. J. Emerg. Med. **17**(6), 671 (2016)

38. Pearce, N.: Traditional epidemiology, modern epidemiology, and public health. Am. J. Public Health **86**(5), 678–683 (1996)

39. Ramteke, J., Shah, S., Godhia, D., Shaikh, A.: Election result prediction using Twitter sentiment analysis. In: 2016 International Conference on Inventive Computation Technologies (ICICT), vol. 1, pp. 1–5. IEEE (2016)

40. Ruiz-Martínez, J.M., Valencia-García, R., García-Sánchez, F., et al.: Semantic-based sentiment analysis in financial news. In: Proceedings of the 1st International Workshop on Finance and Economics on the Semantic Web, pp. 38–51 (2012)

41. Salas-Zárate, M.d.P., Medina-Moreira, J., Lagos-Ortiz, K., Luna-Aveiga, H., Rodriguez-Garcia, M.A., Valencia-Garcia, R.: Sentiment analysis on tweets about Diabetes: an aspect-level approach. Comput. Math. Methods Med. **2017** (2017)

42. Salas-Zárate, M.D.P., Paredes-Valverde, M.A., Limon-Romero, J., Tlapa, D., Baez-Lopez, Y.: Sentiment classification of Spanish reviews: an approach based on feature selection and machine learning methods. J. UCS **22**(5), 691–708 (2016)

43. del Pilar Salas-Zárate, M., Paredes-Valverde, M.A., Rodriguez-García, M.Á., Valencia-García, R., Alor-Hernández, G.: Automatic detection of satire in Twitter: a psycholinguistic-based approach. Knowl. Based Syst. **128**, 20–33 (2017). https://doi.org/10.1016/j.knosys.2017.04.009

44. Saldanha, T.J., Krishnan, M.S.: Organizational adoption of web 2.0 technologies: an empirical analysis. J. Organ. Comput. Electron. Commer. **22**(4), 301–333 (2012)

45. Wolfe, R.M., Sharp, L.K.: Vaccination or immunization? The impact of search terms on the internet. J. Health Commun. **10**(6), 537–551 (2005). https://doi.org/10.1080/10810730500228847. pMID: 16203632

46. Young, T., Hazarika, D., Poria, S., Cambria, E.: Recent trends in deep learning based natural language processing. IEEE Comput. Intell. Mag. **13**(3), 55–75 (2018)

Prediction of Energy Consumption in an Electric Arc Furnace Using Weka

Nury León-Munizaga[1] (✉) [iD], Maritza Aguirre-Munizaga[2] [iD], Katty Lagos-Ortiz[2] [iD], and Javier Del Cioppo-Morstadt[2] [iD]

[1] School of Engineering, Cardiff University Queen's Buildings, The Parade Cardiff, CF24 3AA Cardiff, UK
`leonnc@cardiff.ac.uk`
[2] Universidad Agraria del Ecuador, Facultad de Ciencias Agrarias, Av. 25 de Julio, Guayaquil, Ecuador
`{maguirre,klagos,jdelcioppo}@uagraria.edu.ec`

Abstract. Industry 4.0 and digital transformation have managed to integrate technology into production processes with the aim of improving their automation levels. The purpose of this research was to identify some potentially useful and understandable patterns from the energy consumption data of an Electric Arc Furnace (EAF), starting from the hypothesis that the final energy consumption of an EAF depends on the different types of waste that are used to power the oven. The process was applied as part of the methodology Knowledge Discovery in Databases in order to collect, select and transform data. Then Weka software was used to discover predictive models and rules that were evaluated and interpreted to obtain knowledge. The methodological process to build the appropriate model that fits the collected data is described in this work, able to generate an effective prediction of energy used in steel production processes with an EAF. Through simulations, the prediction models were tested, and some conclusions were reached regarding the accuracy of the models. The results about the models are presented by means of a comparative table, in which the model M5P would have greater accuracy at the time of predicting the energy consumption for identifying which would be the optimal composition of the material to feed the furnace and therefore improve the efficiency of the metal melting process.

Keywords: KDD · Electric arc furnace · Automation · Weka

1 Introduction

Today's industry has an urgent need to dive into digitalization of manufacturing processes, due to the fact that these processes help improve productivity. Industry 4.0 represents the fourth industrial revolution [1], which defines a level of organization, management and control of the value chain of the life cycle of products, and is oriented to the needs of users. This industry consists of interconnecting all the production units of a company, achieving effective automation and obtaining a smarter company, through connectivity, digital information and digital access to the customer. These processes

© Springer Nature Switzerland AG 2020
R. Valencia-García et al. (Eds.): CITI 2020, CCIS 1309, pp. 58–70, 2020.
https://doi.org/10.1007/978-3-030-62015-8_5

include the internet of things IoT, industrial internet, smart manufacturing, cloud-based manufacturing, cyber-physical systems, industrial integration, business architecture, service-oriented architecture, business process management, the integration of industrial information, among other processes [2–5].

In short, because of the aforementioned, companies that are willing to achieve the digital transformation of their production processes must have the ability to interoperability and mass data collection of all the components that are part of their production processes, and must also be able to manage and analyze those massive amounts of data. For this type of analysis, big data, data analytics and data mining technologies must be implemented [6–8], since these technologies and methods can transform data into useful and necessary information, in order to be processed for creating smart and flexible systems.

Figure 1 shows the technologies that are the basis for predictive manufacturing systems (PMS) and their interconnection [9]. Big data and data mining tools play an essential role in the process to find a valid and understandable model that describes patterns according to the information obtained. This methodological process is known as discovery of knowledge in databases (KDD) [10], so are also immersed other techniques that use statistics and intelligent systems such as pattern recognition [11], which can recognize text, number, video or audio patterns.

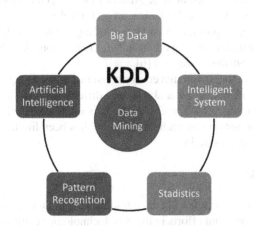

Fig. 1. Predictive manufacturing systems technologies

Product manufacturing systems today use the pattern recognition technique, relying on current pattern behavior to solve future situations. Thus, manufacturing systems nowadays can predict future events during the manufacturing chain or cycle.

The primary purpose of this KDD exercise is to predict the energy consumption while feeding an Electric Arc Furnace (EAF) [1] with different kinds of ferrous scraps during steel production operation. It is based on the datasets collected from a real-world steel mill, which contents 3493 instances and 21 attributes, including raw data from inputs, outputs and parameters. In this research, it is important to try different models and choose the one which can accurately predict the final energy consumption of the EAF [2] and can be fed with the collected datasets.

The working principle of EAFs is to use the heat produced by electric current between graphite electrodes to melt the recycled ferrous scraps, during the process it is blowed oxygen to purify the steel and other metals are added to give the required chemical composition [3]. EAFs are widely used to produce steels, including carbon steels and alloy steels, and according to industrial efficiency technology database [4], "about 1/3 of the steel production in the world is done through recycling of ferrous-scrap with the use of an Electric Arc Furnace."

The advantages of EAFs in the steel industry are quite obvious. Firstly, it uses recycled ferrous scraps to produce new steel, which can help to minimize industrial waste and make a reuse of ferrous scraps. Secondly, compared with other kinds of furnaces, the manufacturing process of the equipment is more straightforward, and it takes less space in the manufacturing floor. However, the process of EAFs consumes a tremendous amount of energy which is mainly used for scrap melting, as well as different chemical reactions. This energy is provided by electric power, which is related with a high cost and results in a low efficiency of the process.

For the purpose of reducing costs, as well as producing better quality of steel, a reliable prediction is required. Luckily, nowadays we have a really powerful tool that is Data Mining for processing massive datasets and making predictions or classifications [5].

Waikato Environment for Knowledge Analysis (WEKA) tool has been used for the application of the miner database. Weka is a project developed by Waiko University in New Zealand, this project provides a collection of algorithms for data pre-processing (filtering) and data mining, including algorithms for regression, classification, grouping, association rules, and attribute selection [6].

In this research, the aim is to predict energy consumption focusing mainly on increasing the efficiency of the process by analyzing the different combinations and compositions of the scrap mix which feeds the furnace. This model is based on the correlation between energy consumption and each attribute and has been limited by boundaries of productivity and energy required [7].

2   Related Work

The steelmaker sector, regardless of being a traditional and mature activity, it's characterized for realizing important efforts in the new technologies camps of fabrication and improvement of products qualities.

Electric arc furnace (EAF) steelmaking technology has been applied for more than one hundred years. For this technology, solid forms of raw materials such as scrap and Ferro alloys are used to produce special grades of steels. Solid raw material was firstly melted through direct arc melting, refined and tapped for further processing. The reaction between raw materials and additives consists of three phases: melting, oxidizing and reducing.

Even though the steel industry it's very common in the use of classic techniques to develop mathematical models that explain the behavior of a product or a process, it is more and more common the use of data mining techniques to obtain a broader knowledge of the fabrication processes and to develop strategies to decrease expenses, improve product quality and increase productivity.

Data mining uses inferences and statistical analysis to extract interesting trends and events that create useful reports, support decision making, etc. Exploit vast amounts of data to achieve business, operational, or scientific goals [8].

The amount of extracted data of production processes have increased exponentially due to the proliferation of detection technologies. When processed and analyzed, the data can provide valuable information and insight into the manufacturing process, production system, and equipment. Previous research is taken as a reference to affirm that, in industries; equipment maintenance is an important key and affects equipment uptime and efficiency. Therefore, it is necessary to identify and solve equipment failures, avoiding stops in production processes [9], many companies aim to act responsibly and set goals for environmental improvement. Therefore, they must measure performance in terms of saving energy and fresh water or reducing waste, released volatile organic compounds and greenhouse gas emissions.

In this context, the research [10] applied a knowledge discovery database (KDD) approach for the analysis within the automotive industry to determine the influence of volatile organic compounds released and greenhouse gas emissions on pollution. Other related research [11] is based on defining a method in the context of data mining, to model stripping data from many records collected by observing fabrication activities. The method allows building a repository to characterize the disassembly time of joining elements (for example, screws) considering different characteristics and conditions, it has been tested to evaluate the most relevant corrective factors in consideration to estimate the unscrewing time of multiple types of screws.

3   Data Understanding

Making the data preprocessing [12] is the essential stage in data mining. For this reason, the next paragraph describes how this process has been carried out with the source data taken from the steel industry.

In the first table, the data was converted to the same unit in Kg or hours, transforming the records that are in numerical form to the nominal form (used for classification and J48 algorithm) by using Weka preprocessing. Once the classification had been carried out, useless data such as Heat Number was eliminated; as shown in Table 1, this action could reduce the number of calculated data samples and increase the precision of data processing in Weka [13].

An example of missing values is shown in Table 2. Between 12 and 28 missing values were detected in the attributes Lime & Dolomite and Dolomite respectively, there are also some missing data [14] gathered in the same attributes. It is widely believed that missing values can lead to difficulties in the algorithm for execution and calculation, so the root cause should be analyzed as it can also represent a problem with the equipment during the data collection process. These attributes with missing data [15] were safely examined and repaired by replacing them with the mean because it was possible to observe that these values were similar in all data sets.

Table 1. Removing useless data

No.	Name
1	Clean bales 1 (Kg)
2	Clean bales 2 (Kg)
3	Steel turnings (Kg)
4	Tin can (Kg)
5	Estructural (Kg)
6	Fragmentized scrap (Kg)
7	Merchant 1 & 2 (Kg)
8	Recovered Scrap (Kg)
9	EAF (MWh)
10	Power on time (min)
11	Secondary oxygen (Kg)
12	Main oxygen (Kg)
13	Natural gas (Kg)
14	Argon (Kg)
15	Carbon injected (Kg)
16	Lime and Dolomite (Kg)

Table 2. Samples with missing values

Steel grade nominal	Secondary oxygen Kg	Main oxygen Kg	Natural gas Kg
KP22	?	?	?
KP18	?	?	?
KP08	942	?	?
KP18	?	?	?

The generation of a good model is based on the fact that the analyzed database contains complete and valid observations so that it is possible to determine the essential characteristics of the data and, therefore, make accurate predictions. To do this, as a stage prior to the modelling of the data, preliminary analysis and debugging is carried out.

A database with 2329 correct samples was obtained from the steel sector. With them, it was tried to get an estimated value of the energy consumption in the EAF. The proposed model has 16 input variables, in the source data the problem is faced, due to human failures due to inaccurate movements, very high currents are produced continuously, which in turn leads to the destruction of many of the system components. Another human error that could be detected in the source data is in the Steel grade attribute, two records presented a date format which is also presented as a human error in the data collection process and it is emphasized that it could be solved by changing the cell format.

4 Methodology

The effective prediction of energy consumption during the steel melting processing is made by using regression algorithms of Machine Learning, which are basically able to predict output values based on input features from the collected datasets.

The first main step in data analysis is understanding the provided data set, this could be completed by doing some research about the context of the supplied data and searching for patterns and missing data. After this deep analysis of the provided data, the following step is to manipulate the data by removing the missing values and ensuring the uniformity in the standard units.

After the data has been manipulated adequately, the data would be uploaded on Weka in the preprocess tab. Preprocess tab is used to study attributes in the data and remove irrelevant and incorrect attributes according to data understanding. The relevance of the attributes is collated through using the ranker method [17] in the "Select Attributes" tab. After this stage, the least relevant attributes should be removed. The data would be filtered as the attribute is transformed from numeric to nominal. Weka software always illustrates the samples as numerical, and the attributes at numerical condition negatively influence the reliability of the result to be acquired.

Moreover, the application in classifiers is called multilayer perceptron. According to previous tutorials and tests, multilayer perception could demonstrate the best accuracy over other classification algorithms. In this classification, the clean data set has 2328 instances, which works with the 90% of it (2096 instances) and save 10% (232 instances) by using the Resample filter and No Replacement feature to assure that the test data set could not content repeated values from the training set. The training data set was used to build the model, and the testing data should be used to set up the accuracy of the model and inspect for outliers.

Finally, visualize classifier errors could identify and clarify the deviation of actual energy consumption and predicted energy usage from the given data set. It is also applied to analyze the relationship between energy consumption and each scrap utilized with input attributes.

4.1 Model Building

After cleaning human error in datasets, feature reduction should be made to improve the accuracy of the algorithm. According to the background of EAFs steel production operation, the "productivity" and "energy requirement per ton" can be used as a metric to set boundaries to help cleaning those infrequent values.

The first one is calculating the Productivity of the EAF, a general formula is used to interpret the efficiency of steel production operation; it is shown as below:

$$\%Procutivity = Billet\ (tons)Total\ Scrap\ Mix\ tons\ \times\ 100 \qquad (1)$$

When this calculation was made, another error was noticed. The number of "Total Scrap Mix" should be bigger than that of "Billet tons", however, there are 76 instances in which the output was bigger than the input, so they were also removed. Figure 5 shows that almost 87% of the batches recorded had an efficiency over 83%, based on it, the batches with the lowest efficiency were removed.

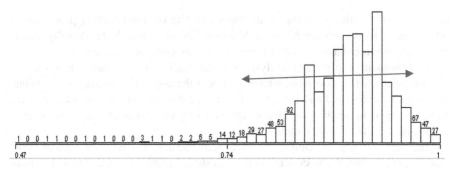

Fig. 2. %Productivity distribution

In addition, energy consumed in one unit was calculated to set boundaries to help reduce the data quantity and improve the accuracy of the algorithm. Energy consumption will change according to the chemical energy reactions produced by the mixed scrap; in other words, it depends on the amount of Total Scrap Mix used as input. As a result, a formula is given as below in Fig. 6 and an optimal range (0.301 to 0.352 MWh/ton) is chosen to make a model (Fig. 3).

$$Energy\ Required\ \left(\frac{MWh}{Tons}\right) = \frac{EAF\ (MWh)}{Total\ Scrap\ Mix\ (tons)} \tag{2}$$

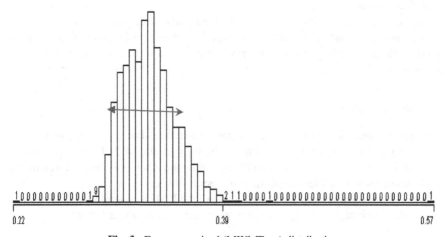

Fig. 3. Energy required (MWh/Tons) distribution

In the next step, for the sake of predicting energy usage in the production process, it is crucial to identify which attributes are more useful and essential. After comparing different evaluators, the "Correlation Attribute" evaluator was applied; and because it requires a nominal data type of EAF, the data type was changed by using the "Discretize filter". Then, an attribute evaluator called "CorrelationAttributeEval" [18] and a search method called "Ranker" with the application of Cross-Validation were used to get insights about the relation between the attributes and the EAF power consumption. Results are shown in Table 3.

Table 3. Correlation attribute evaluation

Average merit	Average rank	Attribute
0.143 ± 0.002	1 ± 0 10	Power on time (min)
0.109 ± 0.002	2.2 ± 0.4 15	Carbon injected (Kg)
0.103 ± 0.003	2.8 ± 0.4 11	Secondary oxygen
0.085 ± 0.002	4.2 ± 0.4 6	Fragmentized scrap
0.081 ± 0.002	4.8 ± 0.4 12	Main oxygen
0.054 ± 0.002	6 ± 0 16	Lime and Dolomite (Kg)
0.038 ± 0.003	7.2 ± 0.6 7	Merchant 1 & 2
0.033 ± 0.002	8.7 ± 0.9 13	Natural gas
0.032 ± 0.002	9.3 ± 1.27 5	Structural
0.031 ± 0.001	9.8 ± 1.08 8	Recovered scrap
0.031 ± 0.003	10.5 ± 1.5 1	Clean bales 1
0.028 ± 0.001	12.1 ± 0.94 4	Tin can
0.028 ± 0.001	12.4 ± 0.66 3	Steel turnings
0.024 ± 0.002	14.2 ± 0.4 2	Clean bales 2
0.02 ± 0.003	14.8 ± 0.4 17	Dolomite (Kg)
0.015 ± 0.001	16 ± 0 14	14 Argon (Kg)

Different correlations between attributes and energy can be seen in Table 3. Combined with the background of EAFs working process, a boundary of 0.028 was set to remove the least four correlated attributes, which are Dolomite, Clean bales 2 and Argon. The purpose of this step was supposed to select the most intimate attributes with energy and increase the accuracy; however, after compared with the result using whole attributes, the correlation coefficient did not improve; as a result, all the attributes were kept.

The data has been well prepared, there are 2328 instances and 17 attributes (including the EAF) left, the next step is to split the clean data to two parts, one is used for building models, and another is used for tests. Finally, a ratio of 9:1 was set, which means training on 90% partition and testing on the remaining 10%. This was implemented by setting in the "filter-resample".

The most important part is to choose suitable algorithms to build models. After comparison, five algorithms J48 [19], linear regression, decision table, multilayer perceptron and M5P model [20] were analyzed and the list narrowed down to the one with the best accuracy based on the correlation coefficient, as shown in Table 4.

Table 4. Accuracy models

Model	Correlation coefficient
M5P	0.8701
J48	0.8481
Multilayer perceptron	0.6812
Linear regression	0.6369
Decision table	0.6005

The advantages and disadvantages of these two algorithms are summarized as below:

1. These two algorithms both can output a high accuracy/correlation (86%/0.85) and a low root mean square error (0.13/1.24) when using a training set, which is useful in the model building process.
2. When using cross-validation, the J48 algorithm shows a sharp falling in the accuracy value which is just 44%, while M5P algorithm performed more stable.
3. J48 has a more complex visualized tree structure than M5P, which is determined by the algorithm's characteristics.

Finally, the algorithm M5P is used to learn and predict energy consumption in this case, it is an efficient and practical method which combined with linear regression and decision tree. It can deal with numeric data type, which is suitable for the energy data type. Some parameters were set to make the model more accurate. For instance, "minNumInstances" was set to 6.0, which can improve the algorithm performance slightly.

4.2   Results, Performance and Evaluation

The model built with the training datasets give us two main parameters to consider, which are the correlation coefficient and the root mean squared error. The former measures the accuracy of the model, while the later represents the discrete degree. In this case, these two numbers are 0.8701 and 1.1874, respectively, which means a good performance of the model.

The next step is using the test dataset to run this model, the results in Fig. 9 shows the correlation coefficient and root mean squared error are stable, which means the model is solid enough (Table 5).

Table 5. Results by test sets

Description	Results
Correlation coefficient	0.8701
Mean absolute error	0.94
Root mean squared error	1.1874
Relative absolute error	46.8832%
Root relative squared error	49.8549
Total number of instances	232

By visualizing classifier errors in the result list, a deviation of energy consumption and predicted energy usage could be seen, the size of the cross represents the deviation between the real figure and predicted figure. From Fig. 2, one cross is selected, whose actual energy consumption is 51.05 MWh while the predicted energy usage is 55.015 MWh. This cross represents the worst situation, as its size is big enough (Fig. 4).

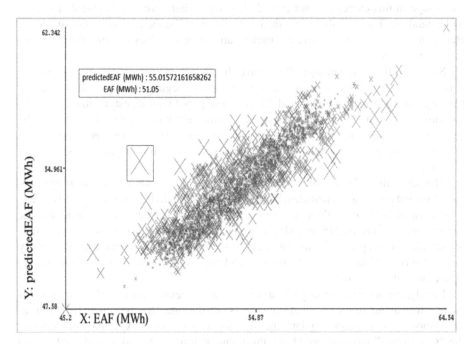

Fig. 4. Classifier errors

Data mining is an analysis process from different perspectives, which allows us to generate useful information such as patterns, associations and relationships among all this data which could be visualized as a descriptive form for decision making. In this paper, Weka was used to make an effective prediction for energy usage in EAF steel production processes. This process is shown in Fig. 11, containing the data preparation, the sample selection, preprocessing of the date and its classification.

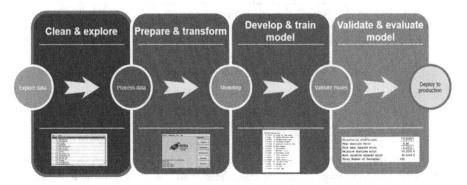

Fig. 5. Workflow for deploying a prediction model.

Firstly, the data preparation and feature selection are important to indicate that the data usage in this exercise is not entirely accurate. Therefore, it was essential to data understanding. There is also some data with lower influence on energy consumption. Hence, it is necessary to remove the useless and missing values in data mining during the preprocessing.

Secondly, the different algorithms have diverse characteristics for the attribute, it is difficult to choose the most appropriate one at the beginning. Some of them could have a good performance in the model building step, but poor in testing, that means the algorithm is very intelligent for meeting the requirement, but it may not be suitable. The data set was divided into the training set and testing set. The training set illustrates the model building and the testing set demonstrates the validation of the testing model's accuracy.

Moreover, the M5P algorithm could establish the relationship between energy consumption and all kinds of attributes. However, it is difficult to find a relationship between energy usage and steel grade, to produce an efficient and correct model. Through some experiments and errors, J48 and M5P were measured and arrived at some conclusions for samples in this paper; the model could make the prediction for the usage in energy which can be used to optimize the process and improve the efficiency of metal melting operation in this steel mill.

Finally, the benefits of using Weka for the data processing are clear because it helps the user to analyze, summarize and get insights into the data. However, there for activities like removing or transforming data, the software didn't work as expected. For example, the "Classifying" tap only could use the nominal form to be calculated, ranked and disposed, it means that the data with numeric form should be converted to nominal form, this process might generate some problems that can confuse the data mining. In addition, when cleaning the data by means of removing useless and missing values and dividing the training and testing data is also a problem in this exercise. Finding options to deal with these challenges in a better way could help to improve the data mining in manufacturing informatics.

Extracting knowledge from Big Data is the process of transforming this data into actionable information. The exponential growth of data has ushered in a myriad of new opportunities and has made data the most valuable production raw material for many organizations. Therefore, in the future, it is expected to carry out a systematic review with tests of the different data mining applications for quality improvement in the steel industry.

References

1. Toulouevski, Yuri N., Zinurov, Ilyaz Y.: Electric Arc Furnace with Flat Bath. SAST. Springer, Cham (2015). https://doi.org/10.1007/978-3-319-15886-0
2. Toulouevski, Y.N., Zinurov, I.Y.: Energy efficiency criteria of EAFs. In: Innovation in Electric Arc Furnaces. pp. 85–97. Springer, Heidelberg (2013). https://doi.org/10.1007/978-3-642-36273-6_5
3. Torres-Rentería, A., Damián-Cuallo, M., Mayo-Maldonado, J., Micheloud-Vernackt, O.: Analysis of electric arc furnaces efficiency via frequency spectrum-based arc coverage detection. Ironmak. Steelmak. **44**, 255–261 (2017). https://doi.org/10.1080/03019233.2016.1210361
4. Lee, B., Sohn, I.: Review of innovative energy savings technology for the electric arc furnace. JOM **66**(9), 1581–1594 (2014). https://doi.org/10.1007/s11837-014-1092-y
5. Harrell, F.E.: Classification vs. Prediction. Statistical Thinking (2018)
6. University of Waikato: Weka 3 - Data Mining with Open Source Machine Learning Software in Java. https://www.cs.waikato.ac.nz/ml/weka/. Accessed 25 Aug 2020
7. Bajpai, A., Fernandes, K.J., Tiwari, M.K.: Modeling, analysis, and improvement of integrated productivity and energy consumption in a serial manufacturing system. J. Clean. Prod. **199**, 296–304 (2018). https://doi.org/10.1016/j.jclepro.2018.07.074
8. Morzy, T., Zakrzewicz, M.: Data mining. In: Błażewicz, J., Kubiak, W., Morzy, T., Rusinkiewicz, M. (eds.) Handbook on Data Management in Information Systems. International Handbooks on Information Systems. Springer, Heidelberg (2003). https://doi.org/10.1007/978-3-540-24742-5_11
9. Carvalho, T.P., Soares, F.A.A.M.N., Vita, R., Francisco, R.P., Basto, J.P., Alcalá, S.G.S.: A systematic literature review of machine learning methods applied to predictive maintenance. Comput. Ind. Eng. **137**, 106024 (2019). https://doi.org/10.1016/j.cie.2019.106024
10. Dehning, P., Lubinetzki, K., Thiede, S., Herrmann, C.: Achieving environmental performance goals - evaluation of impact factors using a knowledge discovery in databases approach. Procedia CIRP **48**, 230–235 (2016). https://doi.org/10.1016/j.procir.2016.03.108
11. Favi, C., Marconi, M., Mandolini, M., Germani, M.: Big data analysis for the estimation of disassembly time and de-manufacturing activity. Procedia CIRP **90**, 617–622 (2020). https://doi.org/10.1016/j.procir.2020.01.072
12. Luengo, J., García-Gil, D., Ramírez-Gallego, S., García, S., Herrera, F.: Big Data Preprocessing. Springer, Cham (2020). https://doi.org/10.1007/978-3-030-39105-8
13. Hall, M., Frank, E., Holmes, G., Pfahringer, B., Reutemann, P., Witten, I.H.: The WEKA data mining software. ACM SIGKDD Explor. Newslett. **11**, 10–18 (2009). https://doi.org/10.1145/1656274.1656278
14. Graham, J.W., Graham, J.W.: Analysis of missing data. In: Missing Data. Statistics for Social and Behavioral Sciences, pp. 47–69. Springer, New York (2012). https://doi.org/10.1007/978-1-4614-4018-5_2
15. Tsiatis, A.: Models and methods for missing data. In: Semiparametric Theory and Missing Data. Springer Series in Statistics, pp. 137–150. Springer, New York (2007). https://doi.org/10.1007/0-387-37345-4_6

16. Yun, J.-T., Yoon, S.-K., Kim, J.-G., Kim, S.-D.: Effective data prediction method for in-memory database applications. J. Supercomput. **76**(1), 580–601 (2019). https://doi.org/10.1007/s11227-019-03050-x
17. Hutter, F., Kotthoff, L., Vanschoren, J. (eds.): Automated Machine Learning. TSSCML. Springer, Cham (2019). https://doi.org/10.1007/978-3-030-05318-5
18. Gnanambal, D., Thangaraj, D., Meenatchi, V.T., Gayathri, D.: Classification algorithms with attribute selection: an evaluation study using WEKA. Int. J. Adv. Netw. Appl. **9**, 3640–3644 (2018)
19. Ymeri, A., Mujovic, S.: Impact of photovoltaic systems placement, sizing on power quality in distribution network. Adv. Electr. Comput. Eng. **18**, 107–112 (2018). https://doi.org/10.4316/AECE.2018.04013
20. Ranganathan, P., Nygard, K.: Smart grid data analytics for decision support. In: 2011 IEEE Electrical Power and Energy Conference, EPEC 2011, pp. 315–321 (2011). https://doi.org/10.1109/EPEC.2011.6070218

ICT for Agronomy and Environment

Towards Automatic Fingerprinting
of Groundwater Aquifers

Antonella Di Roma[1], Estrella Lucena-Sánchez[2,3(✉)], Guido Sciavicco[2],
and Carmela Vaccaro[1]

[1] Department of Physics and Earth Science, University of Ferrara, Ferrara, Italy
{antonella.diroma,carmela.vaccaro}@unife.it
[2] Department of Mathematics and Computer Science,
University of Ferrara, Ferrara, Italy
{estrella.lucenasanchez,guido.sciavicco}@unife.it
[3] Department of Physics, Informatics and Mathematics,
University of Modena and Reggio Emilia, Modena, Italy

Abstract. Geochemical fingerprinting is a rapidly expanding discipline
in the earth and environmental sciences, based on the idea that geological
processes leave behind physical and chemical patterns in the samples. In
recent years, computational statistics and artificial intelligence methods
have started to be used to help the process of geochemical fingerprinting.
In this paper we consider data from 57 wells located in the province of
Ferrara (Italy), all belonging to the same aquifer group and separated
into 4 different aquifers. The aquifer from which each well extracts its
water is known only in 18 of the 57 cases, while in other 39 cases it
can be only hypothesized based on geological considerations. We devise
and test a novel automatic technique for geochemical fingerprinting of
groundwater by means of which we are able to identify the exact aquifer
from which a sample is extracted. Our initial tests returned encouraging
results.

Keywords: Geochemical fingerprinting · Multi-objective optimization
and feature selection

1 Introduction

The increasing exploitation of water resources for human, industrial, and agricultural ends has brought in the last decades great attention toward the quality control of the groundwater. This attention and the complex reality of this
sector has pushed the scientific community to take part in the study and the
management of water resources, to improve the knowledge and to protect every
realistic aspect of their management, to deal with the problems originated by the
variation of volumes and intensity of precipitation due to climate change, over-
exploitation, salinization, anthropic pollution, degradation, and massive irrigation. Many studies have demonstrated that a mindful protection of the existing

© Springer Nature Switzerland AG 2020
R. Valencia-García et al. (Eds.): CITI 2020, CCIS 1309, pp. 73–84, 2020.
https://doi.org/10.1007/978-3-030-62015-8_6

water resources could contribute to the preservation of the availability of fresh water [22,34]. The distribution of the rains is one of the main climatic variables which has a great influence on the ground waters' turnover, on the surface runoff river flows, and on hydroelectricity production as well as on hydrogeological risk. An hydro-geochemistry approach facilitates the understanding of the aquifer reborn, allowing to define the chemical composition of waters, and, through the application of specific models, to suspect and identify the presence of possible mixing between waters of different compositions. The quality and also the geochemical fingerprint of water bodies can be modify to interaction of a plume of polluted waters. A big data geochemical analysis allows to identify the geochemical markers and delimiting the areas of diffusion of the plume and/or the intensity of the contamination in order to quantify the impact and the risks. Geologists usually develop a monitoring network, and, based on the sampling provided, they build a picture of the baseline conceptual hydrogeological model of the studied area, providing a prototype monitoring for continuous data acquisition. Then, *by hand*, sometimes with the help of basic statistical tools, they try to obtain the modeling of multi-aquifer flow in order to increase the knowledge of their hydrogeological characteristic, as well as to find the geochemical fingerprint that represents a specific aquifer level. This process is very expensive and entails an elevated risk of mistake due to potential loss of information, manual loading of data, and prolonged analysis time. But recent innovations in the field of information management with intelligent systems of data acquisition for aquifer features and modeling the seasonal fluctuations of chemical and physical parameters, such as sensor systems and big data algorithms have opened innovative scenarios for the application of computer technology to the environmental monitoring industry. Indeed, machine learning approaches are necessary to streamline the activities, from raw data to artificial intelligence applications; together with an adequate corroboration, and geochemical and geological interpretation of the obtained results, these approaches may allow to automatize activities such as geochemical fingerprint search.

In the recent literature, various statistical methods have been used in the last decades to aid the traditional geochemical investigation to understand pollution sources, possible correlation among elements, and, in some cases, the nature of the contamination [4,16,31]. The recent work focused on protection of groundwater against pollution, deterioration, and for input pollution identification include applying geographical information systems and decision analysis [25,27], logistic regression model learning [21], univariate and multivariate analysis [23], and multiple regression models [10]. More in general, machine learning is emerging as an effective empirical approach for both regression and/or classification of nonlinear systems, ranging from few to thousands of variables, and they are ideal for addressing those problems where our theoretical knowledge is still incomplete but for which we do have a significant number of observations. In the past decades, it has proven useful for a very large number of applications, and among the techniques most commonly used we may mention artificial neural networks [2,18,30,33], support vector machines [3], but also self-organizing map, decision trees, ensemble methods such as random forests, case-based reasoning, neuro-fuzzy networks, and evolutionary algorithms [17]. In this paper we considered 57 water wells located in the province of Ferrara, all belonging to the aquifer group A (the most superficial one), which, in turn, is separated into 4 different aquifers, named from $A1$ to $A4$ [1]. The aquifer from which each well extracts its water is known only in 18 of the 57 cases, while in other 39 cases it can be only hypothesized based on geological considerations; the ultimate purpose of the present study it to devise an automatic, machine learning based method to identify the geochemical fingerprint of each aquifer, so that each unknown well can be assigned an aquifer, and the control network can be improved. The number of possible combinations is exponential in the number of variables, giving rise to a feature selection problem combined with a clusterization problem, which we express as an optimization problem and solve using an evolutionary algorithm. The result can be considered as an approximation to the geochemical fingerprint of each of the four aquifer, expressed in terms of *centroid*, that is, in terms of an ideal, hypothetical set of values for each aquifer of a selection of the indicators, that represents the aquifer itself. By using such a fingerprint, we were able to assign the correct aquifer to each of unknown wells, with a reasonable expected accuracy.

This paper is organized as follows. In the next section, we give the necessary background on fingerprinting, feature selection, and clustering. In Sect. 3 we present our data and give a very simple exploratory analysis. In Sect. 3 we give a short account of our data, and in Sect. 4 we present the mathematical formulation of our technique. Then, in Sect. 5 we present and discuss our results, before concluding.

2   Background

Feature selection is a machine learning technique for data preprocessing, defined as eliminating features from the data base that are irrelevant to the task to be performed [12]. In its original formulation and meaning, feature selection facilitates data understanding, reduces the storage requirements, and lowers the processing time, so that model learning becomes an easier process. Feature selection methods that do not incorporate dependencies between attributes are called *univariate* methods, and they consist in applying some criterion to each pair feature-response, and measuring the individual power of a given feature with respect to the response independently from the other features, so that each feature can be ranked accordingly. In *multivariate* methods, on the other hand, the assessment is performed for subsets of features rather than single features. There are several different approaches to feature selection in the literature. Among them, the most versatile ones are those that define the selection problem as an optimization problem. A *multi-objective optimization problem* (see, e.g. [5]) can be formally defined as the optimization problem of simultaneously minimizing (or maximizing) a set of k arbitrary functions:

$$\begin{cases} \min/\max \ f_1(\bar{x}) \\ \min/\max \ f_2(\bar{x}) \\ \dots \\ \min/\max \ f_k(\bar{x}), \end{cases} \tag{1}$$

where $\bar{x}$ is a vector of decision variables. A multi-objective optimization problem can be *continuous*, in which we look for real values, or *combinatorial*, we look for objects from a countably (in)finite set, typically integers, permutations, or graphs. Maximization and minimization problems can be reduced to each other, so that it is sufficient to consider one type only. A set $\mathcal{F}$ of solutions for a multi-objective problem is *non dominated* (or *Pareto optimal*) if and only if for each $\bar{x} \in \mathcal{F}$, there exists no $\bar{y} \in \mathcal{F}$ such that (i) there exists i $(1 \leq i \leq k)$ that $f_i(\bar{y})$ improves $f_i(\bar{x})$, and (ii) for every j, $(1 \leq j \leq k, j \neq i)$, $f_j(\bar{x})$ does not improve $f_i(\bar{y})$. In other words, a solution $\bar{x}$ *dominates* a solution $\bar{y}$ if and only if $\bar{x}$ is better than $\bar{y}$ in at least one objective, and it is not worse than $\bar{y}$ in the remaining objectives. We say that $\bar{x}$ is *non-dominated* if and only if there is not other solution that dominates it. The set of non dominated solutions from $\mathcal{F}$ is called *Pareto front*. Optimization problems can be approached in several ways; among them, *multi-objective evolutionary algorithms* are a popular choice (see, e.g. [9,14,24]). Feature selection can be seen as a multi-objective optimization problem, in which the solution encodes the selected features, and the objective(s) are designed to evaluate the performances of some model-extraction algorithm; this may entail, for example, instantiating (1) as:

$$\begin{cases} \max \ Performance(\bar{x}) \\ \min \ Cardinality(\bar{x}), \end{cases} \tag{2}$$

where $\bar{x}$ represents the chosen features; Eq. 2 can be referred to as a *wrapper*.

Cluster analysis or *clustering* is the task of grouping a set of objects so that those in the same group, or *cluster* are more similar to each other than to those in other groups. The literature on cluster analysis is very wide, and includes *hierarchical* clustering, *centroid-based* models, *distribution-based* models, *density* models, among many others. Centroid-based models are of particular interest for us, because they are especially useful for numerical, many dimensional objects such as groundwater samples. The concept of centroid is essential in the most well-known centroid-based clustering algorithm, that is, *k-means* [20]: given a group of objects and a notion of distance, its *centroid* is the set of values that describes an object C (which may or may not be a concrete object of the group) such that the geometric mean of the distances between C and every other element of the group is minimal. In the k-means algorithm the groups (and even their number) is not known beforehand (this type of cluster analysis is called *exploratory*), and the algorithm is based on an initial random guessing of the centroid that eventually converges to a local optimum. KNN [6] is a distance-based *classification* algorithm, whose main idea is that close-by objects can be classified in a similar way. In this paper we use both ideas of centroid and distance-based classification in order to systematically extract geochemical fingerprints.

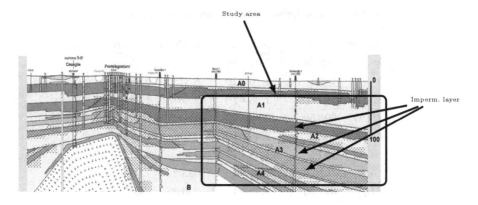

Fig. 1. The area under study, cross-section.

Finally, geochemical fingerprinting is based on the idea that geological processes leave behind physical, chemical and sometimes also isotopic patterns in the samples. Many of these patterns, informally referred to as *geochemical fingerprints*, may differ only in fine details from each other. For this reason, approaching automatic fingerprinting requires highly precise and accurate data analysis [15]. Applications of geochemical fingerprinting range on a wide set of contexts, from studies on ancient artifacts such as glass or ceramics [19], to mineral identification and discovery of Jurassic-age kimberlite [29], to dust transport monitoring [11], to groundwater resources identification and study [28], to the study of the quality of food and beverages, especially wine, as shown in [26]. Because of the statistical nature of geochemical fingerprints, statistical methods are suitable for their identification. In the most recent literature, statistical methods are being progressively integrated and paired with machine learning and artificial intelligence based technology. In this paper, we develop a novel method for groundwater fingerprint identification, based on feature selection, solved as an optimization problem, and implemented via a evolutionary algorithm.

3   Data

The data used for this study consist of 910 samples extracted from 57 wells located in the province of Ferrara, all belonging to the aquifer group A (the most superficial one), from 2010 to 2017. This aquifer group is separated into 4 different aquifers, as it is shown in Fig. 1, named from $A1$ to $A4$ from the most to the least superficial, which present a (probably impermeable) layer in between each pair [1]. The exact aquifer from which each well extracts its water is known only in 18 of the 57 cases, while in other 39 cases it can be only hypothesized based on geological and stratigraphic considerations. Out of the total samples, we selected those which were extracted using *single-filter* pumps (that is, that give the guarantee that the groundwater comes from one aquifer only) and of which the precise aquifer was known, reducing our data set to 229 samples. Each

Table 1. Descriptive statistical analysis of the data.

feature	mean	p-value	kurtosis	skewness
η	469.50	$7.01 * 10^{-20}$	7.18	2.15
T	15.81	$1.16 * 10^{-18}$	5.37	0.55
$E.C.$	1574.00	$1.36 * 10^{-18}$	2.45	1.08
HCO_3^-	606.50	$3.54 * 10^{-11}$	4.44	1.18
Cl^-	56.00	$2.43 * 10^{-21}$	2.81	1.25
SO_4^{2-}	18.05	$1.61 * 10^{-19}$	7.59	2.03
Ca^{2+}	462.70	$1.91 * 10^{-29}$	64.02	7.03
Mg^{2+}	381.33	$2.89 * 10^{-32}$	226.95	15.03
Na^+	183.52	$1.79 * 10^{-18}$	4.02	1.51
K^+	24.39	$1.27 * 10^{-29}$	42.85	6.13
NH_4	2135.61	$2.01 * 10^{-27}$	43.06	5.51
Fe	1501.52	$1.40 * 10^{-27}$	39.20	5.47
As	$3.23 * 10^{-3}$	$1.38 * 10^{-22}$	18.84	3.23

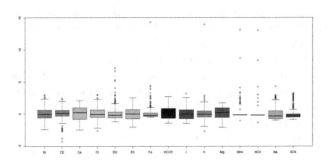

Fig. 2. Distribution statistical analysis of the data.

sample contains 13 chemical-physical indicators: η (hardness), T, $E.C.$, Na^+, K^+, Ca^{2+}, Mg^{2+}, Cl^-, SO_4^{2-}, HCO_3^-, NH_4, Fe, As. Some relevant statistical measures of the different chemical elements are showed in Table 1, correlations between variables are showed in Table 2, and

As it can be observed, none of the variables follows a normal distribution (their p-values are well below 0.05), and they all present very high levels of kurtosis and skewness, being Mg^{2+} and Ca^{2+} the most evident examples. Moreover, Fig. 2 shows as the data contain outliers and anomalous values. As a consequence, applying standard statistical tools such as principal component analysis [32] to identify physical-chemical fingerprints does not make much sense, as such tools usually require a certain statistical well-behaviour, for the results to be reliable [13]. This is a common problem in the analysis of real data, especially of chemical-physical origin. Approaching problems such as fingerprint identification with machine learning tools, instead, tend to bypass this obstacles, at the expenses of a more complex design.

Table 2. Correlation matrix for our variables.

	η	T	E.C.	HCO_3^-	Cl^-	SO_4^{2-}	Ca^{2+}	Mg^{2+}	Na^+	K^+	NH_4	Fe	As
η	1.00	0.13	0.76	0.78	0.62	−0.23	0.14	0.02	0.49	0.14	0.23	0.40	−0.19
T	0.13	1.00	0.05	0.06	0.02	0.20	0.01	0.03	−0.03	0.01	−0.01	0.04	−0.01
E.C.	0.76	0.05	1.00	0.47	0.95	−0.32	0.19	0.10	0.84	0.24	0.27	0.39	−0.20
HCO_3^-	0.78	0.06	0.47	1.00	0.24	−0.34	0.11	−0.01	0.26	0.04	0.21	0.35	−0.07
Cl^-	0.62	0.02	0.95	0.25	1.00	−0.29	0.16	0.13	0.86	0.25	0.24	0.34	−0.21
SO_4^{2-}	−0.23	0.20	−0.33	−0.34	−0.29	1.00	−0.08	−0.04	−0.36	−0.06	−0.15	−0.15	0.03
Ca^{2+}	0.14	0.01	0.19	0.11	0.16	−0.08	1.00	−0.01	−0.09	0.76	−0.06	−0.05	−0.05
Mg^{2+}	0.02	0.04	0.10	−0.02	0.13	−0.04	−0.01	1.00	0.13	−0.01	−0.02	0.03	−0.02
Na^+	0.49	−0.03	0.84	0.26	0.86	−0.36	−0.09	0.13	1.00	−0.09	0.25	0.31	−0.15
K^+	0.14	0.01	0.25	0.05	0.25	−0.06	0.77	−0.01	−0.09	1.00	−0.07	−0.06	−0.05
NH_4	0.23	−0.01	0.28	0.22	0.24	−0.15	−0.06	−0.02	0.25	−0.07	1.00	0.30	−0.01
Fe	0.41	0.05	0.40	0.35	0.34	−0.16	−0.05	0.03	0.31	−0.06	0.30	1.00	−0.02
As	−0.19	−0.01	−0.21	−0.07	−0.21	0.03	−0.05	−0.02	−0.15	−0.04	−0.01	−0.02	1.00

4   Method

Each instance in our data set can be seen as a vector in $\mathbb{R}^d$ (in our case, $d = 13$):

$$
D = \begin{bmatrix}
a_{11} & \cdots & a_{1d} & A1 \\
\cdots & \cdots & \cdots & \\
a_{m_1 1} & \cdots & a_{m_1 d} & A1 \\
a_{(m_1+1)1} & \cdots & a_{(m_1+1)d} & A2 \\
\cdots & \cdots & \cdots & \\
a_{m_2 1} & \cdots & a_{m_2 d} & A2 \\
a_{(m_2+1)1} & \cdots & a_{(m_2+1)d} & A3 \\
\cdots & \cdots & \cdots & \\
a_{m_3 1} & \cdots & a_{m_i d} & A3 \\
a_{(m_3+1)1} & \cdots & a_{(m_3+1)d} & A4 \\
\cdots & \cdots & \cdots & \\
a_{m_4 1} & \cdots & a_{m_4 d} & A4
\end{bmatrix} \tag{3}
$$

In order to evaluate the distance between two instances $I = (a_1, \ldots, a_d)$ and $J = (a'_1, \ldots, a'_d)$, we use the well-known notion of *Euclidean distance*:

$$
dist(I, J) = \sqrt{\Sigma_{i=1}^d (|a_i - a'_i|^2)} \tag{4}
$$

In this way we can compute the distance between any two samples of groundwater. Such a value is strongly influenced by the parameters (the specific subset of the d dimensions) that are taken into consideration. If we choose to represent the instances with a specific subset of parameters, instead of using all of them, the relative distances among different pairs of instances can vary very much. Consequently, the fingerprint extraction problem can be seen as a feature selection problem, that is, the problem of establishing the *best* subset of chemical-physical parameter. However, unlike the classical feature selection problem, selecting the correct classification algorithm (i.e., the correct inference model) is not immediate. We choose to model the fingerprint of an aquifer as the set of values that best represent an (ideal) sample of groundwater from that aquifer, that is, its centroid. Thus, we have a *feature selection for centroid identification* problem, as it is a clusterization problem in which the clusters are already set.

Now, let $\bar{x} = (x_1, \ldots, x_d)$ a vector of solution variables, each taking values in the domain $\{0, 1\}$; as in a classical feature selection problem, each 1 means that the corresponding feature is selected, while 0 means that it is discarded; we denote by $C_j(\bar{x})$ the centroid of the j-th aquifer ($1 \leq j \leq 4$, in our case) computed using precisely the attributes that correspond to $\bar{x}$. In order to adapt (2) to our problem, we need to define how we evaluate the performances of the solution, which, in our case, means defining what classification problem we want to solve. To this end, indicating by $A(I)$ the (true) aquifer to which the instance I correspond, we compute the number of correct predictions as:

$$\#Correct(\bar{x}) = \Sigma_{I \in D} \begin{cases} 1 \text{ if } A(I) = argmin_{A_j} d(I, C_j(\bar{x})) \\ 0 \text{ otherwise} \end{cases} \tag{5}$$

and, consequently, define the *accuracy* of $\bar{x}$ over D as:

$$Acc(\bar{x}) = \frac{\#Correct(\bar{x})}{|D|} \tag{6}$$

The accuracy of a fingerprint selection can be used to reformulate our problem as an optimization problem, as it can be seen as suitable performance indicator. Minimizing the cardinality of the selected features is also correct in fingerprinting selection, as smaller fingerprints are more interpretable. In order to take into account the fact that some geochemical processes are not necessarily linear, we can slightly complicate our formulation by introducing a third objective. As a matter of fact, we can expand the domain of each solution variable x_i to take value in $\mathbb{N}$, instead of $\{0, 1\}$. While we still interpret 0 as discarding the corresponding parameter, we now interpret a positive value as the power to which the corresponding parameter is raised; we simulate, in this way, a sort of dynamic normalization of our data. It is possible to optimize the complexity of the resulting fingerprint in terms of non-linear behaviour, that is, by minimizing the maximum exponent:

$$MaxExp(\bar{x}) = \max_{i=1}^{d} x_i \tag{7}$$

So, in each execution, a vector of solutions variables $\bar{x}$ entails a transformation of the original data set (3) into:

$$D = \begin{bmatrix} a_{11}{}^{x_1} & \cdots & a_{1d}{}^{x_d} & A1 \\ \cdots & \cdots & \cdots & \\ a_{m_11}{}^{x_1} & \cdots & a_{m_1d}{}^{x_d} & A1 \\ a_{11} & \cdots & a_{1d} & A2 \\ \cdots & \cdots & \cdots & \\ a_{m_21}{}^{x_1} & \cdots & a_{m_2d}{}^{x_d} & A2 \\ a_{11} & \cdots & a_{1d}{}^{x_d} & A3 \\ \cdots & \cdots & \cdots & \\ a_{m_31}{}^{x_1} & \cdots & a_{m_1d}{}^{x_d} & A3 \\ a_{11}{}^{x_1} & \cdots & a_{1d}{}^{x_d} & A4 \\ \cdots & \cdots & \cdots & \\ a_{m_41}{}^{x_1} & \cdots & a_{m_2d}{}^{x_d} & A4 \end{bmatrix} \qquad (8)$$

where, for simplicity of notation, we have not shown the case of discarded attributes.

Summing up, we can reformulate (2) for fingerprint extraction as the following optimization problem:

$$\begin{cases} \max \ Acc(\bar{x}) \\ \min \ MaxExp(\bar{x}) \\ \min \ Cardinality(\bar{x}) \end{cases} \qquad (9)$$

5   Implementation and Results

Multi-objective evolutionary algorithms are known to be particularly suitable to perform multi-objective optimization, as they search for multiple optimal solutions in parallel. In this experiment we have chosen the well-known NSGA-II (Non-dominated Sorted Genetic Algorithm) [7] algorithm, which is available as open-source from the suite *jMetal* [8]. NGSA-II is an elitist Pareto-based multi-objective evolutionary algorithm that employs a strategy with a binary tournament selection and a rank-crowding better function, where the rank of an individual in a population is the non-domination level of the individual in the whole population. We used the standard parameters in each experiment, and implemented elementary variants of mutation and crossover to make them specific to our solution format. To cope with the intrinsic unbalancing of our data (over 70% of the samples belong to $A1$), we operated a re-sampling, to obtain a training set with 10 samples per each aquifer ($D_{training}$), and left every other sample for test (D_{test}). Test was performed in the natural way, that is, by applying the accuracy function(s) to D_{test} using the centroid and the selected attributes extracted from the chosen solution. We have executed 10 runs of the model (9), each with a different seed; the population side was 100 in each experiment, and we set each experiment for 100 generations each. A multi-objective optimization problem gives rise to a Pareto front, that is, to a *last* population of (non-dominated) individuals from which one or more individuals can be selected via a decision-making process. The standard approach to decision making is selecting the solution with the best value in the most important among the

Table 3. Test results.

fingerprint		recall			
	acc	A1	A2	A3	A4
$(\eta)^2, HCO_3^-, (NH_4)^3$	0.59	0.55	0.71	1.00	1.00
$(\eta)^3, HCO_3^-, (Fe)^3$	0.60	0.54	0.81	0.90	1.00
$(\eta)^3, (HCO_3^-)^3, (Fe)^3$	0.60	0.53	0.81	1.00	1.00
$(\eta)^2, (HCO_3^-)^3, (NH_4)^2, Fe$	0.60	0.55	0.71	1.00	1.00
$(T)^2, (HCO_3^-)^2, SO_4^{2-}, NH_4$	0.54	0.47	0.81	1.00	1.00
$(\eta)^3, (HCO_3^-)^3, (Fe)^3$	0.60	0.47	0.81	1.00	1.00
$(\eta)^3, (HCO_3^-)^3, (Fe)^3$	0.60	0.53	0.81	1.00	1.00
$(T)^2, \eta, (HCO_3^-)^2$	0.55	0.47	0.81	1.00	1.00
$(\eta)^3, HCO_3^-, (Fe)^3$	0.60	0.55	0.71	1.00	1.00
$(T)^2, \eta, HCO_3^-$	0.55	0.47	0.81	1.00	1.00

objectives; in our case that would be the accuracy. Unfortunately, this strategy gives rise to fingerprints with too many characteristics, which would be too difficult to interpret. Therefore, our decision-making strategy is to select the most accurate solution with strictly less than six chosen characteristics.

The set of chosen results is shown in Table 3. As it can be seen, we reach a level of accuracy between 0.55 and 0.60; taking into account that we have a four-classes problem, we may consider it acceptable. Moreover, the recall level (i.e., the ratio of correct answers) per class, shows that, in general, our fingerprints are able to identify three out of four aquifers in a very precise way. Finally, it can be observed how while different executions have produced different fingerprints, they share many elements, indicating that our approach is stable.

6   Conclusions

In this paper we have considered the results of the geochemical analysis of groundwater samples from 57 water wells located in the province of Ferrara, all belonging to the same aquifer group. We considered the problem of identifying the geochemical fingerprint of each aquifer of the group, so that those wells that extract water from the same group but from an unknown aquifer can be safely assigned one without making decisions based on the depth of the well itself. We proved that our method, based on an artificial intelligence technique which we called feature selection for centroid identification, returns fingerprints with a sufficiently high level of accuracy.

Our method can be improved in many ways. Future directions include considering different optimization functions (e.g., building a *fault-tolerant* accuracy that considers neighbour aquifers as less severe mistake, or optimizing the complexity of the resulting fingerprint in different ways), and using *ratios* among affine elements/characteristics instead of, or in conjunction with, the original variables. Moreover, if we take into account the temporal component of the data, this problem can be seen as a multivariate temporal series classification problem, so to define a fingerprint as a *temporal pattern* instead of a set of values. By doing so, one can set up a completely different set of experiments, to establish by how much, and in which way, fingerprints change over time.

References

1. Amorosi, A., Bruno, L., Rossi, V., Severi, P., Hajdas, I.: Paleosol architecture of a late Quaternary basin-margin sequence and its implications for high-resolution, non-marine sequence stratigraphy. Global Planet. Change **112**, 12–25 (2014)
2. Atkinson, P., Tatnall, A.: Introduction: neural networks in remote sensing. Int. J. Remote Sens. **4**(18), 699–709 (1997)
3. Azamathulla, H., Wu, F.: Support vector machine approach for longitudinal dispersion coefficients in natural streams. Appl. Soft Comput. **2**(11), 2902–2905 (2011)
4. Belkhiri, L., Mouni, L., Narany, T.S., Tiri, A.: Evaluation of potential health risk of heavy metals in groundwater using the integration of indicator kriging and multivariate statistical methods. Groundwater Sustain. Dev. **4**, 12–22 (2017)
5. Collette, Y., Siarry, P.: Multiobjective Optimization: Principles and Case Studies. Springer, Heidelberg (2004). https://doi.org/10.1007/978-3-662-08883-8
6. Dasarathy, B.: Nearest Neighbour (NN) Norms: NN Pattern Classification Techniques. IEEE Computer Society Press, Los Alamitos (1991)
7. Deb, K.: Multi-objective Optimization Using Evolutionary Algorithms. Wiley, London (2001)
8. Durillo, J., Nebro, A.: jMetal: a Java framework for multi-objective optimization. Adv. Eng. Softw. **42**, 760–771 (2011)
9. Emmanouilidis, C., Hunter, A., Macintyre, J., Cox, C.: A multi-objective genetic algorithm approach to feature selection in neural and fuzzy modeling. Evol. Optim. **3**(1), 1–26 (2001)
10. Farhadian, H., Katibeh, H.: New empirical model to evaluate groundwater flow into circular tunnel using multiple regression analysis. Int. J. Min. Sci. Technol. **27**(3), 415–421 (2017)
11. Galleta, S., Jahn, B., Lanoë, B.V.V., Dia, A., Rossello, E.: Loess geochemistry and its implications for particle origin and composition of the upper continental crust. Earth Planet Sci. Lett. **156**, 157–172 (1989)
12. Guyon, I., Elisseeff, A.: An introduction to variable and feature selection. J. Mach. Learn. Res. **3**, 1157–1182 (2003)
13. Jiang, B., Pei, J.: Outlier detection on uncertain data: objects, instances, and inferences. In: Proceedings of the 27th International Conference on Data Engineering, pp. 422–433 (2011)
14. Jiménez, F., Sánchez, G., García, J., Sciavicco, G., Miralles, L.: Multi-objective evolutionary feature selection for online sales forecasting. Neurocomputing **234**, 75–92 (2017)
15. Kamber, B.: Geochemical fingerprinting: 40 years of analytical development and real world applications. Appl. Geochem. **24**(6), 1074–1086 (2009)
16. Kozyatnyk, I., Lövgren, L., Tysklind, M., Haglund, P.: Multivariate assessment of barriers materials for treatment of complex groundwater rich in dissolved organic matter and organic and inorganic contaminants. J. Environ. Chem. Eng. **5**(4), 3075–3082 (2017)

17. Lary, D., Alavi, A., Gandomi, A., Walker, A.: Machine learning in geosciences and remote sensing. Geosci. Front. **7**(1), 3–10 (2016)
18. Lary, D., Muller, M., Mussa, H.: Using neural networks to describe tracer correlations. Atmos. Chem. Phys. **4**, 143–146 (2004)
19. Li, B., et al.: ICP-MS trace element analysis of Song dynasty porcelains from Ding, Jiexiu and Guantai kilns, north China. J. Archaeol. Sci. **32**, 251–259 (2005)
20. MacQueen, J.: Some methods for classification and analysis of multivariate observations. In: Proceedings of the 5th Berkeley Symposium on Mathematical Statistics and Probability, pp. 281–297 (1967)
21. Mair, A., El-Kadi, A.: Logistic regression modeling to assess groundwater vulnerability to contamination in Hawaii, USA. J. Contam. Hydrol. **153**, 1–23 (2013)
22. Martinelli, G., Minissale, A., Verrucchi, C.: Geochemistry of heavily exploited aquifers in the Emilia-Romagna region (Po Valley, Northern Italy). Environ. Geol. **36**, 195–206 (1998). https://doi.org/10.1007/s002540050335
23. Menció, A., et al.: Nitrate pollution of groundwater; all right ..., but nothing else? Sci. Total Environ. **539**, 241–251 (2016)
24. Mukhopadhyay, A., Maulik, U., Bandyopadhyay, S., Coello, C.C.: A survey of multiobjective evolutionary algorithms for data mining: part I. IEEE Trans. Evol. Comput. **18**(1), 4–19 (2014)
25. Ozdemir, A.: GIS-based groundwater spring potential mapping in the Sultan Mountains (Konya, Turkey) using frequency ratio, weights of evidence and logistic regression methods and their comparison. J. Hydrol. **411**(3), 290–308 (2011)
26. Pepi, S., Vaccaro, C.: Geochemical fingerprints of "Prosecco" wine based on major and trace elements. Environ. Geochem. Health **40**, 833–847 (2018). https://doi.org/10.1007/s10653-017-0029-0
27. Pizzol, L., Zabeo, A., Critto, A., Giubilato, E., Marcomini, A.: Risk-based prioritization methodology for the classification of groundwater pollution sources. Sci. Total Environ. **506**, 505–517 (2015)
28. Ranjbar, A., Mahjouri, N., Cherubini, C.: Development of an efficient conjunctive meta-model-based decision-making framework for saltwater intrusion management in coastal aquifers. J. Hydro-environ. Res. **26**, 45–58 (2019)
29. Ross, J., et al.: Sodium in garnet and potassium in clinopyroxene: criteria for classifying mantle eclogites. In: Kimberlites and Related Rocks, pp. 27–832 (1989)
30. Shahin, M., Jaksa, M., Maier, H.: Artificial neural network applications in geotechnical engineering. Aust. Geomech. **1**(36), 49–62 (2001)
31. Singh, C.K., Kumar, A., Shashtri, S., Kumar, A., Kumar, P., Mallick, J.: Multivariate statistical analysis and geochemical modeling for geochemical assessment of groundwater of Delhi. India. J. Geochem. Explor. **175**, 59–71 (2017)
32. Wold, S., Esbensen, K., Geladi, P.: Principal component analysis. Chemometr. Intell. Lab. Syst. **2**(1–3), 37–52 (1987)
33. Yi, J., Prybutok, V.: A neural network model forecasting for prediction of daily maximum ozone concentration in an industrialized urban area. Environ. Pollut. **3**(92), 349–357 (1996)
34. Zuppi, G., Sacchi, E.: Hydrogeology as a climate recorder: Sahara-Sahel (North Africa) and the po plain (Northern Italy). Global Planet. Change **40**, 79–91 (2004)

Search for Damage of the Citrus Miner to the Lemon Leaf, Implementing Artificial Vision Techniques

José Luis Carranza-Flores[1][(✉)] [iD], Miriam Martínez-Arroyo[1] [iD],
José Antonio Montero-Valverde[1] [iD], and José Luis Hernández-Hernández[2] [iD]

[1] Tecnológico Nacional de México/IT de Acapulco, Acapulco, México
jlcflores18@gmail.com, {miriam.ma,jose.mv}@acapulco.tecnm.mx
[2] Tecnológico Nacional de México/IT de Chilpancingo, Chilpancingo, México
joseluis.hernandez@itchilpancingo.edu.mx

Abstract. Computer vision it is a scientific discipline that in recent years it is being widely used in applications via computer. Such discipline includes mechanisms to capture, process, analyze and understand the images from some specific domain. Currently has become a very important tool and powerful in agronomy to monitor growth and fruit development and vegetables that are produced in the Mexican fields. In this investigation digital image processing is applied to pre-process, segment, extract features and classify the marks left by the miner in the leaves of the Mexican lemon. The digital image processing, segment and classify the leaves on the lemon trees, making use of the established color models by Commission Internationale d'Eclairage (CIE). The techniques used in this work to segment and classify the leaves of the lemon tree; are able to process the images even if they have: low lighting, pixel saturation, noise, shades, different shades in the lemon leaves and intrinsic parameters of photographic cameras. There are several investigations in this regard, which have demonstrated how important it is the optimum choice of color model to be used for each specific area. In the present investigation, the color model HSL (Hue, Saturation, Lightness) was considered, which was used in the software MatLab ® for the tests that were carried out.

Keywords: Computer vision · Segmentation · Classification · Crop pests · Citrus miner

1 Introduction

Plant pests and diseases affect food crops and causes significant losses to farmers and threat to production if the pest gets to contaminate a single leaf. It is worth mentioning that the pests and the virus are different things, viruses cause disease and pests cause damage, but both are a risk to any crop [1]. These can easily spread as there are factors that favor them such as the climate, the air, the rain, the heat, etc. Outbreaks can cause huge crop losses, endangering the livelihoods of vulnerable farmers, food security and nutritional of millions of people every year [2, 3, 5].

© Springer Nature Switzerland AG 2020
R. Valencia-García et al. (Eds.): CITI 2020, CCIS 1309, pp. 85–97, 2020.
https://doi.org/10.1007/978-3-030-62015-8_7

Some researchers and software developers have made use of artificial vision testing techniques that offer them a broader picture to quickly detect damage or plant diseases; this in order for the farmers take appropriate measures to protect their parcels, because according to the World Health Organization [4], by 2050 there will be 9.7 billion people living on the planet, this means that farmers shall make use of the technology as a support for crop care.

Mexico is one of the main lemon producers worldwide, due to its high activity in the production of this citrus fruit, a large part of production is destined for domestic consumption because lemon is an important part of Mexican cuisine and another part is exported (United States and European countries). The low productivity of this citrus in the country is due to different pests and/or diseases that attack the lemon tree, some of them if not controlled in time, cause great economic losses [6–8].

Phyllocnistis citrella Stainton (Lepidoptera: Gracillariidae), is known as a citrus leaf miner and it's a plague which has an economic impact on most of the citrus growing regions of the world. It's a plague that affects young lemon plants and especially the tender foliage, creating mines or streamers usually in the lower epidermis, causing the leaves to distort and curl up [9]. The larvae of the lemon miner, consume the epidermal cells of the leaf leaving the remaining leaf tissue behind almost intact with the overlying cuticle of the leaf tissue that protects the larva [10, 11]. This insect forms galleries as it feeds and consequently, brown spots appear and the leaves start to curl until they wilt and they fall down. On the older leaves, brownish patches are formed, that serve as sources of infection for the rest of the leaves of the lemon tree. The attacked leaves twist and/or are bent, but they remain in the plants for a long time and the damage gradually spreads to the fresh leaves of the lemon tree [12, 17]. In Fig. 1, you can see the lemon miner.

Fig. 1. Lemon miner image (Phyllocnistis citrella Staintonr).

The classification of an image, allows to analyze it in a better way since it divides it into several parts or objects, its objective is to simplify representation of an image in an easier one to interpret. The classification is to make the recognition of the damage that produces the lemon miner to the plant.

2 Materials and Methods

The investigation describes development and implementation of techniques and algorithms for the classification of the damages caused by the citrus miner on the Mexican lemon leaf, through the methodology for project development that implement artificial vision techniques. The software was used MatLab ® for image processing and analysis of the information generated.

The methodology consists of the following phases: image acquisition, preprocessing, segmentation, feature extraction and classification; as shown in Fig. 1. In each of the phases, techniques were applied which allowed an optimal result to the required. In the same way, the results obtained are shown in each of the phases when applying algorithms that more suited, since there are methods and techniques that can be applied in each phase, this involves testing each of them to verify that the selected techniques are adequate. The phases used in the methodology, can be seen in Fig. 2.

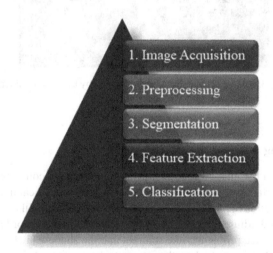

Fig. 2. Phases of the proposed research methodology.

2.1 Image Acquisition

In this phase the images are captured, it should be taken into account that not all images will give a favorable result since consideration should be given to: light intensity, shadow, distance, time, as well as the climate because on many occasions it is cloudy or with rain, due to tropical storms that affect each year. It is recommended to take photographs when there is sunlight, preferably in the morning so that the light is not too intense as shown in Fig. 3.

The images of the leaves of the lemon tree that are taken for research, are obtained with a medium resolution camera. This in order to detect image imperfections and be able to correct them before the process. These images are stored in JPEG image format.

The photos that were obtained for the evidence of the investigation, were taken at a distance between 30 and 40 cm this in order to properly detect the most important features such as: shape, texture, color and size.

Fig. 3. Image on a lemon plant, damaged by the lemon miner.

2.2 Preprocessing

The improvement of the image is one of the important steps of computer vision and has played a very important role in various applications, such as medical imaging, industrial inspection, the detection of plant diseases, etc. The enhancement of the image is a process used to improve and adjust the contrast of the acquired image in order to address the variability of luminance problems, like sunlight and the shadow [13].

The first step that is applied to the image to be processed, is to remove a little brightness and the elimination of noise to obtain the best results in the treatment of the image.

Usually, the image is received in the RGB (Red, Green and Blue) color model and is converted to the HSL color model to analyze channels and determine according to needs, which channel should be taken for the segmentation process. The HSL Color Model, also called HSI (Hue, Saturation, Intensity), define a color model in terms of its constituent components. The HSL color model is graphically represented as a double cone or a double hexagon. The two vertices in the HSL model correspond to black and white, the angle corresponds to the hue and the distance to the axis with the saturation and the distance to the black-white axis correspond to the luminance. Color models HSI and HSV, are a non-linear deformation of the RGB color model.

2.2.1 Conversion from RGB Color Model to HSL

The RGB values must be expressed as numbers from 0 to 1, MAX corresponds to the maximum of the RGB values and MIN is equivalent to the minimum of these values, as shown in Eq. 1.

$$H = \begin{cases} 0, & \text{if } MAX = MIN \\ \left(60 \times \frac{G-B}{MAX-MIN} + 360\right) \bmod 360, & \text{if } MAX = R \\ 60 \times \frac{B-R}{MAX-MIN} + 120, & \text{if } MAX = G \\ 60 \times \frac{R-G}{MAX-MIN} + 240, & \text{if } MAX = B \end{cases}$$

$$L = \frac{1}{2}(MAX + MIN)$$

$$S = \begin{cases} 0, & \text{if } MAX = MIN \\ \frac{MAX-MIN}{MAX+MIN} = \frac{MAX-MIN}{2L}, & \text{if } L \le \frac{1}{2} \\ \frac{MAX-MIN}{2-(MAX+MIN)} = \frac{MAX-MIN}{2-2L}, & \text{if } L > \frac{1}{2} \end{cases} \quad (1)$$

The representation of the HSL color model, you can see in Fig. 4.

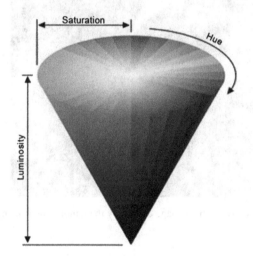

Fig. 4. Representation of the color model used HSL.

Figure 5 shows an image of a lemon tree leaf, converted from RGB to HSL where the RGB image is represented in a range of (0, 1) and the formula of Eq. 1 is applied to obtain the values of each channel.

After analyzing the three channels and having performed multiple tests on different images was decided to use the saturation channel (S) since with such channel better results were obtained for image segmentation. Figure 6 shows the result of applying the HSL filter in channel S; the damage caused by the miner is observed in the image in a darker color compared to the other parts of the image.

Fig. 5. Image of a lemon leaf in the HSL color model.

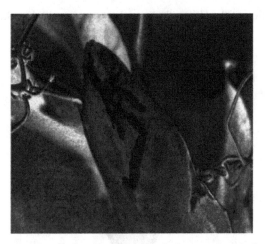

Fig. 6. Image showing the damage caused by the lemon miner (using channel S)

2.3 Segmentation

The main objective in almost all detections of diseases in plants using image processing, is to segment the different pixels that appear on the images into two classes: disease (in the leaves of the tree) and background (it is the rest of the image - soil and waste). Removal of the background is an essential process and has to be done in a proper way to avoid misclassification [14, 15].

Image segmentation is based on decomposing an image into its constituent parts, referencing the main object and in the background of the image, segmentation allows to separate or exclude zones with specific characteristics of shape or color [16]. The basic segmentation attributes are: luminance in monochrome images, the color components in color images, texture, shape, etc. Within this phase are techniques such as: edge detection, thresholding, based on regions and others.

Thresholding is a basic method of binarization that serves to differentiate the object of the image background. It consists of the pixels that are marked with 1, correspond to the image object. If the object is dark with respect to the background, the process is reverse. Figure 7 shows the binarized image; in white color there is information that does not correspond to the damage caused by the miner.

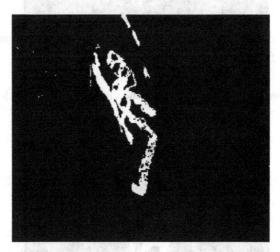

Fig. 7. Threshold image of the damage caused by the lemon miner.

In this segmentation phase, algorithms were tested that obtain the threshold value automatically, the method GRAYTHRESH of the software MatLab ® calculates a global threshold using the OTSU method. The OTSU method chooses a threshold that minimizes intraclass variance of blank pixels and black of the thresholds, receiving the image obtained from the channel S of the HSL color model. Then a cycle is carried out that runs through each of the pixels of the image and according to the threshold value replaces all pixels in the input image with a luminance higher than with the white color, replacing all other pixels with the color black as shown in Fig. 8.

Figure 8 shows the use of the technique REGIÓNPROMP of the software MatLab ®, which is a very useful function for morphological processing of an image, that allows to select the objects that are in the image and in this case they are received from the segmentation. As can be seen from the image threshold, some objects are observed that are not of interest therefore a route is made to eliminate them, indicating that it encloses objects smaller than 500 pixels in a red rectangle as shown in Fig. 8.

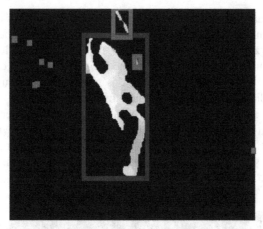

Fig. 8. Object detection through technique REGIONPROMP of the lemon leaf damaged by the miner. (Color figure online)

In Fig. 9 shows the damage caused by the citrus leaf miner enclosed in a green rectangle.

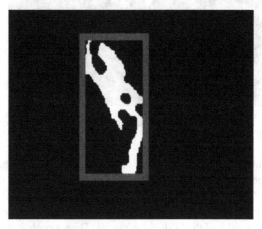

Fig. 9. Obtaining the size of the damage caused by the lemon miner. (Color figure online)

As shown in Fig. 9, the damage of the miner is seen in white and is enclosed in a green circle, also obtained with the technique REGIÓNPROMP you can get the size enclosed.

2.4 Feature Extraction

In this phase, characteristics of the segmented image are obtained through LBP (local Binary Pattern) which is a very efficient texture operator which labels the pixels of an image by threshold neighborhood of each pixel with the value of the central pixel and consider the result as a binary number.

A folder is created that stores a set of segmented images to extract features through LBP and they are saved in a training data file.

The algorithm used to extract the features can be observed in Algorithm 1.

Algorithm 1. Extraction of features from the lemon leaf
1.   for X = 1; X <= 100; X++
2.   Read image of the leaves of the lemon tree
3.   Segmentation to extract damage
4.   Dilate the image to remove noise
5.   Apply erosion to the image
6.   Show image with eroded edges
7.   Label found damage
8.   The structure of the found damage is filled
9.   The segmented image is obtained
10.   The features are stored in a file
11. end for

Two classes are created containing characteristics of 100 images containing plague and 100 images of lemon leaf without plague, according to the MatLab ® software compiler recognition is indicated with the following values:

- The value 110 which is the characteristics of the images that contain damage of the miner.
- The value 121 which are those images of healthy lemon leaf.

In Fig. 10, the characteristics of the images that will be processed are obtained, taking 100 images as input (some with damage from the lemon miner and others healthy).

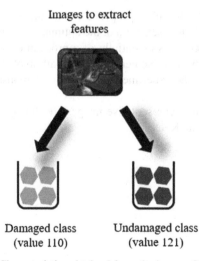

Fig. 10. Characteristics obtained from the images for training.

2.5 Classification

The nearest neighbors it is a supervised classification method used to estimate the density function of the predictions for each class.

To classify a test folder is created which contains over 100 images of plague and non-plague lemon leaves, these are analyzed with MatLab ® software and something similar is obtained as can be seen in Fig. 11. The classified image and the number you provide, corresponds to the class that has a plague as mentioned in the previous phase.

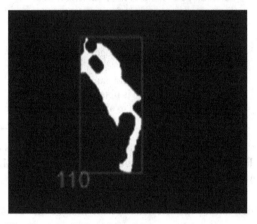

Fig. 11. Image classified with lemon miner damage.

3 Results and Discussion

In this article, an algorithm has been proposed to find the features of an image of the leaves of a lemon tree, including selection of the optimal color space (color model HSL, channel S). The method consists essentially of a procedure to find lemon leaf miner damage. The process has been implemented in the MatLab ® application, designed for digital image processing. The experiments carried out demonstrated the viability and efficacy of the proposal.

In Fig. 12, can be seen 8 representative images are shown of those used in the test for classification through the KNN.

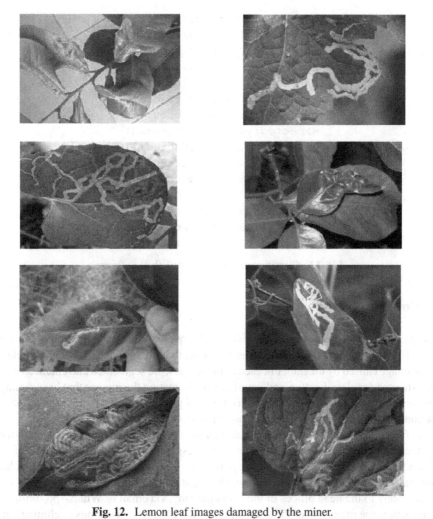

Fig. 12. Lemon leaf images damaged by the miner.

In Fig. 13, the results obtained for each of the images are shown with the legend "expected"; in addition there is the name of the image following it the prediction to the class to which it belongs, as well as explained in the previous phases about the classes.

```
expected:y - predicted:121
expected:y1 - predicted:121
expected:i2 - predicted:121
expected:y6 - predicted:121
expected:y7 - predicted:121
expected:n5 - predicted:110
expected:n6 - predicted:110
expected:y4 - predicted:121
expected:111 - predicted:110
expected:14 - predicted:110
expected:y8 - predicted:121
expected:18 - predicted:110
expected:y9 - predicted:121
expected:19 - predicted:110
expected:y10 - predicted:121
```

Fig. 13. Classifier results, using MatLab ® Software.

4 Conclusions

The present work proposes artificial vision techniques, for the classification of damage caused by the miner pest on citrus leaves that affect the cultivation of the Mexican lemon. The damage caused by the miner in each of the images, are segmented and characteristics are extracted for classification and your training indicating the images that have damage and those that do not. The training dataset gave a positive result when entering images for consultation, being 95% effective, according to the results mentioned above.

A future work to be done, is to develop an App to be used on the site of lemon trees are located and in real time the following process is carried out: take a photo of the lemon tree (leaves), carry out the damage recognition process caused by the citrus leaf miner and store the results on the mobile device (smartphone or tablet). The result is sent immediately to the head offices of the fruit company, via email or WhatsApp. With this information, the managers of the company will make the right decisions to eliminate the citrus leaf miner from their crops.

References

1. Moore, S.D., Duncan, L.W.: Microbial control of insect and mite pests of citrus. In: Lacey, L.A. (ed.) Microbial control of insect and mite pests, pp. 283–298. Academic Press, London (2017)
2. Hu, J., Jiang, J., Wang, N.: Control of citrus Huanglongbing via trunk injection of plant defense activators and antibiotics. Phytopathology **108**(2), 186–195 (2018)
3. Chávez-Almazán, L.A., et al.: Análisis regional de la contaminación por plaguicidas organoclorados en leche humana en Guerrero, México. Revista internacional de contaminación ambiental **34**(2), 225–235 (2018). http://dx.doi.org/10.20937/rica.2018.34.02.04
4. Organización Mundial de la salud (OMS). Programa internacional de seguridad de sustancias químicas; impacto de las sustancias químicas en la salud (2016)

5. Buccini, J., Cortinas, C.: Impacto de la producción y uso de sustancias químicas en la salud y el ambiente. Documento de antecedentes encargado por el Grupo de Tarea sobre Sustentabilidad Ambiental del Proyecto Milenio de las Naciones Unidas Naciones Unidas, Nueva York. siscop. inecc. gob. mx/producción y uso de sustancias químicas consultada el **15**(01), 2014 (2004)

6. Pardo, S., et al.: Insecticide resistance of adults and nymphs of Asian citrus psyllid populations from Apatzingán Valley, Mexico. Pest Manage. Sci. **74**(1), 135–140 (2018)

7. Grajales-Conesa, J., Meléndez-Ramírez, V., Leopoldo, C.L., Sánchez, D.: Native bees in blooming orange (Citrus sinensis) and lemon (C. limon) orchards in Yucatán, Mexico. Acta Zoológica Mexicana (nueva serie) **29**(2), 437–440 (2013)

8. López-Hernández, W.A., Garza-Bueno, L.E., Cruz-Galindo, B., Nieto-Angel, R.: Competitividad del limón persa en la región del Papaloapan, Oaxaca. Revista Mexicana de Ciencias Agrícola. **10**(4), 921–934 (2019). https://doi.org/10.29312/remexca.v10i4.408

9. Pandey, N.D., Pandey, Y.D.: Bionomics of Phyllocnistis citrella Stn. (Lepidoptera: Gracillariidae). Indian J. Entomol. **26**, 417–422 (1964)

10. Sohi, G.S., Verma, G.C.: Feeding habits of Phyllocnistis citrella in relation to the anatomical structure of the leaf. Indian J. Entomol. **27**, 483–485 (1965)

11. Chhetry, M., GUPTA, R., Tara, J.S., Pathania, P.C.: Seasonal abundance of citrus leaf miner Phyllocnistis citrella Stainton (Lepidoptera: gracillariidae) from Jammu and Kashmir. J. Insect Sci. **25**(2), 144–149 (2012)

12. Belasque Júnior, J., Amorim, L.: Dinâmica espacial do cancro cítrico, interação com a larva minadora dos citros (Phyllocnistis citrella) e diversidade genética do seu agente causal (Xanthomonas axonopodis PV. citri) (2005)

13. Jeon, G.: Color image enhancement by histogram equalization in heterogeneous color space. Int. J. Multimedia Ubiquitous Eng. **9**(7), 309–318 (2014). http://dx.doi.org/10.14257/ijmue.2014.9.7.26

14. Hamuda, E., Glavin, M., Jones, E.: A survey of image processing techniques for plant extraction and segmentation in the field. Comput. Electron. Agric. **125**, 184–199 (2016)

15. Woebbecke, D.M., Meyer, G.E., Von Bargen, K., Mortensen, D.: Plant species identification, size, and enumeration using machine vision techniques on nearbinary images. SPIE Opt. Agric. For. **1836**, 208–219 (1992)

16. Hernández-Hernández, J.L., García-Mateos, G., González-Esquiva, J.M., Escarabajal-Henarejos, D., Ruiz-Canales, A., Molina-Martínez, J.M.: Optimal color space selection method for plant/soil segmentation in agriculture. Comput. Electron. Agric. **122**, 124–132 (2016)

17. Schaffer, B., et al.: Citrus leafminer (Lepidoptera: Gracillariidae) in lime: assessment of leaf damage and effects on photosynthesis. Crop Prot. **16**(4), 337–343 (1997)

Temporal Aspects of Chlorophyll-a Presence Prediction Around Galapagos Islands

Fernando Chávez-Castrillón[1,2], Massimo Coltorti[2], Roberta Ivaldi[3],
Estrella Lucena-Sánchez[4,5(✉)], and Guido Sciavicco[5]

[1] Dept. of Educ. and Doct., Ecuadorian Navy, Guayaquil, Ecuador
fchavez@armada.mil.ec
[2] Department of Physics and Earth Science, University of Ferrara, Ferrara, Italy
massimo.coltorti@unife.it
[3] Hydrographic Institute of the Italian Navy, Genoa, Italy
roberta_ivaldi@marina.difesa.it
[4] Department of Physics, Informatics and Mathematics, University of Modena
and Reggio Emilia, Modena, Italy
[5] Department of Mathematics and Computer Science,
University of Ferrara, Ferrara, Italy
{estrella.lucenasanchez,guido.sciavicco}@unife.it

Abstract. Chlorophyll-a is a specific form of chlorophyll used in oxygenic photosynthesis which has been linked to nutrient presence in sea waters, and being able to correctly determine its concentrations may turn out to be a key step in helping preventing and controlling illegal fishing activities in certain areas. In this work, we consider open access data taken from the Copernicus space program (currently used in the European Union for Earth observation and monitoring) that include several physical and biochemical variables and measurements of the ocean surrounding Galapagos Islands (Ecuador). We use such data in an attempt to build a reliable spatial temporal model that can be used to forecasting the presence of Chlorophyll-a, using a novel technique called spatial-temporal regression. Our initial results, that show a probability of certainty in the forecast from 0.75% (5 days ahead prediction) to 82% (1 day ahead prediction), can be used to design a more complex, reliable, and implementable prediction model for real-time forecasting of Chlorophyll-a presence.

Keywords: Chlorophyll-a concentrations · Temporal regression · Illegal fishing prevention

1 Introduction

Oceanography is an important Earth science that studies the physical and biological aspects of the ocean. It requires a large amounts of data for modelling, investigating, predicting and explaining the different natural phenomena. Such

© Springer Nature Switzerland AG 2020
R. Valencia-García et al. (Eds.): CITI 2020, CCIS 1309, pp. 98–110, 2020.
https://doi.org/10.1007/978-3-030-62015-8_8

data is usually provided by scientific instruments like satellites, oceanographic ships, buoys, and others. Because available data are growing in quantity and in complexity, the need is emerging for a *machine learning* approach to integrate, if not substitute, the more classical statistical approach used in oceanographic research. Among the many applications of oceanography to marine resources management, controlling and preventing illegal fishing stands out as a very important one. Illegal, unregulated, and unreported fishing is becoming more sophisticated, and, as it turn out, oceanographic conditions are predominant predictors of the seasonal variations in fishing effort [3]. Being able to automatically identifying favourable fishing zone is one possible strategy for helping illegal fishing activity monitoring and preventing, and, to this end, automatically identifying favourable oceanic conditions in a promising strategy.

Chlorophyll-a is a specific form of chlorophyll used in oxygenic photosynthesis which has been linked to nutrient presence in several different areas [7,8,19]. It is known that certain kind of satellite data can be used to predict the presence of Chlorophyll-a in oceanic areas [7,9]. In this work, we consider open access data taken from the Copernicus space program, currently used in the European Union for Earth observation and monitoring, in an attempt to build a reliable *spatial-temporal* prediction model for Chlorophyll-a presence around Galapagos Islands, particularly, in the Galapagos Marine Reserve (GMR), with the purpose of creating the basis for an *implementable, cost-effective,* and *reliable* model for potential fishing area prediction to be used in illegal fishing control activities. At certain geographical point the presence of Chlorophyll-a, in combination with relevant physical, chemical, and biological variables of the same point can be thought of as a multivariate spatial-temporal series, in which the Chlorophyll-a plays the role of dependent variable. As such, *multivariate spatial-temporal regression* can be used to estimate not only the functional model, but also the temporal component for each predictor. Multivariate spatial-temporal regression is simply a multivariate regression in which the spatial-temporal component are explicitly taken into account via suitable data transformations. In its simplest form, it consists of adding suitable *lagged* data to the original ones so that the temporal history of an element plays a role in the regression; more complex techniques include automatic optimization of lags, such as in [11]. The problem considered in this paper is particularly complex from the spatial-temporal point of view. Therefore, in this work we want to first assess the expected improvement that lagged data can entail, effectively paving the way toward a more systematic exploration and optimization of the possible data transformations that take into account both the space and time components.

This paper is organized as follows. In Sect. 2 we give a short account of the current literature that concerns oceanographic data and learning. In Sect. 3 we give some practical motivations for this work and the problem we want to solve. Then, in Sect. 4 we describe the data that we have used, the mathematical model that we have applied, and discuss our results, before concluding.

2 Related Work

As the quantity, the complexity, and the availability of oceanographic data grows, machine learning-based approaches to their analysis are becoming ever more common [1]. Typical applications range from climate prediction, habitat modelling, and climate change analysis, to species distribution and identification, resource management, and environmental protection (see [18] for a recent review). Examples of concrete applications include species identification [10], automatic detection and classification of ocean pollution, oil spills, alga bloom, plastic pollution [6], as well as several fishing control-related applications. Fishing control, and connected activities, in particular, are of special interest in this work.

The surveillance of illegal fishing activities and the detection of abnormal fishing vessel behaviours are critical issues for the management of marine resources. Machine learning techniques were employed for fishing gear recognition starting from *vessel monitor system* (in short, *VMS*) data to detect abnormal VMS patterns of fishing vessels in Indonesia [14]. Moreover, while the coastal fisheries in national waters are closely monitored, at least by some countries, in high seas, there is a lot of uncertainty. For the automatic control of fishing activities in high seas it is necessary to understand the general behaviour of fishing fleets, to enforce fisheries management and conservation measures worldwide. *Satellite-based automatic information systems* (in short, *S-AISs*) are now commonly installed on the vessels and have the function to control the ships' positions, and have been proposed as a tool for monitoring the movements of fishing fleets in near real-time. Using this data, models have been developed to detect potential fishing activity from trawlers, longliners and purse seiners [17]. However, illegal fishing control is related with ocean resource and habitat management, because it affects the conservation of fishery resources, and taking the correct decisions is often a hard problem, due to the non-availability of specific data. Accordingly [18], machine learning techniques have demonstrated the potential to eliminate data gaps, predict future events, and increase the accuracy of the results. The satellite remote sensing for marine applications started in the early 1960s, with the first pictures of the Earth. Currently, satellites are being used in the indirect detection of fishes, via measuring water temperature, which is the most used environmental parameter in investigations concerning the relationship between environment and fish abundance [16]. Nevertheless, other oceanographic variables exist that can be used to increase the accuracy of the prediction. The lack of datasets that include such oceanographic variables taken directly from permanent observation stations or from ships have contributed to satellite remote sensing playing a pivotal role, considering that satellites offer the opportunity to measure and monitor multiple oceanographic variables at the same time [15]. This approach has been applied on large spatial scales with high temporal resolutions in coastal waters, but while oceanic color satellites suffer of serious limitations, such as the low spatial resolution of sensor systems, using machine learning techniques, such as artificial neural networks and support vector machines, allowed to develop Chlorophyll-a models, for example in [13].

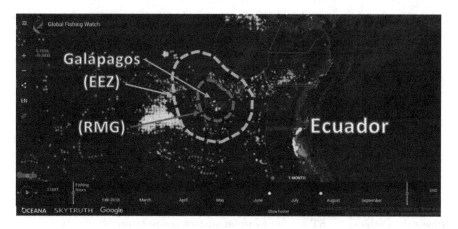

Fig. 1. An aerial view of fishing ships around Galapagos exclusive economic zone. Snapshot taken in August, 2019. Source: http://www.globalfishingwatch.org.

Sea surface temperature and chlorophyll images are considered fundamental for the identification of fishing zones, which in turn is essential for illegal fishing detection. Features such as eddies, gyres, meanders, and upwelling that are indicative of fish abundance areas, can be derived from satellite information. One of the elements that indicate the quality of the water is the concentration of Chlorophyll-a, whose presence is highly correlated with the phytoplankton biomass [7]. Phytoplankton is the base of the food chain in the marine ecosystems, and it is the main responsible for the primary production. A very recent multivariate statistical approach to predict Chlorophyll-a levels in coastal marine ecosystems, taking into account 20 variables from 64 observations is reported in [9]. The main differences between [9] and our approach are that the former uses coastal data extracted from sensor, instead of high sea data from satellite, and, it does not include a spatio-temporal study of the cause-effect relationships.

3 Motivation

Galapagos Islands are located more than $1000kms$ westward of the Ecuador's continental coast. In 1998, the Government of Ecuador created the *Galapagos Marine Reserve* (in short, *GMR*) to preserve the resources of the islands. In 2001, Galapagos was declared a World Heritage by UNESCO. Due to its location, the islands receive, the influence of two currents, the so-called Humboldt's cold current and Panama's warm current from the east, and the so-called cold and deep Cromwell current from the west. These currents carry waters plenty of nutrients from the sea bottom to the surface. Because of this combination, Galapagos has extremely high productivity areas with diverse marine organisms [12], attracting various species towards the exclusive economic zone of the Galapagos and its surroundings. For this reason, it receives pressure from industrial fishing, principally from Asia, as shown in Fig. 1. Very often, the activities around

Table 1. A description of the physical and the biochemical variables used in this experiment.

	Variable	Description	Unit
Biochemical variables	Chl	Total chlorophyll-a	mg/m^3
	Fe	Dissolved iron	$mmol/m^3$
	NO3	Nitrate	$mmol/m^3$
	O2	Dissolved oxygen	$mmol/m^3$
	pH	ph	–
	PO4	Phosphate	$mmol/m^3$
	Si	Dissolved silicate	$mmol/m^3$
	SPCO2	Surface CO2	pa
Physical variables	ST	Sea water surface temperature	°C
	DT	Sea water $-40\,m$ temperature	°C
	So	Salinity	$1/e^3$
	Zos	Sea surface height	m
	Mlotst	Mixed layer depth	m
	Uo	Northward sea current water velocity	m/s
	Vo	Eastward sea current water velocity	m/s

the maritime limits become in illegal fishery, which is very difficult to control due to the immense Galapagos' maritime territory. The effective control of maritime spaces can only be carried out through satellite monitoring; however, an extremely expensive solution. Less expensive solutions require the use of VMSs and S-AISs systems, which are installed onboard the fishing ships, to monitor the position and fishing activities; although, these systems can be disconnected by the ships when performing illegal fishing activities.

An alternative solution to help illegal fishing control while reducing the cost of surveillance is being able to predict the areas where fishing activity may take place. This prediction is related to oceanographic variables, chlorophyll levels and sea temperatures being two of the most important ones. It is in fact known that distribution and migration of species is strongly influenced by these two variables [19]. Therefore, in this research we try to develop a model that can predict chlorophyll levels at open sea, in an attempt to identify the areas where is most probable to find a high concentration of chlorophyll. With this information, law enforcement ships can monitor these areas more closely, looking forward to intercept ships during illegal and unregulated fishing activities.

4   Chlorophyll Prediction

Temporal Regression. Given a data set A with n independent variables $A_1, \ldots, A_n$ and one observed variable B, solving a linear regression problem consists of finding $n + 1$ *parameters* (or *coefficients*) $c_0, c_1, \ldots, c_n$ so that the equation:

$$B = c_0 + \sum_{i=1}^{n} c_i \cdot A_i + \epsilon, \tag{1}$$

where ϵ is a random value, is satisfied. Starting from a data set of observations:

$$A = \begin{bmatrix} a_{11} & a_{12} & \cdots & a_{1n} & b_1 \\ a_{21} & a_{22} & \cdots & a_{2n} & b_2 \\ \cdots & \cdots & \cdots & \cdots & \cdots \\ a_{m1} & a_{m2} & \cdots & a_{mn} & b_m \end{bmatrix} \tag{2}$$

the regression problem is usually solved by suitably estimating the coefficients c_i so that, for each $1 \le j \le m$:

$$b_j \approx c_0 + \sum_{i=1}^{n} c_i \cdot a_{ij} + \epsilon. \tag{3}$$

There are several available, and well-known algorithms to solve such an inverse problem. The performance of such an estimation can be measured in several (standard) ways, such as *correlation, covariance, mean absolute error*, among others. When A is a multivariate time series, composed by n independent and one dependent time series, then data are temporally ordered and associated to a time-stamp:

$$A = \begin{bmatrix} a_{11} & a_{12} & \cdots & a_{1n} & b_1 & t_1 \\ a_{21} & a_{22} & \cdots & a_{2n} & b_2 & t_2 \\ \cdots & \cdots & \cdots & \cdots & \cdots & \cdots \\ a_{m1} & a_{m2} & \cdots & a_{mn} & b_m & t_m \end{bmatrix} \tag{4}$$

Using linear regression to explain B, then, entails that finding optimal coefficients for:

$$B(t) = c_0 + \sum_{i=1}^{n} c_i \cdot A_i(t) + \epsilon, \tag{5}$$

because we aim to explain B at a certain point in time t using the values $A_1(t), \ldots, A_n(t)$. Equations (1) and (5) model exactly the same problem, only in the latter the temporal component is made explicit.

Lag (or *temporal*) (linear) regression consists of solving a more general equation, formulated as:

$$B(t) = c_0 + \sum_{i=1}^{n} \sum_{l=0}^{p_i} c_{i,l} \cdot A_i(t - l) + \epsilon. \tag{6}$$

In other words, we use the value of each independent variable A_i not only at time t, but also at time $t - 1, t - 2, \ldots, t - p_i$, to explain B at time t; each $A_i(t - l)$ is associated to a coefficient $c_{i,l}$, which must be estimated, along with each *maximum lag* p_i. There are available techniques, based on standard regression

Table 2. Basic statistical values of physical and biochemical variables recorded during January, 2018.

	Mean	Median	Maximum	Minimum	Variance	Skewness	Kurtosis	Std Dev.
SPCO2	47.48	47.79	62.06	32.77	9.70	−0.30	0.80	3.12
O2	177.70	188.66	230.27	57.95	1630.82	−0.68	−0.64	40.38
NO3	9.96	8.19	26.88	0.20	32.98	0.63	−0.64	5.74
PO4	1.15	1.09	2.10	0.43	0.08	0.53	−0.08	0.28
Si	7.38	6.77	21.65	2.63	9.79	0.82	−0.01	3.13
pH	7.93	7.95	8.03	7.66	0.00	−1.41	2.01	0.06
Fe	9.8E−05	7.0E−05	6.4E−04	5.2E−06	7.7E−09	1.5E+00	2.2E+00	8.8E−05
Chl	0.45	0.32	2.03	0.13	0.09	1.69	2.47	0.31
Vo	−0.05	−0.03	1.11	−1.42	0.05	−0.51	1.85	0.23
Uo	−0.03	−0.03	1.26	−1.41	0.07	−0.06	1.45	0.27
Mlotst	13.30	9.00	87.30	2.90	103.16	1.83	3.77	10.16
So	34.88	34.96	36.68	32.90	0.19	−0.89	1.21	0.44
Zos	0.21	0.20	0.46	0.04	0.00	0.61	−0.01	0.06
ST	24.35	24.36	29.10	18.35	1.89	−0.02	−0.11	1.37
DT	21.19	21.99	28.18	11.41	9.87	−0.51	−0.82	3.14

algorithms, that allow one to solve the inverse problem associated to (6). The question to be addressed is how to estimate p_i, for each variable A_i. Moreover, our problem presents a further degree of complexity. Even assuming that we have solved (6), it would not be very useful for illegal fishing control, because it would be a prediction for the current day, while it may be necessary more than one day to reach the geographical points with higher Chlorophyll-a predictions (which are candidates for illegal fishing areas). To solve this inconvenience, we use linear temporal *forecasting* regression with a temporal range of k units:

$$B(t + k) = c_0 + \sum_{i=1}^{n} \sum_{l=0}^{p_i} c_{i,l} \cdot A_i(t - l) + \epsilon. \tag{7}$$

In the particular case in which all p_is are equal, which is the case in our experiments, we denote the unique maximum lag of the problem by using p.

Data. The space program that is currently used in the European Union for Earth observation and monitoring is called Copernicus. It encompasses three complete constellations, each one with two satellites plus an additional single satellite. This system provides 150 TB of open access data every day, including fundamental measurements or estimates of several physical, chemical, and biological oceanic variables. Ocean color information of the Sentinel satellites is employed for monitoring water quality through chlorophyll-a and phytoplankton analysis; other oceanic variables such as wave height, tide, sea current, salinity, temperature, nutrient, and oxygen are used to develop hydrodynamic models to forecast the evolution of ocean variables relevant for aquaculture. Moreover, the

Table 3. Correlation matrix for our variables recorded during January, 2018.

	Chl	SPCO2	O2	NO3	PO4	Si	pH	Fe	
	1	−0.15	−0.87	0.88	0.85	0.83	−0.81	0.83	Chl
Chl	1	1	0.22	−0.05	0.08	−0.01	0.07	−0.04	SPCO2
ST	0.22	1	1	−0.94	−0.89	−0.90	0.87	−0.84	O2
DT	−0.48	0.33	1	1	0.97	0.87	−0.88	0.87	NO3
Vo	−0.06	0.07	0.06	1	1	0.85	−0.90	0.83	PO4
Uo	−0.02	0.12	−0.04	−0.05	1	1	−0.75	0.88	Si
Mlotst	−0.42	0.07	0.49		0.04	1	1	−0.68	pH
So	−0.31	−0.43	−0.19	0.14	0.03	0.39	1	1	Fe
Zos	−0.11	0.52	0.58	−0.01	−0.08	0.11	−0.49	1	
	Chl	ST	DT	Vo	Uo	Mlotst	So	Zos	

temperature, salinity, mixed layer thickness, wind, sea currents, wave heights, mixed layer thickness, chlorophyll, phytoplankton, zooplankton, and nutrients are used to develop models related with oceanic conditions and fish's habitat spatial distribution [2]. Since our ultimate goal is to build a spatial-temporal model that explains, and therefore predicts, Chlorophyll-a concentrations, phytoplankton-related values have been excluded from this analysis, as they can be considered *effects* of Chlorophyll-a presence, rather than *causes*.

Our research area is located around the Galapagos Islands, namely between 6°N and 10°S and between 85° W and 116°W. Our data come from the data base Global Analysis Forecast-PHY-CPL-001-012, containing the values of physical variables, and the data base Global Analysis Forecast-BIO-001-028, containing biochemical variables (see [4,5]). A summary of the considered variable can be found in Table 1. Our data set was constructed with daily mean values of these variables during January, 2018 (we call this data set $A_{training}$) and during February, 2018 (A_{test}), with a spatial granularity of $\frac{1}{4}$ nautical mile in every direction, for a total of 8125 geographically distinct points per day. Our data contained no missing values. Basic statistical values of all 14 physical and biochemical variables can be found in Table 2, and their one-to-one correlation can be found in Table 3. As it can be appreciated, Chlorophyll-a presents a high positive correlation with nutrients (NO3, PO4, Si, Fe), and some negative correlation with oxygen, pH, temperature, and mixed layer depth. Other parameters like surface CO2, salinity, sea surface height, and sea current water velocity seem to have a low correlation.

Our Strategy. Our strategy consists of the following three steps:

1. Estimate the maximum lag p using a selection of 1000 randomly chosen geographical points from the data set $A_{training}$, so that the average correlation for temporal forecasting regression with k units, with $1 \leq k \leq 5$ is sufficiently high.

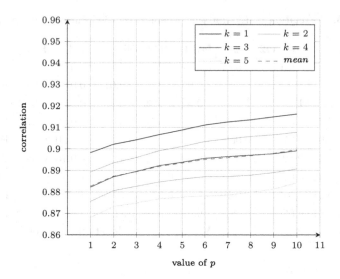

Fig. 2. Estimating the best value of p - full training mode.

2. Evaluate the decision by applying temporal forecasting regression with k units, with $1 \leq k \leq 5$, with maximum lag p using the data set $A_{training}$ with all available points recorded during January, 2018.
3. Validate the obtained model by testing it with $1 \leq k \leq 5$ on the data set A_{test} with all available points recorded during February, 2018.

Experiments. In our first experiment, 1000 random samples were selected from the $A_{training}$ to fit a multivariate regression model to estimate the levels of Chlorophyll-a, and, in particular, to evaluate the effect on the predicting capabilities of our model of adding longer histories to each of our variables. Thus, we instantiate (7) with p from 1 to 10, and with k from 1 to 5. Our goal is to establish how the 10-fold cross-validation values for each value of k increases as p increases. The results can be found in Figs. 2 and 3, in which we also show the average results among the five groups. As it can be seen, the improvement is clearly visible for p from 1 to 7, and becomes less marked afterwards, but still present at least up to $p = 10$. We conclude that using $p > 10$ is not justified, and we fix the remaining experiments to the value $p = 10$.

Following our strategy, we applied a 10-days lag transformation to the data set $A_{training}$, and evaluated the correlation, the determination index, the root squared error, mean absolute error, and root mean squared error of multivariate regression in 10-folds cross-validation mode. The results are shown in Table 4, top. Then, we validated our approach on the set A_{test}, and the results are shown in Table 4, bottom.

Discussion. In the first experiment, as we have explained, we evaluated the optimal value of p. Using a random choice of geographical points we guarantee

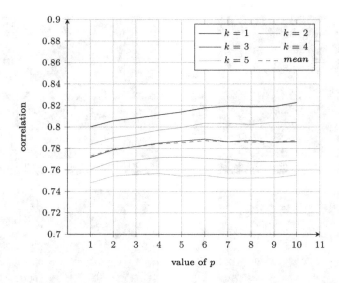

Fig. 3. Estimating the best value of p - 10-folds cross validation mode.

Table 4. Results of Chlorophyll-a forecasting. Full-training mode (top), and test mode (bottom).

	Value of k	Deter. ind.	r.s.m. err.	m.a. err.	Max err.	Corr. ind.
10-folds cv $A_{training}$	1	0.8079	0.0161	0.0836	1.1830	0.8214
	2	0.7861	0.0177	0.0884	1.0985	0.8033
	3	0.7632	0.0191	0.0928	1.0539	0.7836
	4	0.7389	0.0206	0.0965	1.0314	0.7656
	5	0.7188	0.0218	0.0995	1.0751	0.7508
Test mode A_{test}	1	0.7301	0.0149	0.0863	0.6514	0.8728
	2	0.7215	0.0153	0.0887	0.6233	0.8670
	3	0.6910	0.0170	0.0937	0.6338	0.8550
	4	0.6018	0.0213	0.1025	0.7468	0.8296
	5	0.5721	0.0223	0.1037	0.7675	0.8264

that the value of p is not biased by local conditions, and using only a small subset of the available points we guarantee that our methodology is, in fact, applicable. As we have seen, the resulting graph has the classical *elbow*-shaped aspect, allowing one to estimate at which point adding new variables is not worth the expected improvement. Also, we can see how our results are consistent for different values of k, suggesting that our approach is stable. In the second experiment, we set $p = 10$. This means that for one specific prediction we considered 10 days of history per each variable. With our training data, recorder on January, 2018, our multivariate linear regression model shows interesting correlation values ranging from 0.75 (5 days ahead prediction) to 0.82 (1 day ahead

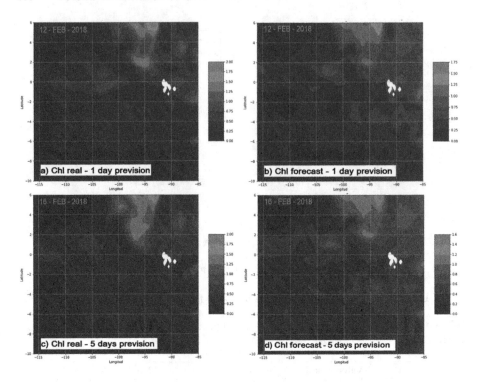

Fig. 4. Real and forecast chlorophyll map in the study area.

prediction). In order to establish the validity of our approach, the computed model was tested on our data set A_{test}, with values recorded during February, 2018. As it turned out, the correlation values are consistent, ranging from 0.82 to 0.87. In Fig. 4, we show how the error in the prediction is geographically distributed on a particular, random, day in February, 2018. As it can be seen, the 'bulk' of the concentration of Chlorophyll-a is correctly predicted even in the 5-days ahead model; the longer the forecast, however, the more difficult is to predict the correct values in low-level concentration areas.

5   Conclusions

In this work we have designed a first prediction model for Chlorophyll-a concentration in the waters surrounding Galapagos Islands, Ecuador. The main motivation behind this study is the design of an implementable, cost-effective system that allows naval forces to guess possible illegal fishing areas with enough time to intervene, and enough accuracy to minimize false alarms. The initial results show a certainty in the forecast from 0.75% (5 days ahead prediction) to 82% (1 day ahead prediction). These results allow to create a model to identify with a period of anticipation from 1 to 5 days, the areas with favourable conditions to fishing maintaining a certainty from 82% to 75%. This information can help to a better and quickly planification of the maritime surveillance's rules. Strengths of our approach are the use of open access high sea data from satellite and to tack this problem as a spatial-temporal multivariate linear regression problem focusing, to begin with, on the temporal component. On the other hand, weaknesses of our approach are that while the results seem encouraging, the role of the spatial and the temporal component of this problem are yet to be identified clearly. The ultimate goal of this project is, indeed, to build a long-term explanation/prediction model, so that naval operations can be planned in a proper way.

As future work, we want to experiment with more complex techniques of data transformation and optimization, in order to establish optimal lags for each independent variables, but also optimal spatial relationships between neighboring geographical points.

References

1. Ahmad, H.: Machine learning applications in oceanography. Aquat. Res. **2**(3), 161–169 (2019)
2. ao, R.S.: Blue Book - Copernicus for a sustainable ocean. Mercator Ocean International (2019)
3. Cimino, M.A., Anderson, M., Schramek, T., Merrifield, S., Terrill, E.J.: Towards a fishing pressure prediction system for a western Pacific EEZ. Sci. Rep. **9**(1), 1–10 (2019)
4. COPERNICUS: Product User Manual for Global Biogeochemical Analysis and Forecasting Product. Marine Environment Monitoring Service (2019). https://resources.marine.copernicus.eu/
5. COPERNICUS: Product User Manual for Global Physical Analysis and Coupled System Forecasting Product. Marine Environment Monitoring Service (2020). https://resources.marine.copernicus.eu/
6. Del Frate, F., Petrocchi, A., Lichtenegger, J., Calabresi, G.: Neural networks for oil spill detection using ERS-SAR data. IEEE Trans. Geosci. Remote Sens. **38**(5), 2282–2287 (2000)
7. Desortová, B.: Relationship between Chlorophyll-α concentration and phytoplankton biomass in several reservoirs in Czechoslovakia. Internationale Revue der gesamten Hydrobiologie und Hydrographie **66**(2), 153–169 (1981)
8. Dutta, S., Chanda, A., Akhand, A., Hazra, S.: Correlation of phytoplankton biomass (Chlorophyll-a) and nutrients with the catch per unit effort in the PFZ forecast areas of northern bay of bengal during simultaneous validation of winter fishing season. Turk. J. Fish. Aquat. Sci. **16**, 767–777 (2016)
9. Franklin, J.B., Sathish, T., Vinithkumar, N.V., Kirubagaran, R.: A novel approach to predict Chlorophyll-a in coastal-marine ecosystems using multiple linear regression and principal component scores. Mar. Pollut. Bull. **152**, 110902 (2020)
10. Guisande, C., et al.: IPez: an expert system for the taxonomic identification of fishes based on machine learning techniques. Fish. Res. **102**(3), 240–247 (2010)
11. Jiménez, F., Kamínska, J., Lucena-Sánchez, E., Palma, J., Sciavicco, G.: Multi-objective evolutionary optimization for time series lag regression. In: Proceedings of the 6th International Conference on Time Series and Forecasting (ITISE), pp. 373–384 (2019)

12. Jones, P.J.: A governance analysis of the Galápagos Marine Reserve. Mar. Policy **41**, 65–71 (2013)
13. Kwon, Y.S., et al.: Monitoring coastal Chlorophyll-a concentrations in coastal areas using machine learning models. Water **10**(8), 1020 (2018)
14. Marzuki, M.I., Gaspar, P., Garello, R., Kerbaol, V., Fablet, R.: Fishing gear identification from vessel-monitoring-system-based fishing vessel trajectories. IEEE J. Oceanic Eng. **43**(3), 689–699 (2017)
15. Monolisha, S., George, G., Platt, T.: Fisheries oceanography-established links in the eastern Arabian sea (2017)
16. Santos, A.M.P.: Fisheries oceanography using satellite and airborne remote sensing methods: a review. Fish. Res. **49**(1), 1–20 (2000)
17. de Souza, E.N., Boerder, K., Matwin, S., Worm, B.: Improving fishing pattern detection from satellite AIS using data mining and machine learning. PLoS ONE **11**(7), e0163760 (2016)
18. Thessen, A.: Adoption of machine learning techniques in ecology and earth science. One Ecosyst. **1**, e8621 (2016)
19. Zainuddin, M.: Skipjack tuna in relation to sea surface temperature and Chlorophyll-a concentration of Bone Bay using remotely sensed satellite data. Jurnal Ilmu dan Teknologi Kelautan Tropis **3**(1), 82–90 (2011)

Recognition of the Damage Caused by the Cogollero Worm to the Corn Plant, Using Artificial Vision

José Luis Bravo-Reyna[1](✉) [iD], José Antonio Montero-Valverde[1] [iD],
Miriam Martínez-Arroyo[1] [iD], and José Luis Hernández-Hernández[2] [iD]

[1] Tecnológico Nacional de México/IT de Acapulco, Acapulco, México
jlbreyna18@gmail.com, {jose.mv,miriam.ma}@acapulco.tecnm.mx
[2] Tecnológico Nacional de México/IT de Chilpancingo, Chilpancingo, México
joseluis.hernandez@itchilpancingo.edu.mx

Abstract. The vision by computer has become a very important tool and powerful in the area of agriculture and agronomy for monitoring and automatic handling of the different agricultural processes. Digital processing of images is used to segment and classify leaves in the corn fields of the Mexican fields making use of color models. The techniques of segmentation and classification using color, they are capable of processing trivial features such as: shadows, noise, pixel saturation, low light, different crop varieties and intrinsic camera parameters. Several previous investigations, have shown the importance to select the optimal color space for each specific area. In the present investigation the HSI color model is used, which was used in the software MatLab ® demonstrating the practical feasibility of the project.

Keywords: Intelligent systems · Artificial vision · Digital image processing · Crop pests · Cogollero worm

1 Introduction

The diseases and pests in crops reduce harvests, decrease the quality of the product and limit the availability of food and raw materials; the impact this has on people who depend on agriculture is very large [1]. The damages that pests can cause in crops are diverse, can cause crop losses endangering the livelihoods of vulnerable farmers, food security and nutritional of millions of people [2].

The main problem that limits corn production in the state of Guerrero is the presence of pests. Particularly corn is attacked by the cogollero worm which devastates entire crops in a few days. The cogollero worm is native to the American continent and is a pest which is found in corn, sorghum and grass; attacks around 60 species of plants [3, 4].

The cogollero worm causes scratches in the tender foliage which then appear as translucent areas being the optimal time for your control. Later the damage affects the bud and when the foliage unfolds, perforations are detected by the leaf blade or damaged

© Springer Nature Switzerland AG 2020
R. Valencia-García et al. (Eds.): CITI 2020, CCIS 1309, pp. 111–122, 2020.
https://doi.org/10.1007/978-3-030-62015-8_9

areas and in this phase excrement of the pest is observed in the form of sawdust. Serious damage to the corn plant occurs when it has a height between 35 and 60 cm; and an age under 25 days [5–7].

Really, Mexico is the center of origin and domestication of corn [8], with a great diversity of ecosystems that is why there is a high possibility of finding associated native natural enemies such as the cogollero worm [9].

Your control based on chemical insecticides has occasioned that this species acquired resistance, their natural enemies are eliminated and affect the environment [10].

In recent years, artificial vision systems have provided a non-invasive automated alternative and profitable, replacing traditional manual inspection methods and have become a simple answer and effective to different problems in agriculture.

2 Materials and Methods

To apply the different techniques based on artificial vision for digital image processing and the implementation of the image classification model. A methodology has been implemented consisting of 5 stages and which have as their end, find the damages that cause the cogollero worm in the corn fields of the agricultural parcels of Mexico. This methodology is shown in Fig. 1.

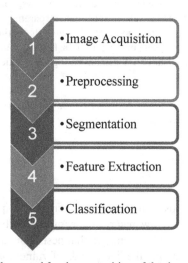

Fig. 1. Methodology implemented for the recognition of the damage of the cogollero worm.

2.1 Image Acquisition

It is the process through which you get a digital image of corn cultivation. For capturing images climate conditions must be taken into account (rain, cloudy sky, shadows, lots of light, etc.) because a non-visible image can be obtained and with noise; for this purpose the catch must be made in an environment with sunlight to facilitate the process disease detection; preferably among the 9:00 y 12:00 h. The photos that were obtained for the evidence of the investigation, were taken at a distance between 20 and 30 cm this in order to properly detect the most important features such as: color, texture, shape and size.

For testing of the research project, 100 images were taken. In Fig. 2, only some of them are shown.

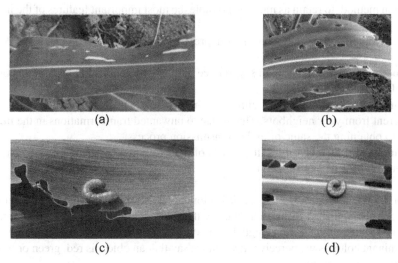

Fig. 2. Images taken from the leaves of the corn plant. (a) Little damage to the blade, (b) Perforated leaves of corn, (c) and (d) Cogollero worm in corn plants.

Vulgarly known as *"worm/isoca cogollero"* - for its action in the bud of the plant - or *"late military caterpillar"* as, if the food becomes scarce, the larvae are transferred to other crops moving in mass as a *"regiment"* causing various damages [11].

It is a polyphage plague which causes severe losses if not controlled in a timely manner. According to the behavior in the agricultural fields, is found in the group of constant pests, which can cause economic damage annually because it is present throughout the crop cycle. Its main features are shown in Fig. 3.

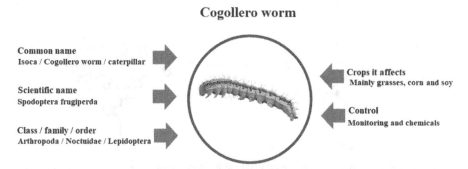

Fig. 3. Main characteristics of the Cogollero worm.

2.2 Preprocessing

This stage, includes techniques such as noise reduction, detail enhancement, remove a lot of light and lighten dark areas; for this, spatial domain methods are used.

The noise, is unwanted information that contaminates the image; this appears during the process of acquisition and digitization, making it necessary to implement a noise reduction method, to retain as much as possible the most important features of the image [12–14].

The main objectives that are sought in preprocessing are:

- **Smooth the Image**. That is to say, reduce intensity variations between neighboring pixels.
- **Eliminate Noise**. What is to eliminate those pixels whose intensity level is very different from your neighbors. This is due to unwanted transformations in the image due to obtaining the same or in the transmission process.
- **Enhance and Detect Edges**. It consists of detecting pixels where a sudden change occurs in the intensity function.

For digital image processing, the HSI color model was used [15]. In this color model, colors are distinguished from each other by their hue, intensity and saturation. Tone is associated with dominant wavelength in a mixture of light waves. So, the tone represents the dominant color as we perceive it; when we say that an object is red, green or brown we're indicating your tone.

The intensity represents the perceived illumination. The intensity gives the feeling that some object reflects more light. This attribute we can see it clearly on a black and white television. Saturation refers to the amount of white light mixed with the dominant color. Saturation is an attribute that differentiates an intense color from a pale one.

Each of the primary colors has its highest saturation value before being mixed with other colors. So, the sky blue color is very clear (less saturated), while the navy blue color is more opaque (more saturated). Another example, is the color pink (Red and white) which is less saturated; while the color red is fully saturated. In Fig. 4, a representation of the HSI color model is shown and its transformation from the RGB color model.

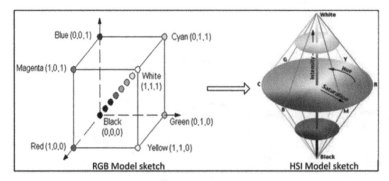

Fig. 4. HSI color model, transformed from the RGB color model. (Color figure online)

To carry out the transformation of an image of the RGB color model to the color model HSI, Eqs. 1, 2 and 3 are implemented.

$$I = \frac{R + G + B}{3} \tag{1}$$

$$S = 1 - \frac{3}{(R + G + B)} \min(R, G, B) \tag{2}$$

$$H = \cos^{-1} \sqrt{\frac{\frac{1}{2}((R - G) + (R - B))}{(R - G)^2 + (R - B)(G - B)}} \tag{3}$$

An image was processed using the HSI color model and channel I was used, obtaining the image shown in Fig. 5.

Fig. 5. Channel of interest I, from the HSI color model.

2.3 Segmentation

Segmentation subdivide an image into its constituent parts or objects, in order to separate the parts of interest from the rest of the image, therefore, the level at which this subdivision is carried out depends on the problem to solve. In the process to detect parts in an image borders of the image are identified or segmented into regions, lines, curves, etc. Another definition considers segmentation as the classification of the image points (pixels), indicating the classes to which the different pixels belong. The basic segmentation attributes of an image are: luminance in monochromatic images, the components of color images, texture, shape, etc. [16]

Thresholding is a simple segmentation technique and efficient which allows to separate pixels from an image in grayscale in two categories from a threshold value of intensity. The fixed global threshold or global T, is the one that is unique over the whole image as shown in Eq. 4.

$$f1(x, y) = \left. \begin{array}{l} 0 \\ 1 \end{array} \right\} \begin{array}{l} sif(x, y) < t \\ sif(x, y) \geq t \end{array} \tag{4}$$

Otsu is another method of thresholding that uses the probability distribution, average and variance of the intensities to define the optimal threshold.

Starting from the premise of the existence of two classes: background and objects. Using an initial threshold, two probability distributions are defined.

The threshold value methods are a group of algorithms whose purpose is to segment raster graphics, that is, separate the objects of an image that interests us from the rest of it. With the help of threshold value methods in the simplest situations, you can decide which pixels make up the objects you are looking for and what pixels are only the environment of these objects.

This method is especially useful to separate the text of a document from the background of the image (beige paper, with stains and wrinkles for example) and so we can carry out optical text recognition (OCR) with more guarantee of obtaining the correct text. This is especially useful if we want to digitize old books, in which the contrast between the text (that lost part of its pigments) and paper (obscured by time) it's not too high [17].

As with all segmentation methods is about assigning each pixel to a certain group, commonly called "segment". The image to be segmented, like any raster graphic, is composed of numerical values (one or more color values for each pixel). The belonging of a pixel to a certain segment is decided by comparing your gray level (or other one-dimensional value) with a certain threshold value. The gray level of a pixel is equivalent to its luminosity level; the rest of the color information not taken into account. Since this comparison of values is made individually for each pixel, to the threshold value method it is considered a pixel oriented segmentation method [18].

The binarization of an image consists of a process reduction of the information of the same, in which only two values persist: true and false. In a digital image, this values, true and false, can be represented by the values 0 and 1 or more frequently, for the black colors (gray value 0) and white (gray value 255).

In processing and image analysis, the binarization is used to separate the regions or objects of interest from the rest of an image. The binary images are used in Boolean operations or logical to individually identify objects of interest or to create masks over regions.

In many cases, a binary image is the result of a segmentation by gray levels or of a segmentation by selection of a certain color range.

For the image segmentation thresholding is performed [19, 20], resulting in the image shown in Fig. 6.

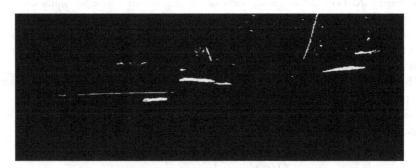

Fig. 6. Binary image of channel I, from the HSI color model.

Later, the image is binarized and small objects are removed so that the regions can be obtained of the pixels of the size considered of the damage caused by the cogollero worm.

For said process, the following method is used: BW (Binary Weight) which serves to eliminate all connected components (objects) they have fewer pixels than the binary image, producing another binary image as shown in Fig. 7.

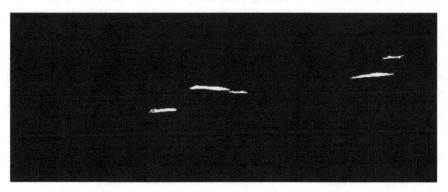

Fig. 7. Segmented image of the region of interest.

The following process to define the features, the properties of the regions shall be measured of the image of each object and limiting them by rectangles, which allows us to know the size of the region to determine the length for your classification. These objects limitations can be seen in green in Fig. 8.

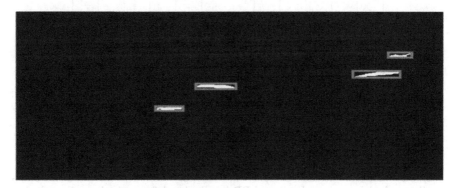

Fig. 8. Identifying the regions of interest of the damage caused. (Color figure online)

The following methods of the MatLab ® software were used for this:

a) Function REGIONPROPS, returns measurements for the set of specific properties of each component (object) in the binary image, it's an array structure containing a data structure, for each object in the image.

b) Properties BWSTATS, that can be used in contiguous regions and non-contiguous regions, depending on the case study.

2.4 Feature Extraction

Feature extraction, is a set of methods that assign input entities to new exit entities. Many feature extraction methods use learning without supervision to extract features.

A typical use of entity extraction, is to find entities in the images. Using these features can lead for better classification accuracy.

Local Binary Patterns (LBP) it is a highly effective descriptive technique for object classification within the artificial vision filtering the adjacent pixels through certain considerations and get a representative binary value. Encodes the ratio of the central pixel with the color intensity of the surrounding pixels. Due to its high discriminatory capacity, is a standard approximation for solving a multitude of problems. Probably one of its most important features is robustness [21, 22].

The LBP operator is unaffected by any monotonic gray-scale transformation which preserves the pixel intensity order in a local neighborhood, as can be seen in Fig. 9.

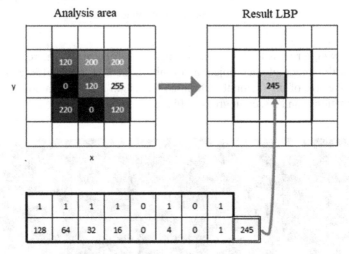

Fig. 9. Function of LBP for object classification.

Initially for the LBP algorithm you should only work with one image channel, normally worked in gray scale or an LBP is calculated for each channel; a pixel is selected which will be the axis of the analysis, an additional order of comparison is determined, which can be any that the user requires, as long as, is kept constant in all analyzes related by this technique [23, 24].

Some of the basic features that were obtained from the images, specifically in the regions of interest are: area, length and texture; which can be seen in Fig. 10.

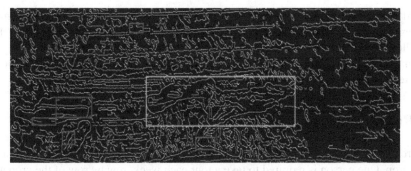

Fig. 10. Extraction of characteristics of the corn leaf damaged by the cogollero worm.

In Fig. 11, the features extracted from the images are shown. The values are observed of some characteristics that when extracted are stored in a file for further training.

The algorithm used to extract the features can be observed in algorithm 1.

Algorithm 1. Feature extraction
1.   for X = 1; X <= 100; X++
2.   Read photo of corn crop
3.   Segmentation of the region to use
4.   Dilate the region
5.   Close region
6.   Apply erosion to the region
7.   Show image with eroded edges
8.   Label found regions
9.   The structure of found regions is filled
10.   The region of the segmented image is obtained
11.   The characteristics are stored in a file
12. end for

2.5   Classification

The classification it is a process to know the identity of some pixels, that are located within the training areas, are used to classify pixels of unknown identity. The supervised classification involves the following steps:

- Training stage
- Selection of appropriate classification algorithm
- Post classification operations

In the training stage the analyst selects areas of known identity of land cover of interest (crops, afforestation's, soils, plants, fruits, etc.) outlining them on the digital image under the shape of rectangles or polygons whose numerical data are stored in the computer as regions of interest constituting the "sample training data".

At the algorithm selection stage, the most appropriate classification algorithm is chosen in order to obtain the best recognition results of the damage caused by the cogollero worm.

In the last stage that is post classification, is thresholding in order to eliminate noise or pixels out there lost in the image.

3   Results and Discussion

The research results are very encouraging, because they can be implemented in a large corn crop. One person is required to take a tour each week, row by row of the crop and take photos to detect the existence of cogollero worm. When finding the worm or larvae, immediately apply a commercial powder insecticide or in liquid form to remove larvae or worm.

Figure 11 shows the sample images with the damage caused by the bollworm in the corn crop.

Fig. 11. Sample images of the damage caused by the cogollero worm, on the leaves of the corn crop plant.

4   Conclusions

Digital image processing has proven to be an effective tool and very powerful for analysis in various fields and applications. It has been very useful to detect the damage caused by the cogollero worm in the corn leaves of the fields of Mexican crops.

The systems of artificial vision, they are powerful tools for automatic recognition of damage in the corn plant, including classification by parameters internal and external that determine the quality of the product. Further, these systems favor appropriate strategies for automatic monitoring to detect post-harvest processes, until the corn reaches the final consumer. The artificial systems they not only replace human recognition, they also improve accurate classification in real time and at the corn cultivation site.

In this investigation, the MatLab ® software was used, because it provides a set of functions digital image processing, as well as preprocessing analysis functions, segmentation and feature extraction from images.

Processing was implemented in a desktop application, using Windows ® 10 Operating System. In the experiments carried out, viability has been verified and the efficiency of the method. The segmentation method is based on the color of the corn plant leaf.

A future work to be done, is to develop an App to be used on the site of corn cultivation and in real time the following process is carried out: take photo of corn crop, carry out the process of recognizing the damage caused by the cogollero worm and store results on mobile device (smartphone or tablet). The result is immediately sent to the head offices of the agricultural company, via email or WhatsApp. With this information, the directors of the company they will make the right decisions to eliminate cogollero worm their crops.

References

1. SIAP, Servicio de Información Agroalimentaria y Pesquera. Anuario estadístico de la producción agrícola (2016)
2. Subirats-Coll, I.: La web semántica y su aplicación en servicios de información: El caso de la Organización de las Naciones Unidas para la Alimentación y la Agricultura (2013). http://hdl.handle.net/10760/22452
3. Andrews, K.L.: Latin american research on Spodoptera frugiperda (Lepidoptera: Noctuidae). Flo. Entomol. **71**, 630–653 (1988). https://doi.org/10.2307/3495022. https://www.jstor.org/stable/3495022
4. Cruz, I., Figueiredo, M.L.C., Oliveira, A.C., Vasconcelos, C.A.: Damage of Spodoptera frugiperda (Smith) in different maize genotypes cultivated in soil under three levels of aluminium saturation. Int. J. Pest Manage. **45**(4), 293–296 (1999)
5. Banda, T.J.F., Enkerlin, S.D., De Alba, F.G., Garza, B.L.E.: Importancia económica de Heliothis zea (Boddie) y determinación del umbral económico, distribución matemática y muestreo secuencial de Spodoptera frugiperda [J. E. Smith] en maíz criollo. Fitófilo **85**, 101–118 (1981)
6. Lezama, R., et al.: Efecto del hongo entomopatógeno Metarhizium anisopliae sobre el control del gusano cogollero del maíz en campo. Avances en Investigación Agropecuaria **9**(1) (2005)
7. Harrison, F.P.: Observations on the infestation of corn by fall armyworm (Lepidoptera: Noctuidae) with reference to plant maturity. Flo. Entomol. **67**, 333–335 (1984)
8. Mangelsdorf, P.C., Reeves, R.G.: The origin of maize. Proc. Natl. Acad. Sci. U.S.A. **24**, 303–312 (1938)
9. Williams, T., Arredondo-Bernal, H.C., Rodríguez-del-Bosque, L.A.: Biological pest control in Mexico. Ann. Rev. Entomol. **58**, 119–140 (2013)
10. Sánchez, S.J.A., et al.: Control biológico de las principales plagas de lepidópteros en pastos con Trichogramma pretiosum (Hymenoptera: Trichogrammatidae). In: Rodríguez, L.E., Escobar, A.J.J., (eds.) Proceedings of the Memorias del XXII Congreso Nacional de Control Biológico, Texcoco, Estado de México, México, 28–29 Octubre 1999. Sociedad Mexicana de Control Biológico: Montecillo, Estado de México, México, pp. 183–185 (1999)
11. Veliz, F., Alexi, B.: Efectos de la aplicación de insecticidas de última generación en el control del Gusano cogollero (Spodoptera frugiperda Smith) en el cultivo del maíz (Zea mays L.) (Bachelor's thesis, BABAHOYO; UTB, 2019) (2019)

12. Kalia, R., Lee, K.D., Samir, B.V.R., Je, S.K., Oh, W.G.: An analysis of the effect of different image preprocessing techniques on the performance of SURF: speeded up robust features. In: 2011 17th Korea-Japan Joint Workshop on Frontiers of Computer Vision (FCV), pp. 1–6. IEEE, February 2011. https://doi.org/10.1109/fcv.2011.5739756

13. Chaki, J., Dey, N.: A Beginner's Guide to Image Preprocessing Techniques. CRC Press, Boca Raton (2018)

14. Hernández-Hernández, J.L., Hernández-Hernández, M., Feliciano-Morales, S., Álvarez-Hilario, V., Herrera-Miranda, I.: Search for optimum color space for the recognition of oranges in agricultural fields. In: Valencia-García, R., Lagos-Ortiz, K., Alcaraz-Mármol, G., Del Cioppo, J., Vera-Lucio, N., Bucaram-Leverone, M., (eds.) International Conference on Technologies and Innovation, pp. 296–307. Springer, Cham (2017)

15. García-Mateos, G., Hernández-Hernández, J.L., Escarabajal-Henarejos, D., Jaén-Terrones, S., Molina-Martínez, J.M.: Study and comparison of color models for automatic image analysis in irrigation management applications. Agric. Water Manage. **151**, 158–166 (2015)

16. Senthilkumaran, N., Vaithegi, S.: Image segmentation by using thresholding techniques for medical images. Comput. Sci. Eng. Int. J. **6**(1), 1–13 (2016)

17. Kandwal, R., Kumar, A., Bhargava, S.: Existing image segmentation techniques. Int. J. Adv. Res. Comput. Sci. Softw. Eng. **4**(4) (2014)

18. Yogamangalam, R., Karthikeyan, B.: Segmentation techniques comparison in image processing. Int. J. Eng. Technol. (IJET) **5**(1), 307–313 (2013)

19. Hammouche, K., Diaf, M., Siarry, P.: A comparative study of various meta-heuristic techniques applied to the multilevel thresholding problem. Eng. Appl. Artif. Intell. **23**(5), 676–688 (2010)

20. Kurban, T., Civicioglu, P., Kurban, R., Besdok, E.: Comparison of evolutionary and swarm based computational techniques for multilevel color image thresholding. Appl. Soft Comput. **23**, 128–143 (2014)

21. Heusch, G., Rodriguez, Y., Marcel, S.: Local binary patterns as an image preprocessing for face authentication. In: 7th International Conference on Automatic Face and Gesture Recognition (FGR06), p. 6. IEEE, April 2006

22. Trefný, J., Matas, J.: Extended set of local binary patterns for rapid object detection. In: Computer Vision Winter Workshop, pp. 1–7, February 2010

23. Yang, L., et al.: A boosting framework for visuality-preserving distance metric learning and its application to medical image retrieval. IEEE Trans. Pattern Anal. Mach. Intell. **32**(1), 33–44 (2010)

24. Ahonen, T., Hadid, A., Pietikäinen, M.: Face recognition with local binary patterns. In: Pajdla, T., Matas, J. (eds.) ECCV 2004. LNCS, vol. 3021, pp. 469–481. Springer, Heidelberg (2004). https://doi.org/10.1007/978-3-540-24670-1_36

Integrated System for the Improvement of Precision Agriculture Based on IoT

Roberto Cabezas-Cabezas$^{(\boxtimes)}$ (ID), Jomar Guzmán-Seraquive, Kevin Gómez-Gómez, and Corima Martínez-Villacís

Facultad de Ciencias Agrarias, Escuela de Ingeniería en Computación e Informática, Universidad Agraria del Ecuador, Av. 25 de Julio y Pío Jaramillo, P.O. BOX 09-04100, Guayaquil, Ecuador
{rcabezas,kgomez}@uagraria.edu.ec, elizagusser@gmail.com,
corinamartinez1984@gmail.com

Abstract. This research presents a proposal for an integrated system focused on the improvement of precision agriculture based on Internet of Things technologies, with the objective of monitoring and evaluating in a better way the behavior of climatic variables such as humidity and temperature, integrating different devices so that the user can monitor these activities remotely and receive alerts of the conditions. For the validation of this proposal, a prototype based on this architecture is implemented for the census and monitoring of humidity and temperature in a rose greenhouse at Hacienda La Silvia located on El Triunfo - General Antonio Elizalde Bucay road; results are evaluated based on the time and precision of the data that the prototype emits, which are controlled by a desktop application.

Keywords: Agriculture · IoT · Technologies

1 Introduction

Agricultural production in Ecuador is undoubtedly one of the main sources of income for the same, currently, the agricultural sector is based on the management and control of data that are obtained concerning the soil and its properties, which is why the application of appropriate techniques of information management has become a necessity in this industry, with the sole objective of improving performance and operation. In the coastal region, in cities like Milagro or its surroundings, nurseries are a common method of agricultural production. One of the main characteristics of these centers is the need to generate an artificial ecosystem that meets the needs of the plantation, so it is necessary to talk about precision agriculture.

The overall objective of precision agriculture is to integrate spatial and temporal management of production through Global Positioning Systems (GPS), Geographic Information Systems (GIS), sensor technologies, and land mapping [1].

As the authors state, the integration of Information and Communication Technologies for obtaining and analyzing data of interest is no longer a field outside agriculture. Global positioning systems (GPS), telemetry management, the use of drones, or the integration of sensors are increasingly common practices in agriculture.

© Springer Nature Switzerland AG 2020
R. Valencia-García et al. (Eds.): CITI 2020, CCIS 1309, pp. 123–136, 2020.
https://doi.org/10.1007/978-3-030-62015-8_10

Several technologies have provided sustainable alternatives for precision agriculture, such as the development of the Internet of Things or telemetry; the Internet of Things (or also known as IoT) is one of the most mentioned technologies nowadays because of its ability to connect all kinds of devices to the Internet [2].

The Internet of Things (IoT), has positioned itself as one of the methodologies with greater resources and impact in terms of the integration of technological alternatives for the agricultural sector; the integration of sensors for real-time monitoring of climatic conditions is one of the many applications that the IoT can have, it allows to obtain the precise information and even predict these conditions.

The constant advances in science and technology have enabled different aspects or processes in the daily life of human beings to be improved. agriculture has been no stranger to this computer revolution.

For countries like Ecuador, agriculture is of significant importance, which is why for a long time ago, we have been working on solutions focused on the optimization of processes that improve or increase production, which allow us to know the status of crops such as soil and air humidity, ecosystem temperature, and levels of light or radiation.

The integration of tools related to the Internet of Things has significantly collaborated in the effective collection of information, allowing for more efficient monitoring and analysis of the plantation or crop.

The rest of the article is divided into four sections; point number two details works and research related to the progress and projection of the Internet of Things, precision agriculture, and the widespread use of technological tools in agricultural processes. Section three describes the architecture used in the prototype and reference models for application of the Internet of Things, the main microcontrollers, sensors, and actuators. In section four, the validation of the proposed architecture is carried out through the implementation of the prototype as a case study. The main results obtained are detailed, proving that time and efficiency in the control of climate variables have been improved. The fifth section refers to an evaluation, comparing the results obtained with those of other articles and research. The final section presents the conclusions obtained in comparison with other research and the improvements and future work that can be developed based on the proposed architecture.

2 Related Work

The Internet of Things is currently booming, so it is possible to see more and more projects and solutions related to this area, and agriculture has been one of the areas where most of these applications have proliferated, allowing more efficient planning and control.

Several investigations reflect that some of the great projects of monitoring of agronomic variables such as COMMON-Sense or Sensorscope, are projects that use the standards 802.15.4 for WSN, and 802.11 for (WiFi) [3]. One of the main disadvantages of production systems such as nurseries or greenhouses is the control of climatic variables. To improve the productivity of the plantation, it is essential to have efficient data on the agronomic variables of both the environment and the soil [4]. Here the authors refer to the advances that have been made in the collection, analysis, and distribution of information related to climatic conditions and the monitoring of environmental variables, especially in diversity studies.

The main methods used in the monitoring of variables have been through the integration of sensors and wireless controller boards, however, in other investigations, the use of DigMesh is observed [5]. These use XBEE transmission methods that allow easy deployment of wireless networks.

Process automation based on IoT can generate large amounts of information due to the number of devices that are interconnected; information that must be managed by the company or personnel requiring the information. The adoption of IoT would have been a complex process if a structure based on Big Data [6]. This technology allows the analysis of large amounts of data. The IoT encompasses various possibilities due to the connectivity it allows between devices, for the Big Data, this connectivity, and the process flow generate data in real-time, making it ideal for controlling agricultural processes.

Over time, there has been high growth in the automation of agricultural work; this modernization has positioned the agro-industrial sector as one of the strongest candidates for the integration of IoT tools [7]. These solutions are presented as a support in the management and control of complex processes [8]; so, there is considerable demand in the agricultural sector. Various studies confirm that, at present, the key to increasing agricultural production is considered to be the application of new technologies based on IoT [9]; which would be capable of increasing production by up to 70%, generating a more than positive impact in the coming years.

Different works related to the development and implementation of IoT technologies in the agricultural sector define structures based on layers, such as a perception or data capture layer, a transport or network layer and an application layer [10]. Usually, both hardware and software components such as sensors, actuators, embedded systems, RF devices, or monitoring elements are integrated into each of these levels [11]. The network layer is an important element in these systems, allowing the secure transfer of information generated in the capture module, in which communication protocols are incorporated that interact directly with the application layer.

One of the main applications of IoT technologies in the agricultural sector has been the monitoring of climate variables; its combination with other tools such as cloud computing has facilitated the task of processing and analyzing data in real-time.

Several works have focused their objectives on monitoring physical variables such as soil temperature or moisture applied to precision agriculture [12]. Other research has proposed IoT-based architectures that allow control of water consumption, integrating monitoring elements such as mobile technology or cloud computing [13].

Each of these proposals is based on the integration and interconnection of different devices to achieve process control; most of these applications generate large amounts of information that are processed in their systems.

[14] Real-time analysis is the common factor in these investigations, checking the variability of the environmental state through sensor networks to minimize production risks.

Each of these works focuses on a specific problem, however, the proposal seeks to propose an architecture that is not only applied in this area but can be taken as a reference model for the automation of any other process based on the integration of different devices.

3   Prototype – Soil Moisture and Temperature Monitoring System Un a Mini-Rose Greenhouse

3.1   Architecture

When talking about the Internet of things, architecture refers to the design either logical or physical of the solution including aspects such as "things" services or communication protocols.

There are different reference architectures for the Internet of Things, like the IoT ARM, which was thought by a group of expert researchers in the area to provide architectural foundations focused on the Internet of Things.

However, at present, with the constant development of IoT systems, different schemes have been specified, among which the following stand out.

Intel IoT, which proposes a simplified scheme where connectivity and security prevail [15], presents six main layers which are communication, analysis, management, control, security, and application.

IoT Simple is perhaps one of the most used reference models, it integrates five layers in its architecture which are census layer, gateways, network layer, analysis layer, and Big Data layer.

The IoTWF model (Internet of Things World Forum) is made up of companies such as Cisco, Rockwell Automation, and IBM [16]. It is organized in seven functional layers where drivers, connection layer, edge computing, data accumulation, abstraction, application layer, and process layer are detailed.

The IEEE model, not an approved standard, is rather generic [17]. It is a reference framework that allows variations in its layers improving the implementation of the IoT system. It integrates application, communication, and census layers.

Next, Fig. 1 shows the implementation model of the architecture selected for the prototype, it is based on the Intel IoT and Simple IoT models; four layers are defined that interact with each other, in this one we observe 1 segmentation and integration of layers like perception or census, storage layer, processing layer, and the cloud or application layer. Each one of these layers communicates and works together and with persistence, allowing the analysis of information in an efficient way.

The perception layer represents each of the hardware devices of the platform, it is made up of a set of sensors, actuators, and microcontrollers. For precision agriculture, a series of sensors are used to measure environmental variables such as humidity and temperature. Likewise, depending on the information collected, the prototype has the functionality to execute different actions such as turning on fans or an irrigation system; these actions are carried out through mechanical actuators.

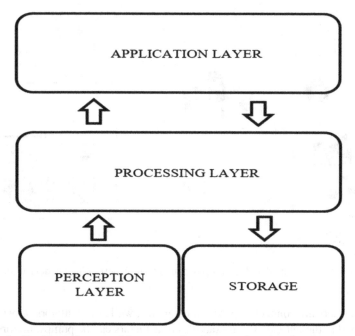

Fig. 1. The block diagram of the proposed architecture based on four layers model.

The network layer allows the communication and transmission of data collected in the census module, these are sent to the storage layer for processing. The proposed architecture allows the integration of various communication mechanisms, such as wireless communication via ZigBee, Wifi communication, or network cables.

Processing is the responsible module for managing each of the actions that are executed based on the analysis of the collected data; this layer is implemented in a cloud server and presents services such as information storage, data visualization, statistical reports from data analysis.

The cloud or application layer allows interaction between the user and the platform, the information is visualized in a desktop application, however, with the use of the HTTP protocol and formats such as JSON and XML it will be possible to access this data from dynamic web applications based on HTML5 and JQuery.

Figure 2 below presents a logic model of the structure used to detail the peripherals and processes that take place in each layer and provide a better understanding of it.

For this proposal, the application layer integrates a system based on Visual.Net that is in charge of reading and presenting the analyzed information in a structured and easy way to be interpreted by the users.

3.2 Sensors and Actuators

Sensors and actuators are peripheral devices that convert hydraulic, pneumatic, or electrical energy into the activation or control of a process [18]. They can be classified according to their output data into digital, analog, and bus communication.

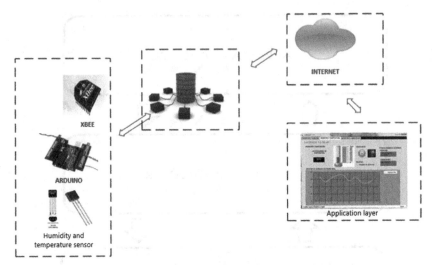

Fig. 2. Implementation model of the proposed architecture, describing the devices involved.

These sensors are connected at Arduino's inputs, while the actuators or peripherals are connected at the outputs, some examples of actuators can be pumps, motors, pneumatics, among others. For the prototype, the DTH11 sensor was used. It has a complex temperature sensor with a calibrated digital signal output. By using the unique digital signal acquisition technique and the temperature and humidity detection technology, which ensures high reliability and excellent long-term stability [19]. One of the main advantages that this sensor will offer is that it has the digital signal calibrated in such a way that it provides great quality and a lot of confidence throughout its use, this is due

```
 sketch_aug30a.ino        ReadMe.adoc          ▼
  dht.begin();
}

void loop() {
  // WAIT BETWEEN MEASUREMENTS, NECESSARY FOR GOOD OPERATION
  delay(2000);

  // READ THE HUMIDITY USING THE READHUMIDITY METER
  float h = dht.readHumidity();
  // READ THE TEMPERATURE USING THE READTEMPERATURE METER
  float t = dht.readTemperature();

  // CHECK THAT THE RESULTS ARE VALID NUMERICAL VALUES, INDICATING THAT THE COMMUNICATION IS CORRECT
  if (isnan(h) || isnan(t)) {
    Serial.println("Failed to read DHT11 sensor!");
    return;
  }

  // PRINT RESULT TO SERIAL MONITOR
  Serial.print("Humidity: ");
  Serial.print(h);
  Serial.print(" % ");
  Serial.print("Temperature: ");
  Serial.print(t);
  Serial.println(" *C");
}
```

Fig. 3. Arduino board configuration, humidity, and temperature control node.

to its 8-bit microcontroller that is integrated. Arduino Mega has been used as a microcontroller. It is an open-source platform, which is based on free hardware and software, it is flexible and easy to use, it allows to integrate different types of microcomputers in a single board [20]. It also provides consistent software in a development environment that has the characteristic of being simple and easy to use. To extract the data, the Arduino board is configured directly in the development ID that it integrates as shown in Fig. 3:

The data recorded in the perception layer are sent via a communication module to a MySQL database. Figure 4 shows the general architecture of the census node and the interrelationship of the different hardware components that are part of the architecture, it details the operation of this node and how it captures, validates, and processes the data in the initial layer and how it integrates with the storage and processing layer to generate visible and understandable results for the user; this allows among other things to streamline the process and limit the use of resources as will be seen in the results section of this research.

An Arduino Mega board is used, quite functional in IoT applications, it allows integration and communication via Wi-Fi, an aspect used to send data on climate variables wirelessly to the persistence and processing layers. DHT11 and Sen92355P sensors are integrated for this proposal due to their low cost, this being another added value of the project since no major expenses are incurred, allowing small farmers the opportunity to integrate this technology into their processes.

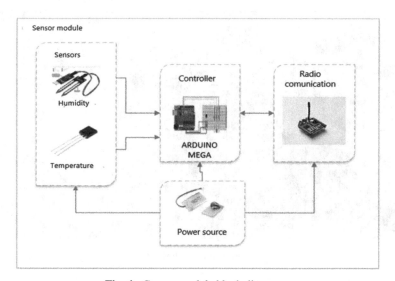

Fig. 4. Census module block diagrams.

4 Verification

To test the prototype and the proposed architecture, a small scenario is made where the module is placed and integrated with the necessary actuators to improve the control of climate variables as shown in Fig. 5:

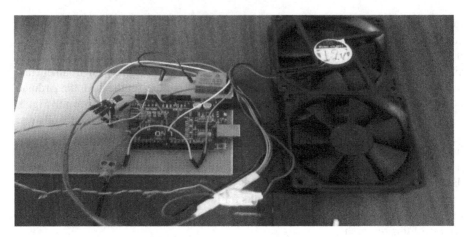

Fig. 5. Prototype controller system

This prototype was integrated into one of the rose greenhouses at Hacienda La Silvia to carry out a test with the different sensors and thus check the operation of the actuators as shown in Fig. 6.

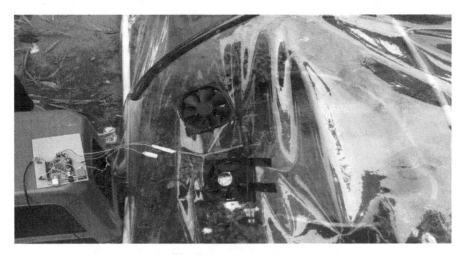

Fig. 6. Prototype testing.

Data validation is performed during a whole working day by storing and tracking temperature sensor records as shown in Table 1. According to the results obtained in the testing days on the automated greenhouse prototype, the values show that the system is capable of controlling temperature in the greenhouse, there was no adverse effect on the cultivation of the nursery.

Table 1. Temperature sensor tracking

	Hour	Values obtained during the day (temperature)	Setpoint
Día 1	11:15	17°	27°
	15:20	28°	27°
Día 2	9:10	19°	27°
	14:20	28°	27°

We can see the values generated in the prototype greenhouse, where the interaction of the system, the temperature sensor, and the actuators used is recorded. This interaction could also be reviewed utilizing a graph that allowed the effective visualization of the temperature changes as shown in Fig. 7. It shows the variations and the state of the actuators.

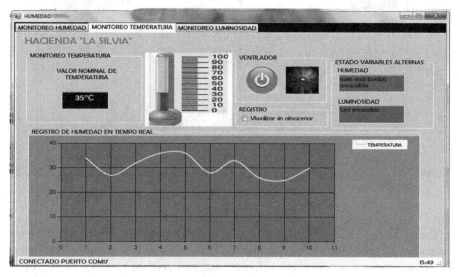

Fig. 7. Temperature monitoring

In the same way, it was possible to check the soil humidity, verifying the alerts when the actuators, in this case, an irrigation pump, were turned on according to the ranges obtained by the sensor as shown in Table 2.

This information can also be viewed from the interface proposed as a cloud layer. Figure 8 shows the variations and values generated by the humidity sensor, as well as the status of the irrigation pump that switches on automatically according to the specified ranges.

Table 2. Humidity sensor monitoring

	Hora	Promedio de valores obtenidos en el día (Humedad)	Set point
Día 1	16:00	600	300–600
	16:10	350	300–600
Día 2	17:00	601	300–600
	17:10	300	300–600

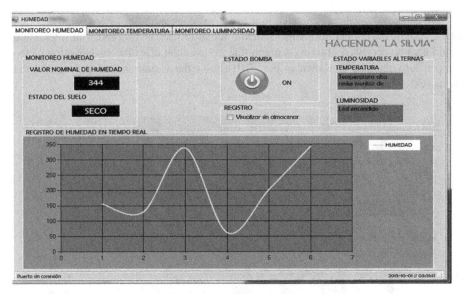

Fig. 8. Moisture monitoring

These data generated allowed an analysis related to the effectiveness of the prototype concerning the time of action as described in Table 3. There is an improvement in the time it takes to carry out the check before the integration of the prototype; it is proven that there is a clear reduction in the time it takes the person in charge to review and check the data in the greenhouse.

Significant savings were made in human resources, as a minimum of 4 people were needed to look after the greenhouse. With the implementation of this system, this factor was reduced to a minimum, and the time spent on controlling these processes is less than that used in a manually controlled greenhouse.

The implemented monitoring system has a friendly and intuitive interface and effectively shows the events taking place in the greenhouse. It also has the possibility of sending alerts to users when the records reach out of range.

Table 3. Comparison between an un-automated and an automated greenhouse (time/human resource ratio)

Invernadero sin automatizar			Invernadero automatizado	
Recuso humano		Tiempo	Recuso humano	Tiempo
Control de iluminación	2	Cinco horas	1	2 s
Control de temperatura	2	15	1	8 a 10 min
Control de humedad	3	20	1	10 min

5 Case Study Evaluation

The IoT architecture proposed in the case study meets the needs of precision and analysis that the industrial sector presents, in the work presented by Hadj et al. [6] the theme of IoT reference architectures based on cognition and BigData technologies is addressed; The authors also propose a four-layer architecture, however, replacing database persistence with real-time extraction and recognition technologies; this procedure can be very beneficial in cases of image or pattern evaluation, such as biometric systems or optical character recognition.

Like the proposed architecture, the one implemented by [6] also guarantees the handling of a variety of perception devices, which represents a great advantage.

Although a layer for data storage is integrated, this does not slow down or minimize performance on processing capacity, since data evaluation is also done in real-time, and is supported by data storage and persistence.

Cloud services have also made an essential contribution to the development of IoT applications, as specified in the work done by [14]; These services have been fundamental in improving the performance of the cloud or application layers of the different IoT services, minimizing the costs of implementing technological structures, making them available to small businesses.

As far as quality assessment is concerned, there are no clearly proposed attributes, most of the proposals found are based on the ISO/IEC 25000 quality model, however, this does not fully fit into IoT applications because of the nature of these systems, as they are very different from conventional systems. In works such as [9], [7], and [8] quality characteristics are mentioned where usability and functional suitability stand out, another characteristic that is mentioned is interoperability, it can be said that this aspect is more in line with what IoT systems represent since it focuses on the compatibility of elements; in this sense, it is concluded that the proposed architecture presents adequate levels of acceptance about the mentioned characteristics.

6   Conclusion and Future Work

The implemented IoT architecture offers the necessary levels of security, performance, and efficiency that allow a robust, functional, and high-performance application.

The agricultural processes present diverse alternatives and needs that can be solved with the integration of this type of technological tools, which makes viable and justifies projects of this nature.

The reference models allow for the integration of various hardware and software components that would facilitate the control of various processes related to agriculture or any other field in which real-time information analysis is needed. Different investigations have focused on this type of proposal [21].

One of the main limitations that are evident in the implemented prototype can be the application implemented in the cloud layer, this can be improved by integrating a web or mobile application [22].

The Arduino Mega data acquisition board is extremely useful in the elaboration of systems that combine hardware and software, the actuators allow the regulation of climatic variables such as humidity and temperature in an automatic way inside the greenhouse which represents a great advantage.

The implemented interface allows the user to visualize in a striking way and in real-time the humidity and temperature levels that are presented in the greenhouse, the alerts are timely and efficient.

As future work, it is proposed to integrate a mobile application, so that monitoring can be done at any time and from any place, providing added value to the benefits already mentioned [23].

As in the proposals, it is possible in the future to include Machine Learning and artificial intelligence technologies for data processing; this is because both technologies have become the engine of data analysis and decision making from them; the more devices are connected, the more data will be generated, which is why it is important to integrate tools for interpretation and analysis; through these technologies, errors are minimized, can be applied to different industries and provides the ability to optimize resources.

References

1. Orozco, Ó.A., Ramírez, G.L: Sistemas de información enfocados en tecnologías de agricultura de precisión y aplicables a la caña de azúcar, una revisión. Rev. Ing. Univ. Medellín, 83–102 (2015). https://doi.org/10.22395/rium.v15n28a6
2. Alvear, V., Rosero, P., Peluffo, D., Pijal, J.: Internet de las cosas y visión artificial, funcionamiento y aplicaciones: revisión de literatura. Enfoque UTE **8**, 244–256 (2017). https://doi.org/10.29019/enfoqueute.v8n1.121
3. Cama, A., Gil, F., Gómez, J., García, A., Manzano, F.: Sistema inalámbrico de monitorización para cultivos en invernadero. Dyna **81**, 164–170 (2014). https://doi.org/10.15446/dyna.v81n184.37034
4. Quiñones, M., González, V., Torres, R., Jumbo, M.: Monitoring system of environmental variables using a wireless sensor network and platforms of internet of things. Enfoque UTE **7**(1), 329–343 (2017). https://doi.org/10.29019/enfoqueute.v8n1.139

5. Casado-Vara, R., Vale, Z., Prieto, J., Corchado, J.M.: Fault-tolerant temperature control algorithm for IoT networks in smart buildings. Energies **11**(12) (2018). https://doi.org/10.3390/en11123430
6. Hadj, M., Ghozzi, F., Chaari, L.: A new architecture for cognitive internet of things and big data. Procedia Comput. Sci., 534–543 (2019). https://doi.org/10.1016/j.procs.2019.09.208
7. Tovar, J., De los Santos, J., Badillo, A., Rodríguez, O.: Internet of things applied to agriculture: actual state. Lámpsakos **22**, 86–105 (2019). https://doi.org/10.21501/21454086.3253
8. Talavera, J.M., et al.: Review of IoT applications in agro-industrial and environmental fields. Comput. Electron. Agric. **142**, 283–297 (2017). https://doi.org/10.1016/j.compag.2017.09.015
9. Medela, A., Cendón, B., González, L., Crespo, R., Nevares, I.: IoT multiplatform networking to monitor and control wineries and vineyards. In: Future Network & Mobile Summit, Lisboa, pp. 1–10 (2013)
10. Cambra, C., Sendra, S., Lloret, J., Garcia, L.: An IoT service-oriented system for agriculture monitoring. In: IEEE International Conference on Communications (2017). https://doi.org/10.1109/ICC.2017.7996640
11. Suprem, A., Mahalik, N., Kim, K.: A review on application of technology systems, standards and interfaces for agriculture and food sector. Comput. Stan. Interfaces, 255–364 (2013). https://doi.org/10.1016/j.csi.2012.09.002
12. Khattab, A., Abdelgawad, A., Yelmarthi, K.: Design and implementation of a cloud-based IoT scheme for precision agriculture. In: 28th International Conference on Microelectronics (ICM), Giza, pp. 201–204 (2016). https://doi.org/10.1109/icm.2016.7847850
13. Navarro, H., Sánchez, R., Soto, F., Albaladejo, C., López, J., Domingo, R.: A wireless sensors architecture for efficient irrigation water management. Agric. Water Manag. **151**, 64–74 (2015). https://doi.org/10.1016/j.agwat.2014.10.022
14. López, J., Pavón, N., Navarro, H., Soto, F., Torres, R.: A software architecture based on FIWARE cloud for precision agriculture. Agric. Water Manag. **183**, 123–135 (2017). https://doi.org/10.1016/j.agwat.2016.10.020
15. Kang, D.H., et al.: Room temperature control and fire alarm/suppression IoT service using MQTT on AWS. In: 2017 International Conference on Platform Technology and Service (PlatCon), pp. 1–15. IEEE (2017). https://doi.org/10.1109/platcon.2017.7883724
16. Guth, J., Breitenbücher, U., Falkenthal, M., Leymann, F., Reinfurt, L.: Comparison of IoT platform architectures: a field study based on a reference architecture. In: Comparison of IoT Platform Architectures: A Field Study Based on a Reference Architecture, pp. 1–6. IEEE (2016). https://doi.org/10.1109/ciot.2016.7872918
17. Guth, J., et al.: A detailed analysis of IoT platform architectures: concepts, similarities, and differences. In: Di Martino, B., Li, K.-C., Yang, L.T., Esposito, A. (eds.) Internet of Everything. IT, pp. 81–101. Springer, Singapore (2018). https://doi.org/10.1007/978-981-10-5861-5_4
18. Shah, N., Mahmood, F.S., Pasha, G.R.: Remote home temperature control using IoT and fuzzy logic. J. ISOSS, 91–104 (2018). https://doi.org/10.1016/j.future.2016.11.02
19. D-Robotics. DHT11 Humidity & Temperature Sensor 9 (2010)
20. Rajkumar, M.N., Abinaya, S., Kumar, V.V.: Intelligent irrigation system—an IOT based approach. In: International Conference on Innovations in Green Energy and Healthcare Technologies (IGEHT), pp. 1–5. IEEE, Coimbotare (2017). https://doi.org/10.1109/igeht.2017.8094057
21. Mamani, M., Villalobos, M., Herrera, R.: Sistema web de bajo costo para monitorear y controlar un invernadero agrícola. Ingeniare Rev. Chil. Ing. **25**(4), 599–618 (2017). https://doi.org/10.4067/S0718-33052017000400599

22. Ascencios, D., Meza, K., Lluen, J., Simon, G.: Calibración, validación y automatización del sistema de riego por goteo subterráneo usando un microcontrolador Arduino. Rev. Inv. Altoandinas **22**(1), 95–105 (2020). https://doi.org/10.18271/ria.2020.540

23. Lugo, O., Villavicencio, G., Díaz, S.: Paquete tecnológico para el monitoreo ambiental en invernaderos con el uso de hardware y software libre. Terra Latinoam. **32**(1), 77–84 (2014)

Mobile and Collaborative Technologies

IntelihOgarT: A Smart Platform to Contribute Comfort in Intelligent Home Environments by Using Internet of Things Paradigm and Machine Learning

Josimar Reyes-Campos[1]([✉]), Giner Alor-Hernández[1], Isaac Machorro-Cano[1],
José Luis Sánchez-Cervantes[2], Hilarión Muñoz-Contreras[1],
and José Oscar Olmedo-Aguirre[3]

[1] Tecnológico Nacional de México/I. T. Orizaba, Av. Oriente 9, 852. Col. Emiliano Zapata, 94320 Orizaba, Veracruz, Mexico
josi.reyescampos@gmail.com, {galor,hmnoz}@ito-depi.edu.mx, imachorro@gmail.com
[2] CONACYT- Instituto Tecnológico de Orizaba, Av. Oriente 9 no. 852. Col. Emiliano Zapata, 94320 Orizaba, Veracruz, Mexico
jsanchezc@ito-depi.edu.mx
[3] Department of Electrical Engineering, CINVESTAV-IPN, Av. Instituto Politécnico Nacional 2, Col. San Pedro Zacatenco 508, Delegación Gustavo A. Madero, 07360 Mexico City, Mexico
oolmedo@cinvestav.mx

Abstract. Nowadays, a large amount of people has access to the use of emerging information and communication technologies. These technologies allow interaction among people and communication between devices that can be monitored or even controlled without the need for being physically in the same place as the user. From this perspective, Internet of Things (IoT) and Machine Learning have emerged as technologies that allow monitoring, controlling (in person or remotely) devices installed in houses or buildings in order to detect behavior patterns to suggest feasible scenarios of comfort in smart houses. For this reason, intelligent configuration approaches for home automation control systems are required. Taking this into account, this work presents the development of a mobile application that performs the process of smart configuration of comfort in the field of home automation by using Machine Learning and IoT.

Keywords: Automatic configuration · Home automation · Internet of Things · Machine learning

1 Introduction

According to Krishna et al. [1], the Internet of Things (IoT) consists of interconnected physical devices and software components. These connected things or objects exchange information to provide a service to the end user. Currently, there are a large number of

© Springer Nature Switzerland AG 2020
R. Valencia-García et al. (Eds.): CITI 2020, CCIS 1309, pp. 139–150, 2020.
https://doi.org/10.1007/978-3-030-62015-8_11

devices for daily use with the aforementioned interconnection capacity, such as smartphones, sensors, actuators, smart televisions, cameras, among others. IoT is considered within the domain of domotics application, which is concerned with the realization of intelligent home environments. IoT is a novel field which can highly benefit from solutions inspired by service-oriented principles to enhance the convenience and security of modern home residents [2]. Also known as home automation, domotic is a set of techniques aimed to achieve the automatic control of a home, considering security, energy management, welfare or communications schemes. Comfort is essential in a home automation system and it is based on the actions taken to improve the well-being and comfort of an environment.

The application of domotic in the IoT faces certain challenges such as the lack of platforms that allow communication between devices, the development and implementation of security protocols that protect the privacy of users or the establishment of automatic configurations through smart schemes that analyze the tastes and usage history of the users [3].

In the Encyclopedia of Computer Science [4] Machine Learning is defined as the study of methods for constructing and improving software systems by analyzing examples of their desired behavior rather than by directly programming them. Machine Learning methods are appropriate in application settings where people are unable to provide precise specifications for desired program behavior, but where examples of this behavior are available. Machine Learning has been widely applied successfully to different domains such as Natural Language Processing [5, 6], energy saving [7–9], health care, particularly in the investigation of behavior patterns to determine control measures for overweight and obesity [10], between others. In the literature there are various research efforts focused on domotic and smart homes in the IoT paradigm. However, such efforts do not consider intelligent customization of comfort for the benefit of the user.

This paper proposes a mobile application (called IntelihOgarT) that performs the process of intelligent comfort through Machine Learning and IoT. The proposed application makes use of classification algorithms, which allow predicting one or more discrete variables, based on attributes of a data set. This work is structured as follows: Sect. 2 presents a review and comparison of related research works. Section 3 describes the architecture and functionality of IntelihOgarT. Finally, Sect. 4 presents conclusions generated based on the results obtained and future work.

2   Related Work

In response to the need for the development of a robust and updated context that addresses the area of domotics, IoT and Machine Learning, several works were consulted. These works were selected for having one or more characteristics similar to the solution proposed in this paper and that have been published within a maximum margin of 10 years.

Filho et al. [11] proposed STORm (Smart Solution for Decision Making in a Residential Environment), a solution that combines fog computing and computational intelligence. The solution was able to recover, treat, disseminate, detect and control the information generated by the sensors installed in the residential scenario to apply it to the decision-making process. In some cases, IoT implementations are complicated due to the exorbitant number of devices, sensors or actuators that can be used. Each device is based on hard-ware platforms that regularly differ widely. Silva et al. [12] proposed a multi-criteria model and a framework to analyze the most appropriate solution for the design of an IoT System. They tested the framework in an industrial scenario. The results presented showed that the proposed methodology helped in the selection of an IoT System, considering criteria such as energy consumption, implementation time, difficulty of use, cost, among other attributes.

In addition, the main idea of IoT is to connect as many objects as possible to the Internet, always seeking to improve people's way of life. However, connecting personal objects to the Internet opens up new security risks. Malina et al. [3] presented a security framework for the Message Queuing Transport Telemetry (MQTT) protocol that allow to improve the security and privacy services of the Internet of Things. Aditionally, Castro-Antonio et al. [13] presented an approach based on Robotics Operation Systems (ROS) that integrated different types of services into an Intelligent House Services System (IHSS). The central idea of the system was to provide services in smart homes without the need to have recognized the entire house through a collection of sensors and cameras. Current advances in IoT have achieved the introduction of connected devices with enhanced intelligence. The power of these devices can be exploited with the use of semantic connection layers that facilitate goal-oriented collaboration between devices and with meaningful interaction with humans. Kasnesis et al. [14] proposed an integrated platform that allows dynamic injections of automation rules based on semantic Web technologies within a collective intelligent environment.

On the other hand, home automation seeks to provide comfort solutions and manage energy, security and communication schemes. This includes the intelligent management of all electrical functions through the use of computing devices and emerging technologies. Saba et al. [15] presented a contribution to the modeling and simulation of multi-agent systems for a residence powered by a hybrid renewable energy system, whose objective was to reduce energy consumption. Currently, embedded systems produce a large number of information that needs to be stored and processed. The administration and control of so much information can be relegated to cloud computing systems. Frontoni et al. [16] developed a framework to allow the rapid development of complex hardware and software systems, the integration of new device classes into existing systems and the control and centralization of information.

Besides, Chacon-Troya et al. [17] explained the design of an intelligent residence application for the control and monitoring of electricity quotas. A hybrid application that combines Web and native technology was developed. The application monitors the voltage, energy consumption, ignition and other criteria, which allows to estimate the cost in money of the devices of the residence. Buono et al. [18] presented the use of a cheap and easy-to-apply Non-Intrusive Load Monitoring System (NILM) that shows, in mobile devices, historical and real-time energy consumption and sends alerts if it is about to occur an energy overload. Current home security needs can be improved with the use of IoT and home au-tomation devices. Lanfor and Perez [19] implemented a security system that uses video streaming to monitor the environments where the installation was applied.

Additionally, Li et al. [20] investigated the use of supervised Machine Learning algorithms for predicting patterns of device usage and made a comparison of the predictions accuracies of commonly used supervised algorithms in order to demonstrate that user preferences can be learned and predicted. Hong et al. [21] performed a study to demonstrate how Machine Learning has been applied at different stages of building life cycle by conducting a literature search on the Web of Knowledge platform where no study was found using Machine Learning in building commissioning.

Table 1 presents a comparative analysis between the most relevant discussed papers covering direct relationship with home automation and IoT configuration schemes.

Table 1. Comparative analysis in relation to home automation and IoT.

Research work	A	B	C	D	E
Filho et al. [11]	Yes	Yes	Yes	No	No
Silva et al. [12]	No	No	No	No	No
Malina et al. [3]	No	No	Yes	No	No
Castro et al. [13]	No	Yes	Yes	No	No
Kasnesis et al. [14]	No	Yes	No	No	No
Saba et al. [15]	No	Yes	Yes	No	No
Frontoni et al. [16]	No	Yes	No	No	No
Chacón et al. [17]	No	Yes	Yes	No	No
Buono et al. [18]	No	Yes	No	No	No
Lanfor et al. [19]	No	Yes	Yes	No	No
Li et al. [20]	Yes	Yes	Yes	No	Yes
Hong et al. [21]	Yes	No	No	No	No

A) Usage of Machine Learning
B) Monitoring smart devices
C) Controlling smart devices
D) Mobile application for domotic administration
E) Domotic automatic configuration with computational learning

The works were selected for having characteristics related to the proposal of this paper. This work proposes the development of IntelihOgarT, a smart home automation configuration platform that stands out for having five main characteristics listed in Table 1, which is included to demonstrate the similarities and differences between the related works and IntelihOgarT. Taking this into account, it was identified that the works address various issues of configuration, security and communication of home automation systems, but none have an integration between intelligent configuration scheme based on the user's historical use and the development of a mobile application for domotic control.

Additionally, as an object of interest of this work, information regarding Machine Learning algorithms was consulted. Singh et al. [22] identified CART (Classification and Regression Trees) as a proposal that contemplates multiple dichotomies and that adjusts decision trees to the type of parameters selected for predictive analysis. It develops regression and classification trees taking into account whether the dependent variable is continuous or qualitative, respectively. CART is a fast and simple classification algorithm, which allows having clear and understandable previews of constructed tree. Quinlan [23] proposed C4.5 in 1993, it is an algorithm that makes use of an "Information Gain". C4.5 begins with large sets of cases that belong to known classes. The cases, described by a mixture of numerical and nominal properties, are scrutinized for patterns that allow classes to be reliably discriminated. These patterns are then expressed as models, in the form of decision trees or sets of conditional rules, which are used to classify new cases, with an emphasis on making the models understandable as well as precise. Finally, Orellana [24] defined Random Forest as a decision tree assembler, made up of a group of weaker predictive models. Useful for regression and classification tasks, it improves the precision and stability of the results of a prediction process through the ability to combine one or more types of classifiers to reduce the variance of the predictions. It aroused as a response to the need to solve bias and variance problems caused by the overfitting of the predictive models that is generated when working with a high volume of data and conditionals.

Taking this into account, IntelihOgarT is a solution, implemented through a mobile application, capable of analyzing the historical interaction of residents with their devices. Useful behavioral patterns are recognized from this analysis that makes possible to automate home configurations. For these reasons, IntelihOgarT is an effective tool that extends and improves the functions of a home automation system. The following section describes the architecture and functionality of IntelihOgarT.

3   IntelihOgarT: Architecture and Functionality

The development of a paradigm of intelligent configuration for domotic devices that makes use of computational learning, arises from the need to have an automatic configuration scheme that analyzes the historical data of users, so that it can accurately predict the actions that would take the user if he/she had manual control of the system. In order to develop this scheme, IntelihOgarT, a mobile application capable of applying classification algorithms to a system of sensors and actuators connected to a physical home automation control system was developed.

3.1   Architecture

An architecture was designed considering the use of a previously developed physical home automation system, which includes all the necessary hardware technology for the control and monitoring of home automation devices. The home automation system is composed of sensors and actuators that act as face-to-face agents in the facilities where the intelligent system is implemented and that fulfill the function of collecting real-time information on the environmental conditions and controlling the connected devices. In turn, the home automation system has a set of Web Services that allow obtaining the data coming from the sensors, as well as activating the specific control functions of the actuators.

The IntelihOgarT architecture contemplates a module for the acquisition and analysis of information that, through the use of Web Services, obtains the data from the sensors, validates them and ensures their integrity to finally redirect them to a data mining sub-module that at the same time, analyzes the information and determines its usefulness, storing a history of information that serves as input for the modules of presentation of historical and real-time information, in addition to directly feeding the necessary inputs for the operation of the automatic configuration module. Also, a user control is contemplated that represents the mobile application from which information can be consulted, control the devices or turn on the automatic configuration scheme. This control consists of four modules: 1) Module for presenting acquired information, 2) Module for presenting historical information, 3) Automatic configuration module and 4) Manual control module.

The main functions of the architecture elements of the proposed solution are described below.

- **Physical devices:** includes all the necessary hardware technology for the control and monitoring of domotic devices. This domotic system is located at the place where the intelligent system is implemented.

  - **Sensors:** devices that are used to detect and record the presence of something (gaseous elements, light, people, among other things) in the environment of the home automation system or that there are changes in its conditions.
  - **Actuators:** devices that are (generally) part of more complex devices (automatic doors, air conditioning, among others), receive control instructions and execute the relevant actions for the different complex devices connected to the system.

- **Web Services set:** contain services that work as a communication interface between the physical devices and the mobile application. They allow the collection of data from the sensors and the sending of instructions to the actuators.
- **Information acquisition and analysis module:** includes the data preprocessing of the physical devices.

  - **Sensor data reading:** receive data from the sensors to validate them, ensure their integrity and finally redirect them to the data mining sub-module.
  - **Data mining module:** analyzes the information, determines its usefulness and stores a history of information that serve as input for the modules of presentation of historical and real-time information in addition to directly feeding the automatic configuration module.

- **User control:** represents the application to which a user has access, from which he can consult information, control his devices or let the system make decisions for him.

- **Acquired information presentation module:** it is a real-time monitor, whose only functionality is to present the information obtained from the sensors connected to the system.
- **Historical information presentation module:** it aims to present the information previously processed and stored by the data mining module. The ordering and structured visualization of the data history allow users to keep track of the use they give to the system.
- **Automatic configuration module:** is responsible for processing the data provided by the data mining module. Making use of prediction algorithms, specifically decision trees with the C4.5 algorithm [25], the module will be able to predict a user comfort setting considering its usage history of domotic devices. The C4.5 algorithm was selected for its ability to avoid overtraining or overclassing data. It addresses such issues through a one-step pruning process and has the ability to work with discrete and continuous data, in addition to handling incomplete data problems.
- **Manual control module:** is responsible for providing the user with a friendly interface from which it is possible to issue direct orders to the actuators connected to the system. This module does not use prediction models.

Below, the IntelihOgarT's architecture is shown in Fig. 1, where the modules and their relationship are depicted.

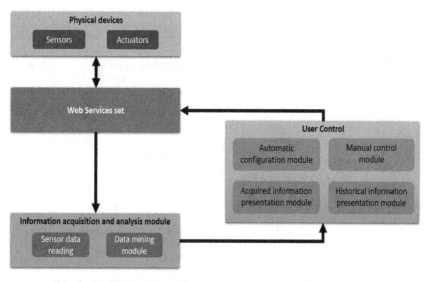

Fig. 1. IntelihOgarT's architecture with smart configuration scheme.

3.2 Automatic Configuration Module

The IntelihOgarT automatic configuration module uses the supervised approach of C4.5 algorithm to generate the correct configurations based on the usage history of the devices.

This is a Machine Learning algorithm that makes use of classification rules to generate decision trees. The application of classification algorithms is very broad, as they can be used in areas ranging from economic and financial frameworks to health and safety services, where they have even been highlighted as tools that facilitate the diagnosis of diseases such as cancer [26] or tumor detection [27]. Likewise, C4.5 has established itself as a reliable algorithm and whose performance surpasses other algorithms, such as CART and Random Forest [28]. For optimal operation, it is necessary to obtain and store the data of the actions that the user executes in the IntelihOgarT on a daily basis. Once a usage history is obtained for each device, the predictive algorithm uses the data to perform the configuration automatically: C4.5 begins with large sets of sensors readings that belong to known settings. The readings, described by a combination of numerical and nominal properties, are examined for behavior patterns identification that allow settings to be reliably discriminated. These behavior patterns are then expressed as models, in the form of decision trees or sets of conditional rules, which are used to classify new readings [23] and establish the correct settings. It is worth mentioning that the more the IntelihOgarT is used manually by the user, the more and better usage data will be obtained, which will allow the automatic configuration module to be trained more precisely, thus obtaining more accurate automatic configurations.

Figure 2 shows the manual configuration interfaces for a room and for an individual device. The constant use of the user allows IntelihOgarT to obtain data that serve for the analysis and subsequent prediction of automatic configurations for each device.

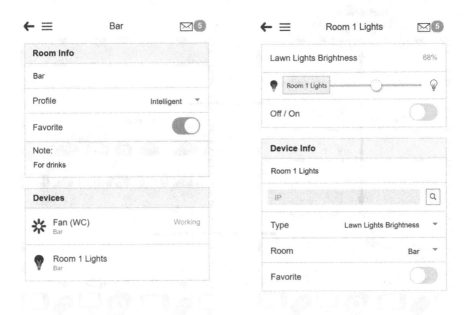

Fig. 2. IntelihOgarT interface for configuring a room and devices manually.

Figure 3 shows the interface from which the entire house can be set in intelligent mode according to the user's behavior patterns (for example, the hours the bedroom lights are turned on or off, the temperature of the air conditioning at night, among other settings). The automatic configuration module uses the C4.5 prediction algorithm to analyze data from home automation devices and establish usage patterns. These patterns function as training values to predict future configurations without the user needing to interact with IntelihOgarT.

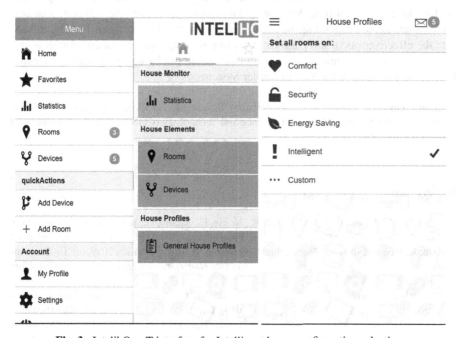

Fig. 3. IntelihOgarT interface for Intelligent home configuration selection.

4   Conclusion and Future Work

In this work, a smart mobile application (called IntelihOgarT) to provide comfort in smart home environments using the Internet of Things and Machine Learning paradigm was proposed. IntelihOgarT contemplates a module for the acquisition and analysis of information that, through the use of Web Services, obtains the data from the sensors and stores a history of information that serves as input for the modules of presentation of historical and real-time information, in addition to directly feeding the necessary inputs for the operation of the automatic configuration module. Also, a user control was contemplated from which information can be consulted, control the devices or turn on the automatic configuration scheme. The automatic configuration module, making use of C4.5 algorithm, is able to predict a user comfort setting considering its usage history of domotic devices.

This work benefit in first instance other researchers and developers who address the need to establish intelligent and personalized automation schemes to meet the needs of each particular user, so the benefits will be extended to users of home automation systems that seek to improve its comfort schemes, releasing the burden of supervising and controlling the devices connected in a smart house.

As future work, we are considering to incorporate to IntelihOgarT different configuration scenarios of domotic control, such as intelligent energy saving or security scenarios, which will allow to establish the rules needed by the automatic configuration module for correct real-time decision making, so the user can select the one that best suits his/her needs, depending on his/her current particular situation. Finally, to validate the effectiveness of the platform regarding the improvement of comfort at home, a User-Centered Evaluation is intended to be carried out by applying the User-Centric Evaluation Framework for Recommender Systems.

Acknowledgments. This work was supported by Tecnológico Nacional de México (TecNM) and sponsored by the National Council of Science and Technology (CONACYT), the Secretariat of Public Education (SEP).

References

1. Krishna, A., Le Pallec, M., Mateescu, R., Noirie, L., Salaun, G.: IoT composer: composition and deployment of IoT applications. In: Proceedings - 2019 IEEE/ACM 41st International Conference on Software Engineering: Companion, ICSE-Companion 2019, pp. 19–22. Institute of Electrical and Electronics Engineers Inc. (2019). https://doi.org/10.1109/ICSE-Com panion.2019.00028
2. Kaldeli, E., Warriach, E.U., Lazovik, A., Aiello, M.: Coordinating the web of services for a smart home. ACM Trans. Web. **7**, 1–40 (2013). https://doi.org/10.1145/2460383.2460389
3. Malina, L., Srivastava, G., Dzurenda, P., Hajny, J., Fujdiak, R.: A secure publish/subscribe protocol for internet of things. In: ACM International Conference Proceeding Series, pp. 1–10. Association for Computing Machinery, New York (2019). https://doi.org/10.1145/3339252. 3340503
4. Reilly, E.D., Ralston, A., Hemmendinger, D.: Encyclopedia of Computer Science. Nature Publishing Group, London (2000)
5. del Pilar Salas-Zárate, M., Alor-Hernández, G., Sánchez-Cervantes, J.L., Paredes-Valverde, M.A., García-Alcaraz, J.L., Valencia-García, R.: Review of English literature on figurative language applied to social networks. Knowl. Inf. Syst. **62**(6), 2105–2137 (2019). https://doi. org/10.1007/s10115-019-01425-3
6. del Pilar Salas-Zárate, M., Paredes-Valverde, M.A., Rodriguez-García, M.Á., Valencia-García, R., Alor-Hernández, G.: Automatic detection of satire in Twitter: a psycholinguistic based approach. Knowl.-Based Syst. **128**, 20–33 (2017). https://doi.org/10.1016/j.knosys. 2017.04.009
7. Machorro-Cano, I., Alor-Hernández, G., Paredes-Valverde, M.A., Rodríguez-Mazahua, L., Sánchez-Cervantes, J.L., Olmedo-Aguirre, J.O.: HEMS-IoT: a big data and machine learning-based smart home system for energy saving. Energies **13**, 1097 (2020). https://doi.org/10. 3390/en13051097

8. Paredes-Valverde, M.A., Alor-Hernández, G., García-Alcaráz, J.L., del Pilar Salas-Zárate, M., Colombo-Mendoza, L.O., Sánchez-Cervantes, J.L.: IntelliHome: an internet of things-based system for electrical energy saving in smart home environment. Comput. Intell. **36**, 203–224 (2020). https://doi.org/10.1111/coin.12252

9. Machorro-Cano, I., Paredes-Valverde, M.A., Alor-Hernandez, G., del Pilar Salas-Zárate, M., Segura-Ozuna, M.G., Sánchez-Cervantes, J.L.: PESSHIoT: smart platform for monitoring and controlling smart home devices and sensors. In: Valencia-García, R., Alcaraz-Mármol, G., Del Cioppo-Morstadt, J., Vera-Lucio, N., Bucaram-Leverone, M. (eds.) CITI 2019. CCIS, vol. 1124, pp. 137–150. Springer, Cham (2019). https://doi.org/10.1007/978-3-030-34989-9_11

10. Machorro-Cano, I., Alor-Hernández, G., Paredes-Valverde, M.A., Ramos-Deonati, U., Sánchez-Cervantes, J.L., Rodríguez-Mazahua, L.: PISIoT: a machine learning and IoT-based smart health platform for overweight and obesity control. Appl. Sci. **9**, 3037 (2019). https://doi.org/10.3390/app9153037

11. Filho, G.P.R., Mano, L.Y., Valejo, A.D.B., Villas, L.A., Ueyama, J.: A low-cost smart home automation to enhance decision-making based on fog computing and computational intelligence. IEEE Lat. Am. Trans. **16**, 186–191 (2018). https://doi.org/10.1109/TLA.2018.8291472

12. Silva, E.M., Agostinho, C., Jardim-Goncalves, R.: A multi-criteria decision model for the selection of a more suitable Internet-of-Things device. In: 2017 International Conference on Engineering, Technology and Innovation: Engineering, Technology and Innovation Management Beyond 2020: New Challenges, New Approaches, ICE/ITMC 2017 – Proceedings, pp. 1268–1276. Institute of Electrical and Electronics Engineers Inc. (2018). https://doi.org/10.1109/ICE.2017.8280026

13. Castro-Antonio, M.K., Carmona-Arroyo, G., Herrera-Luna, I., Marin-Hernandez, A., Rios-Figueroa, H. V., Rechy-Ramirez, E.J.: An approach based on a robotics operation system for the implementation of integrated intelligent house services system. In: CONIELECOMP 2019 - 2019 International Conference on Electronics, Communications and Computers. pp. 182–186. Institute of Electrical and Electronics Engineers Inc. (2019). https://doi.org/10.1109/CONIELECOMP.2019.8673166

14. Kasnesis, P., Patrikakis, C.Z., Venieris, I.S.: Collective domotic intelligence through dynamic injection of semantic rules. In: IEEE International Conference on Communications, pp. 592–597. Institute of Electrical and Electronics Engineers Inc. (2015). https://doi.org/10.1109/ICC.2015.7248386

15. Saba, D., Degha, H.E., Berbaoui, B., Laallam, F.Z., Maouedj, R.: Contribution to the modeling and simulation of multiagent systems for energy saving in the habitat. In: Proceedings of the 2017 International Conference on Mathematics and Information Technology, ICMIT 2017, pp. 204–208. Institute of Electrical and Electronics Engineers Inc. (2017). https://doi.org/10.1109/MATHIT.2017.8259718

16. Frontoni, E., Liciotti, D., Paolanti, M., Pollini, R., Zingaretti, P.: Design of an interoperable framework with domotic sensors network integration. In: IEEE International Conference on Consumer Electronics - Berlin, ICCE-Berlin, pp. 49–50. IEEE Computer Society (2017). https://doi.org/10.1109/ICCE-Berlin.2017.8210586

17. Chacón-Troya, D.P., González, O.O., Campoverde, P.C.: Domotic application for the monitoring and control of residential electrical loads. In: 2017 IEEE 37th Central America and Panama Convention, CONCAPAN 2017, pp. 1–6. Institute of Electrical and Electronics Engineers Inc. (2018). https://doi.org/10.1109/CONCAPAN.2017.8278471

18. Buono, P., Balducci, F., Cassano, F., Piccinno, A.: EnergyAware: a non-intrusive load monitoring system to improve the domestic energy consumption awareness. In: EnSEmble 2019 - Proceedings of the 2nd ACM SIGSOFT International Workshop on Ensemble-Based Software Engineering for Modern Computing Platforms, co-located with ESEC/FSE 2019, pp. 1–8. Association for Computing Machinery, Inc., New York (2019). https://doi.org/10.1145/334 0436.3342726

19. Lanfor, O.G.F., Perez, J.F.P.: Implementación de un sistema de seguridad independiente y automatización de una residencia por medio del internet de las cosas. In: 2017 IEEE Central America and Panama Student Conference, CONESCAPAN 2017, pp. 1–5. Institute of Electrical and Electronics Engineers Inc. (2018). https://doi.org/10.1109/CONESCAPAN.2017. 8277600

20. Li, B., Gangadhar, S., Cheng, S., Verma, P.K.: Predicting user comfort level using machine learning for smart grid environments. In: IEEE PES Innovative Smart Grid Technologies Conference Europe, ISGT Europe (2011). https://doi.org/10.1109/ISGT.2011.5759178

21. Hong, T., Wang, Z., Luo, X., Zhang, W.: State-of-the-art on research and applications of machine learning in the building life cycle (2020). https://doi.org/10.1016/j.enbuild.2020. 109831

22. Singh, S., Gupta, P.: Comparative study ID3, cart and C4.5 decision tree algorithm: a survey. Int. J. Adv. Inf. Sci. Technol. **27** (2014)

23. Quinlan, J.R.: C4.5: programs for machine learning. Morgan Kaufmann Publishers, San Francisco (1993)

24. Orellana Alvear, J.: Arboles de decision y Random Forest, https://bookdown.org/content/ 2031/. Accessed 27 Mar 2020

25. Saha, S.: What is the C4.5 algorithm and how does it work? - Towards Data Science, https://towardsdatascience.com/what-is-the-c4-5-algorithm-and-how-does-it-work-2b971a9e7db0. Accessed 03 Apr 2020

26. Pattanapairoj, S., et al.: Improve discrimination power of serum markers for diagnosis of cholangiocarcinoma using data mining-based approach. Clin. Biochem. **48**, 668–673 (2015). https://doi.org/10.1016/j.clinbiochem.2015.03.022

27. Mutaz, A., Abdalla, M., Dress, S., Zaki, N.: Detection of masses in digital mammogram using second order statistics and artificial neural network. Int. J. Comput. Sci. Inf. Technol. **3** (2011). https://doi.org/10.5121/ijcsit.2011.3312

28. Kureshi, N., Abidi, S.S.R., Blouin, C.: A predictive model for personalized therapeutic interventions in non-small cell lung cancer. IEEE J. Biomed. Heal. Informatics. **20**, 424–431 (2016). https://doi.org/10.1109/JBHI.2014.2377517

Analysis of the Services Generated Through Mobile Applications for an Accurate Diagnosis of Epidemiological Metrics Related to Covid-19

Katty Lagos-Ortiz$^{(\boxtimes)}$ ⓘ, Emma Jácome-Murillo ⓘ, Maritza Aguirre-Munizaga ⓘ, and José Medina-Moreira ⓘ

Universidad Agraria del Ecuador, Facultad de Ciencias Agrarias, Av. 25 de Julio, Guayaquil, Ecuador
{klagos,ejacome,maguirre,jmedina}@uagraria.edu.ec

Abstract. The World Health Organization (WHO) declared SARS-CoV-2, the cause of COVID-19, the coronavirus disease as a global pandemic [1] that affects millions of people due to its high rate of spread and its severity. So far, COVID-19 has reached almost every country in the world with no effective treatment or vaccine to eradicate it. The growing and accelerated curve of infections of Covid-19 has brought with it innumerable problems, and this has triggered zonal governments to establish prevention and control mechanisms, such as quarantines, closings of establishments with influxes of people, including schools, colleges, cinemas, gyms, among others, triggering a severe stopping in economic activities [2]. The aforementioned leads to an emotional alteration of people due to the uncertainty caused by this pandemic, the use of computer applications oriented to e-health or telemedicine (use of information and communication technologies in the area of medicine) today allows in a certain way to control health care and allows application users to enter data on the symptoms presented and recommend prevention and control treatments for those symptoms, being useful for patients as it helps to mitigate their anxiety. The present research is based on the analysis of 97 existing mobile applications used for the control and monitoring of the disease COVID-19 caused by SARS-CoV-2 virus, evaluating the characteristics presented by each one, both for the Android and iOS operating systems. The Scoping methodology was adapted in order to identify the reseach question, select the relevant applications, plot the data, compare, summarize and present the findings.

Keywords: COVID-19 · Mobile applications · Artificial intelligence · Digital technology

1 Introduction

COVID-19 is an infectious disease that usually causes respiratory diseases that can range from the common cold to severe acute respiratory syndrome (SARS) that is induced by a virus recently discovered, SARS-CoV-2. Many infected people have mild symptoms that after treatment recovers without long-term secuels, however the elderly or people

© Springer Nature Switzerland AG 2020
R. Valencia-García et al. (Eds.): CITI 2020, CCIS 1309, pp. 151–165, 2020.
https://doi.org/10.1007/978-3-030-62015-8_12

with cronic health problems, such as respiratory, cardiovascular, diabetes, or cancer tend to develop the disease much faster and could even cause death [3]. As it is shown in Fig. 1 according to the WHO [4] it can be observed a world map of coronavirus: more than 12.9 million cases detected and more than 570,000 deaths worldwide. Countries with the highest intensity colors are those with the highest number of infected people.[1]

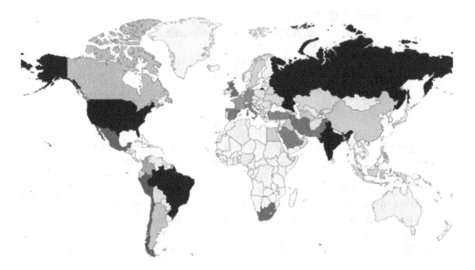

Fig. 1. Coronavirus in the world

As a consequence, the high levels of spread of the virus have led local governments to take radical measures to counter contagions. Among the measures taken, people are not able to leave home, they can't attend social gatherings such as weddings, baptisms, and funerals, also any kind of event which gathers a multitude of people were suspended such as sports events, cinemas, gyms, concerts, among others, as well as attendance at colleges and universities.

Also, governments have promoted home isolation so that nobody leaves their places except in urgent or high need situations. There are even patrols on the streets, preventing people from walking around without a valid justification. Information updated as of July 10, 2020.

According to the information published by the WHO [4] the most affected country is the United States, with more than 3.3 million infections and more than 135,000 deaths, then Brazil, which exceeds 1.8 million cases and more than 72,000 deaths. India with more than 878,000 infections and 23,100 deaths. Below are Russia, which exceeds 732,000 infected and registers more than 11,400 deaths; Peru, which already exceeds 326,000 cases; Chile, with more than 317,000 cases; Mexico, with 300,000 cases; and the United Kingdom, with more than 291,000 infections.

Spain, Iran, South Africa, Pakistan, Saudi Arabia, and Italy have around 250,000 cases, Saudi Arabia, Turkey and Germany already exceeded 200,000 cases. There are

---

[1] Information updated as of July 10, 2020.

also cases in countries like Bangladesh, France, Colombia, Canada, Qatar, and Argentina. And China, the epicenter of the pandemic in December 2019, has just over 83,600 infected people.

As a result of the spread of the virus, more than half of the world's population has been subjected to some form of confinement, also social distancing has been imposed, and displacement has been paralyzed, just as economic activities, causing a severe downturn across the globe. With data presented by Johns Hopkins University, it can be visualized that until August 31st, one of the most affected countries per 100,000 inhabitants was Peru, followed by Chile, Brazil and the United States. The aforementioned can be seen in Fig. 2.

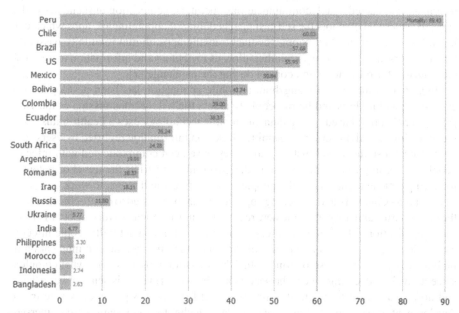

Fig. 2. Number of deaths per 100.000 population, information until, Monday, August 31, 2020, Source: Johns Hopkins University data

Health systems worldwide have been greatly affected due to the high levels of contagion of the virus and the increasing number of infected people, in many cases health institutions have been forced to rather attend to those infected by Covid-19 than attending many other different cases like ailments, controls, consultations and/or operations already scheduled, due to their lack of clinical resources and space [5]. The high death rate worldwide has brought consequences in the relatives and friends of those affected, to the point that many patients avoid approaching a health home in case of presenting any symptoms for fear of being infected more severely, so they prefer to use home remedies to help alleviate their ailments.

It is important to recognize that zonal governments, together with Ministries of Health and institutions involved with technology, have decided to propose the use of digital technology in order to help mitigate the impact caused by this pandemic. By making use of informatics applications, users can have a tool at hand that allows them to recognize the first symptoms of the disease and obtain helpful recommendations for care and prevention. Additionally, with these informatic applications, it is possible to educate people on the importance of establishing and practicing appropriate biosecurity standards in their daily behavior [6].

The use of computer applications, in addition to allowing the user to recognize the disease, could help reduce the number of patients accessing hospital homes, as well as alleviate the clinical burden on doctors, since consultations by telemedicine or online doctors could be performed.

Several applications try to contribute positively to cope and fight against the pandemic. For this reason, these applications offer services such as geolocation through information collected by telecommunications operators, geolocation in social networks, apps, websites and chatbots for self-test or scheduling of appointments, apps which collect information of infected people, contact tracking apps, digital immunity passports, among others that in one way or another allow us to obtain valid information to establish mechanisms for prevention and control during the pandemic [7].

In China, in the city of Hangzhou, a mobile application has been developed, it is easy to use and it alerts and helps people to assess the risk of transmission of the virus [8], this application based on big data and mobile technology uses a health status code: green, yellow or red; the colors are emitted based on information reported by users such as their health status, travel history and if they have been communicated with infected people. According to the classification, the government restricts the travel of potential infected people and allows healthy people to travel freely and return to work.

In Spain - Canary Islands, tracking applications are being used to control the spread of the coronavirus, and are part of the new reality in countries such as Norway or Australia. These applications allow alerting users who have been in contact with people infected by the Covid-19 to avoid a recurrence of the pandemic; through the communication of mobile devices with the use of Bluetooth. The technology used is somewhat complex, since it involves deciding where the servers are, how information is sent between them, and how data is sent to where it is finally stored [9]. The US plays a key role in the development of these technologies since its large technology companies are immersed.

On the other hand, the Internet of Things (IoT) has been used worldwide as a useful tool for creating applications that allow monitoring patients with Covid-19, using interconnected networks, thus increasing patient satisfaction and decreasing the number of hospital admissions; among other benefits it is considered reducing the cost of medical care and improving patient referrals [10]. Applications with IoT allow the patient to control the heart rate, their blood pressure, the glucometer, tracking the health status of the elderly, among other activities. These characteristics improve the flow of the patient's treatment and are also useful for the decision-making process in more complex cases.

According to the author [11], the tracking of digital contacts is also an effective strategy to avoid an outbreak of the disease, since it allows to speed up the tracking process. Among the suggestions is to create adapted applications that are based on GPS tracking and those that are based on token exchange via Bluetooth. For the WHO [12], contact tracking occurs in three steps: 1. Contact identification: based on positive cases already confirmed, and with which the patient had contact. 2. Contact list: Keep a record of possible contacts of infected patients. And 3. Contact follow-up: A necessary follow-up of patients who have come into contact with infected people and who are positive.

On the other hand, a group of researchers considers that the data obtained from mobile phones provide valuable information during the cycle of this disease that has affected humanity. For example, the fingerprints of mobile phones can be used to determine human mobility and its interactions, as well as call logs, GPS data, general data on the use of mobile applications, among others [13]. Despite the conclusion that the use of metrics obtained by mobile phone data by local authorities is not regulated, it is important to highlight that all this information would play a very important role in creating efficient technologies that would help to control the spread of this pandemic.

From the above, it can be deduced that many countries worldwide have created technological tools that allow patients to have a first-hand application that helps to emotionally stabilize users, either with the use of telemedicine or recommendation systems, using forms of home care, thus avoiding the mobilization of patients to hospital institutions, considering the current demand and scarce attention from medical services.

This document presents an evaluation and a comparative study of existing applications for both iOS and Android operating systems, in order to specify the main characteristics and data requested by the applications, and which are used by patients who try to have a guide to control, to get knowledge, self-education, and recommendations to cope with the crisis caused by Covid-19 disease. This section presents a brief introduction to the worldwide implementation of mobile applications which have relationship with Covid-19 disease, in section two the applications were classified according to their category based on the most relevant functionalities found in the research. Then in section three, the criteria of functionality and acceptance of the selected applications were analized and that allowed to collaborate, validate and conclude the revised characteristics to identify the 38 applications best rated worldwide.

2   Mobile Apps for Covid-19

Globally, people face unprecedented challenges as a result of the coronavirus pandemic; in this sense, research has been carried out on various mobile applications deployed worldwide. Taking as a sample 64 countries worldwide and after a thorough analysis of 97 applications developed especially to respond to the spread of Covid-19 for understandable public health reasons, the most relevant functionalities of these tools were analyzed.

In the search for information, applications and websites have been taken into account that are currently part of the technological tools that are focused on various functionalities such as telemedicine, monitoring and evaluating the symptoms of the disease, geolocation of cases, as well as the presentation of other useful data for people who currently suffer from the disease or users who make efforts to prevent the spread.

Additionally, it is also necessary to reflect on the interest aroused by the use of the application, therefore the methodological framework [14] was adapted to identify the applications that were most relevant based on their score and the characteristics offered. There were 97 applications selected, then data was collected from each of them in order to compare the characteristics, summarize and finally present the findings.

Most applications aim to reduce patient flow in health services institutions and provide a monitoring service that includes epidemiological data about the behavior of the disease. Various technologies are used in monitoring, for example Blue trace [15], which is a protocol to facilitate the follow-up of contacts, and through Bluetooth connection it protects the personal data of the users. Other software used for monitoring is the one created by the Pan-European Privacy-Preserving Proximity Tracing (PEPP-PT) [16] this technology allows the authorities to interrupt new SARS-CoV-2 transmission chains quickly and effectively by informing potentially exposed people. In the context of the investigation, standards, technology and services have been created for various countries and developers.

Governments see mobile location data as a key component of measures to contain the spread of Covid-19, and other components are used as well, such as webcams to determine the percentage of crowding and issue measures to help control social distancing. In Ecuador, it has been announced the implementation of an app named "Distacia2", the platform which was created by the Inter-American Development Bank and it determines in real-time the number of people infected and how far they are from each other by using computer vision technologies. This information does not include personal data and is immediately analyzed using artificial intelligence algorithms to produce indicators such as the percentage of agglomeration.

In this investigation, it was possible to detect that certain applications go beyond privacy accesses [16], publishing the database of symptoms registered by users. Apple and Google keep this privacy agreement with the user by generating lists of keys associated with the names provided by infected people, which are related to close contacts in encrypted form to provide heat maps that help contagions to be mitigated.

Figure 3 shows that this data collection also generates a classification of the applications that nowadays exist for Covid-19, taking the European Emergency Number Association (EENA) research as a reference [17], where some concerns have been raised regarding the privacy of citizens.

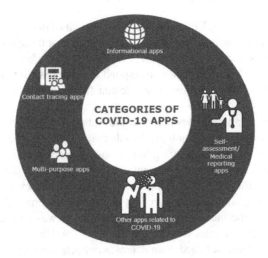

Fig. 3. Categories of Covid-19 apps, Source: Authors

2.1 Informational Apps

In this category, applications which stands out are those which publish information on topics related to several diseases, such as symptoms and how to prevent them, also what to do in case of suspicion or infection. At the same time, infographics on the epidemiological situation of the localities are usually generated.

According to the research carried out, the application named "Appvalència" [18] can be located on this category, it has been running since 2015 and administered by the Valencia City Council. However, with the pandemic generated by Covid-19, the application launched an update in June 2020 to incorporate relevant notices for citizens, such as those related to tax deferrals, administrative procedures or street disinfection.

Another application found in this category is "Open health" published by the government of Belize, as part of the published data, it tracks how the coronavirus situation evolves throughout the globe and provides regular updates to help citizens make informed decisions about their travel plans to Belize and various protocols to protect themselves from Covid-19.

2.2 Self-assessment

These types of applications stand out because they combine their reports with software algorithms, which help predict who has the virus by analyzing the symptoms provided by users. They can also include telemedicine options so that infected people have access to a medical consultation remotely.

For this category, it can be taken as an example the application called "Self-quarantine safety protection" [19], which has been developed by the Ministry of Interior and Security of South Korea, where users can report on the development of any symptoms. This technology prevents the collapse of health centers and an uncontrolled spread of the virus since doctors can give recommendations directly from a distance and with a simple mobile phone. In Ecuador, it was launched an application called "Salud Ec" [20], which allows an evaluation of symptoms that may be from Covid-19, establishing if it is necessary if a citizen requires medical attention, in which case the case is transferred with a call to 911.

2.3 Multi-purpose Apps

Multipurpose applications manage to capture different user data in order to provide local governments with epidemiological and sociodemographic information that helps decision-making regarding isolation measures, as well as generating a social network for registered people to view activities of their close circle of friends and neighbors.

The Basque Government, together with the company EricTel, developed the application COVID-19.EUS [21], aimed at creating a citizen social network that helps stop the coronavirus. The app allows you to add a self-diagnosis to your health status and share it with your close circle of family, friends, co-workers, and/or classmates. In this way, the entire associated network receives periodic recommendations, and they can monitor their health. and track the situation of others. This will help prevent disease.

COVIDOM [22], an application launched in France serves as a reinforcement for the work of the epidemiological teams; in fact, within its functionalities it allows locating where the cases are and, if necessary, carrying out more individualized diagnostic and monitoring interventions in areas of high transmission of the virus.

2.4 Contact Tracking Apps

In these applications, the location of the users is monitored and it is used to geo-reference and estimate the average number of contacts that have been affected by the disease, some use the Bluetooth and others the GPS of the smartphone where the application is installed.

Some countries have adopted or implemented their contact tracking applications, in this scenario are found applications such as "TraceTogether" from Singapore and "Stopp Corona" [23] from Australia, highlighting that contact tracking through mobile applications is a new and relatively unproven technology, but it potentially enables faster and more accurate tracking because it uses automated data collection and analysis. Research has indicated that COVID-19 propagation is too fast in order to be contained by manual contact tracing alone, but it also is shown that containment would be possible using a more efficient method involving a mobile application.

These applications can help to estimate the number of patients with COVID-19 and, for example, quickly visualize the heat maps in a certain spot. The most suitable example for this category is COVTRACER [24], an application developed in the UK that would not track or access personal data or location, instead it follows the proximity of users to each other through Bluetooth functions. Once registered as positive or symptoms presented, the app could track the people you were in contact with in the last seven days. If you were one of those people, the app would alert you and advise self-isolation.

Another application in this category is the one published in the Czech Republic called "eRouška" [25], it is open source and uses Bluetooth to scan the area around the device and find other eRouška users. Once the location is captured, it saves the data of these encounters, its development was approved by the Ministry of Health of the Czech Republic and is inspired by apps like Singapore OpenTrace, ProteGO app from Poland and Covid World developed in Slovakia.

2.5 Other Apps Related to COVID-19

This category includes applications that have been working before the pandemic and have stood out for adding functionalities so that users can find resources during the time of confinement, which have helped to mitigate the psychological effects and collateral damage that can cause disease. Among these applications, the Triumf digital health platform stands out, which has added options that can be used free of charge to provide high-quality and evidence-based psychological support for children.

In Guayaquil-Ecuador the Sosafe application [26] was launched, the same that had been working in other cities in Latin America and was implemented in the framework of the national emergency by the company Claro Ecuador and the Municipality of Guayaquil to generate a social network of citizen emergencies. Through the geolocation system of the cell phone, each person can report robberies at home, riots, traffic accidents, among other incidents.

3   Analysis of Mobile Apps Related to COVID-19

In the exploratory search carried out of mobile applications related to Covid-19 and Coronavirus, it is determined that many of them have been created by the governmental or sectional entities of each country, through their areas of health and the ministries of technologies and information. On the other hand, there are initiatives by private companies, research centers, and universities that have joined the use of technology to support the advancement and control of the pandemic.

According to its functionality and acceptance, 38 applications stand out, which have been evaluated for their compatibility with the main Android and mobile operating systems. However, 7 applications use specifically a web environment.

Table 1. Applications analyzed

N°	NAME	COUNTRY	COMPATIBILITY	NUMBER OF DOWNLOADS	AVERAGE REVIEW
1	APPVALÈNCIA	SPAIN	IOS, ANDROID	10k	3,4
2	ASISTENCIACOVID19	SPAIN	IOS, ANDROID	10k	3,2
3	CORONA-DATENSPENDE	GERMANY	WEB	–	–
4	CORON-APP-COLOMBIA	COLOMBIA	IOS, ANDROID	9,000k	3,8
5	CORONAVIRUS (COVID-19) - APPLE AND CDC	UNITED STATES	IOS, WEB	–	–
6	COVID AP-HM	FRANCE	IOS, ANDROID	4k	–
7	COVID SYMPTOM STUDY	UK	IOS, ANDROID	3,839k	4,7
8	COVID-19 NI	UK	IOS, ANDROID	10k	
9	COVID-19.EUS	BASQUE COUNTRY	IOS, ANDROID	10k	3,5
10	COVID-19-INFOCU	CUBA	ANDROID	50k	–
11	COVID-19MX	MEXICO	IOS, ANDROID	10k	–
12	COVIDOM	FRANCE	ANDROID	50k	3,2
13	COVID TRACKER IRELAND	IRELAND	IOS, ANDROID	500k	4,4
14	COVTRACER	UK	ANDROID	1k	–
15	CUIDAR COVID-19 ARGENTINA	ARGENTINA	ANDROID	5,000k	3,1
16	EROUŠKA	CZECH REPUBLIC	IOS, ANDROID	100k	–
17	IORESTOACASA	ITALY	IOS, ANDROID	5k	3,3
18	KWARANTANNA DOMOWA	POLAND	IOS, ANDROID, HUAWEI	10k	1,6
19	MOVEUP.CARE	BELGIUM	IOS, ANDROID	500	4,8
20	OLVG CORONA CHEQUE	NETHERLANDS	IOS, ANDROID	10k	–

(continued)

Table 1. (*continued*)

N°	NAME	COUNTRY	COMPATIBILITY	NUMBER OF DOWNLOADS	AVERAGE REVIEW
21	OPEN CORONAVIRUS	SPAIN	IOS, ANDROID		–
22	OPEN HEALTH BELIZE	BELIZE	IOS, ANDROID		–
23	PRIVATE KIT: SAFE PATHS	UNITED STATES	IOS, ANDROID	10k	3,2
24	RAKNING C-19	ICELAND	IOS, ANDROID	50k	4,3
25	SALUD EC	ECUADOR	IOS, ANDROID	100k	2,4
26	SELF-QUARANTINE SAFETY PROTECTION	SOUTH KOREA	ANDROID	100k	1,6
27	SER + CONTRA COVID	SPAIN	IOS, ANDROID	100	5
28	SICILIA SI CURA	ITALY	IOS, ANDROID	50k	–
29	SMITTESTOPP	NORWAY			–
30	SOSAFE	ECUADOR	IOS, ANDROID	500k	4,4
31	STOP COVID CAT	SPAIN	IOS, ANDROID	500k	3,2
32	STOPP CORONA	AUSTRIA	ANDROID	100k	3,2
33	TRACECOVID-19	PORTUGAL	WEB		–
34	TRACETOGETHER	SINGAPORE	IOS, ANDROID	1,000k	3,8
35	TRIUMF HEALTH	ESTONIA	WEB	–	–
36	VICINO @ TE	ITALY	WEB	–	–
37	DISTANCIA2	ECUADOR	WEB	–	–
38	MEDIKTOR	SPAIN	ANDROID, IOS, WEB	50k	3,8

Table 1 lists the main applications reviewed, considering their acceptance by the users, as well as the number of downloads. In the case of the self-quarantine safety protection application, which has a low acceptance number, it is necessary to emphasize that its use is mainly directed for people who enter the territory of the country of origin whether they are citizens or foreigners and allows monitoring an adequate quarantine in the designated areas. Its use is mandatory in that country, and failure to comply with its measures may lead to legal sanctions for the citizens involved. The apps are mostly available for both Android and iOS operating systems.

In the case of the Covid Symptomstudy app, which has the highest level of acceptance 4.7 and almost 4 million downloads, it is characterized by its simplicity of use. Registration of the user's information takes less than two minutes, allowing registration of the patient profile by asking a few objective questions about the symptoms, as well as shows updated information on the cases in the area where the user makes the query.

Table 2. Application functionalities

	NAME	EVALUATION OF SYMPTOMS	GEOLOCATION	MEDICAL APPOINTMENTS	SOCIAL NETWORK	REPORT EMERGENCIES
1	APPVALÈNCIA	X	✓	x	x	x
2	ASISTENCIACOVID19	✓	x	x	x	x
3	CORONA-DATENSPENDE	✓	✓	x	x	x
4	CORON-APP-COLOMBIA	✓	✓	x	x	x
5	CORONAVIRUS (COVID-19) - APPLE AND CDC	✓	✓	x	x	x
6	COVID AP-HM	✓	✓	✓	x	✓
7	COVID SYMPTOM STUDY	✓	x	x	x	x
8	COVID-19 NI	✓	x	x	✓	x
9	COVID-19.EUS	✓	✓	x	✓	✓
10	COVID-19-INFOCU	✓	x	x	x	x
11	COVID-19MX	✓	✓	x	x	x
12	COVIDOM	✓	✓	x	✓	✓
13	COVID TRACKER IRELAND	✓	✓	x	x	x
14	COVTRACER	✓	✓	x	x	x
15	CUIDAR COVID-19 ARGENTINA	✓	x	x	x	x
16	EROUŠKA	✓	x	x	x	x
17	IORESTOACASA	✓	x	x	x	x
18	KWARANTANNA DOMOWA	✓	✓	x	x	x
19	MOVEUP.CARE	✓	✓	✓	x	✓
20	OLVG CORONA CHEQUE	✓	✓	✓	x	✓
21	OPEN CORONAVIRUS	✓	✓	x	x	x

(continued)

Table 2. (*continued*)

	NAME	EVALUATION OF SYMPTOMS	GEOLOCATION	MEDICAL APPOINTMENTS	SOCIAL NETWORK	REPORT EMERGENCIES
22	OPEN HEALTH BELIZE	✓	✗	✗	✗	✗
23	PRIVATE KIT: SAFE PATHS	✓	✓	✗	✓	✗
24	RAKNING C-19	✓	✓	✗	✗	✗
25	SALUD EC	✓	✗	✓	✗	✓
26	SELF-QUARANTINE SAFETY PROTECTION	✓	✓	✗	✓	✗
27	SER + CONTRA COVID	✗	✗	✗	✗	✗
28	SICILIA SI CURA	✓	✓	✗	✗	✓
29	SMITTESTOPP	✓	✓	✗	✗	✗
30	SOSAFE	✗	✓	✗	✓	✓
31	STOP COVID CAT	✓	✓	✗	✗	✗
32	STOPP CORONA	✓	✓	✗	✓	✗
33	TRACECOVID-19	✓	✓	✗	✗	✓
34	TRACETOGETHER	✗	✓	✗	✓	✗
35	TRIUMF HEALTH	✗	✗	✗	✗	✗
36	VICINO @ TE	✗	✗	✓	✗	✗
37	DISTANCIA2	✗	✓	✗	✗	✗
38	MEDIKTOR	✓	✓	✗	✗	✗

In the following table we observe the main functionalities of the studied software applications, which are:

- Symptom assessment for Covid-19.
- Geolocation of spaces and concentrations of people with Covid-19 symptoms.
- Medical appointments option that allows you to book an agenda with a doctor if the patient has Covid symptoms.
- Social Network that integrates people who want to be informed regarding news related to the Covid-19.
- Report to emergencies.

With the information in Table 2, we can determine that none of the applications has the 5 five desired characteristics and that only 5 applications have 4 of the 5 functionalities; these applications are Covid Ap-hm, Covid-19. Eus, Covidom, Moveup.care, Olvg Corono Check. The rest of them have 2 and 3 functionalities and finally, we observe that at least 7 applications have only 1 functionality.

4   Conclusions and Future Work

Efforts to mitigate the spread of Covid-19 is a priority initiative of countries that have proven cases of the disease. Globally, public and private organizations have joint efforts to control this pandemic, however, beyond the biosanitary recommendations, the use of technological tools has proven to be an effective way to control Covid-19. This study has evidenced the interest of international communities in the development of new applications that comply with the regulations and conditions of each country. The use of the cloud computing for registering people with symptoms related to the disease, geolocation of people with symptoms or outbreaks of contagion and agglomeration of people, as well as the permanent information to the citizens of the latest news of the disease spread allows to have a vision and make a better projection regarding the care and availability of medical resources for the disease as well as the overflow of health capacities in some countries. Finally, countries with a scarce digital infrastructure are more vulnerable to having adequate control and prevention of Covid-19.

For future considerations, it is necessary to take into account an application that evaluates pharmacological treatment once clinical tests have demonstrated its efficacy, thus determining the evolution of the patient until recovery, taking into account the various risks and vulnerability factors, that is, a smart system that allows through the knowledge acquired by medical experts in the current context to transfer it to future scenarios with similar diseases. It is also considered convenient to incorporate an application that determines the mood and psychological aspects of the patients who contracted the disease [27], as well as indirectly affected people who had a family loss as a result of the pandemic.

References

1. Cucinotta, D., Vanelli, M.: WHO declares COVID-19 a pandemic (2020). https://doi.org/10.23750/abm.v91i1.9397
2. Fauci, A.S., Lane, H.C., Redfield, R.R.: Covid-19 - navigating the uncharted. N. Engl. J. Med. **382**, 1268–1269 (2020). https://doi.org/10.1056/NEJMe2002387
3. Mehta, P., McAuley, D.F., Brown, M., Sanchez, E., Tattersall, R.S., Manson, J.J., HLH Across Speciality Collaboration, UK: COVID-19: consider cytokine storm syndromes and immuno-suppression. Lancet (London, England) **395**, 1033 (2020). https://doi.org/10.1016/S0140-6736(20)30628-0
4. OMS: Nuevo coronavirus (2019)
5. Emanuel, E.J., et al.: Fair allocation of scarce medical resources in the time of COVID-19. N. Engl. J. Med. **382**, 2049–2055 (2020). https://doi.org/10.1056/NEJMsb2005114
6. Ting, D.S.W., Carin, L., Dzau, V., Wong, T.Y.: Digital technology and COVID-19 (2020). https://doi.org/10.1038/s41591-020-0824-5
7. Juan, J.: The use of technologies in the fight against COVID19. An analysis of costs and benefits (2020)
8. Xiao-Ben, P.: Application of personal-oriented digital technology in preventing transmission of COVID-19, China. Ir. J. Med. Sci. **1** (2020). https://doi.org/10.1007/s11845-020-02215-5
9. García, J.G.: Coronavirus: Las 'apps' de rastreo de contagios refuerzan a las tecnológicas de Estados Unidos (2020)
10. Singh, R.P., Javaid, M., Haleem, A., Suman, R.: Internet of things (IoT) applications to fight against COVID-19 pandemic. Diabetes Metab. Syndr. Clin. Res. Rev. **14**, 521–524 (2020). https://doi.org/10.1016/j.dsx.2020.04.041
11. Dar, A.B., Lone, H., Zahoor, S., Amin Khan, A., Naaz, R.: Applicability of Mobile Contact Tracing in Fighting Pandemic (COVID-19): Issues, Challenges and Solutions (2020)
12. Raskar, R., et al.: Apps gone rogue: maintaining personal privacy in an epidemic. arXiv Prepr. arXiv2003.08567 (2020)
13. Oliver, N., et al.: Mobile phone data and COVID-19: missing an opportunity? Comput. Soc. (2020)
14. Arksey, H., O'Malley, L.: Scoping studies: towards a methodological framework. Int. J. Soc. Res. Methodol. Theory Pract. **8**, 19–32 (2005). https://doi.org/10.1080/1364557032000119616
15. Bay, J., et al.: BlueTrace: a privacy-preserving protocol for community-driven contact tracing across borders (2020)
16. HOME| PEPP-PT. https://www.pepp-pt.org/. Accessed 08 July 2020
17. Marta, A.S.: COVID-19 Apps (2020)
18. AppValència - Apps en Google Play. https://play.google.com/store/apps/details?id=es.valencia.lanzadera&hl=es_BO. Accessed 31 Aug 2020
19. Ministry of the Interior and Safety: National Disaster Safety Portal. http://www.safekorea.go.kr/idsiSFK/neo/main/main.html. Accessed 01 Sept 2020
20. SaludEC - Apps en Google Play. https://play.google.com/store/apps/details?id=com.phuyusalud.movil&hl=es_BO. Accessed 31 Aug 2020
21. APP COVID-19.EUS. https://www.euskadi.eus/koronabirusa-app-covid-eus/web01-a2korona/eu/. Accessed 31 Aug 2020
22. Covidom Community - EIT Health. https://eithealth.eu/project/covidom-community/. Accessed 31 Aug 2020
23. Stopp Corona en App Store. https://apps.apple.com/ec/app/stopp-corona/id1503717224. Accessed 31 Aug 2020
24. CovTracer. https://covid-19.rise.org.cy/en/. Accessed 31 Aug 2020

25. eRouška – chráním sebe, chráním tebe. https://erouska.cz/. Accessed 31 Aug 2020
26. SOSAFEl App de seguridad ciudadana. https://www.sosafeapp.com/es/index.html. Accessed 31 Aug 2020
27. Apolinario, Ó., Medina-Moreira, J., Lagos-Ortiz, K., Luna-Aveiga, H., Antonio García-Díaz, J., Valencia-García, R.: Tecnologías inteligentes para la autogestión de la salud Intelligent technologies for health self-management. journal.sepln.org. **61**, 159–162 (2018). https://doi.org/10.26342/2018-61-22

Tourism 3.0 and Indigenous Food Cultures: Case Study Pilahuín

Cristina Páez-Quinde$^{(\boxtimes)}$ ⓘ, Francisco Torres-Oñate ⓘ, Danny Rivera-Flores ⓘ, and Mayorie Chimbo-Cáceres

Facultad de Ciencias Humanas y de la Educación, Universidad Técnica de Ambato, Ambato, Ecuador

{mc.paez,cf.torres,dannygriveraf,elsamchimboc}@uta.edu.ec

Abstract. The present investigation makes an exploratory-experimental study within Ecuador, where it can be shown that it maintains its cultural and gastronomic traditions in almost all its territory. The cultural representation that can be found in the community of Pilahuín includes the typical dishes that are usually prepared with the vegetables and tubers harvested by the same inhabitants of the community. In this research project, information was collected on the community of Pilahuín through an information card of the Food Heritage Atlas of Ecuador. For the development of the mobile application (App) two methodologies were used: ADDIE and TAM. The first one was used since it has an educational concept. It encompasses five stages. In the first stage, the analysis was done through a survey given to the residents of the community. The second stage refers to the design through sketches of the primary and secondary screens of the App. The third stage has to do with the development. At this stage, the Mobincube software was used to create the App. The fourth stage is implementation. Here the application was introduced in the initial version in the Android software application store so that users can access it directly. Finally, in the fifth stage which includes evaluation, the TAM methodology was applied for the measurement of technological acceptability. This acceptance was measured through a survey of several potential users taken by random probabilistic sampling. As a result, it was obtained that the community of Pilahuín mostly agreed to offer digital tourism, which is a significant contribution to the development of tourism trends appropriate to the digital era.

Keywords: Tourism 3.0 · ICT · App · Food cultures · Gastronomy

1 Introduction

When talking about Tourism, reference is made to someone's motivation to share information, which is consistent in the type of sensational, political, and informal information, which is to share the impression of the users of social networks on an issue. Additional research can develop a motivational analysis of information exchange activities by observing the relationship between the user's profile and the motivation to share information or the credibility factor of information [1]. The arrival of virtual reality augmented reality and mixed reality technologies are shaping a new environment in which

© Springer Nature Switzerland AG 2020
R. Valencia-García et al. (Eds.): CITI 2020, CCIS 1309, pp. 166–178, 2020.
https://doi.org/10.1007/978-3-030-62015-8_13

physical and virtual objects are integrated at different levels [2]. Due to the development of portable and corporate devices, along with virtual and highly interactive connections, the landscape of the customer experience is evolving towards new types of hybrid experiences. Research allows academics and managers to classify all technologies, current and potential, that can support or enhance customer experiences, but can also generate new experiences throughout the client's journey. Recent technological developments are changing the ways how people experience physical and virtual environments. Specifically, Virtual Reality (VR) is likely to play a key role in several industries [3]. The wave of megatrends, including the rapid change in globalization and technological advances, is creating new market forces. For any organization to survive and thrive in that environment, innovation is essential. Innovation is about the actual implementation of new ideas or technologies to create new value in ways fundamentally different from those of the past [4].

The use of smart tourism technologies such as travel-related websites, social networks, and smartphones in travel planning has been widespread and growing [5]. By adopting the exploration and exploitation framework and identifying the background that promotes and prohibits such uses, we find that the attributes of smart tourism technologies promote exploratory and exploitative use; while user security and privacy concerns have a negative effect [6]. Besides, the exploratory use has a great influence on the overall satisfaction of the travel experience, and the exploitative use mainly improves the satisfaction of the transaction. Tourists generate a huge amount of data when they visit cities. These data sources can be used to track their presence through their activities [7]. It is not enough to use a data source to analyze the presence of tourists in cities. Several must be used in a complementary way. The smart trip has many features that can make it easier for all tourists to recognize any tourist attraction. Then, the smart travel application is really useful for local or foreign tourists, especially the image recognition function that can automatically recognize tourist attractions with great performance [8]. The main factors that influence the potential for changing the needs of identified customers are digital services, digital marketing, and data mining, and online travel communities. The results of the study show that a personalized approach for the client in digital communication channels represents an essential requirement in the future provision of services [9]. Tourism service providers can benefit sustainably through the application of data mining, which results in the possibility of approaching clients in a personalized way through the integration of social networks, inherent influencers, and bloggers. Companies, however, must prepare their products and services digitally to achieve a growing customer appeal and loyalty.

1.1 Identification of the Main Characteristics of the Indigenous Food Cultures Existing in the Pilahuín Community

Currently in Ecuador, its cultural and gastronomic traditions are maintained in almost all its territory, this in the province of Tungurahua is not the exception because in each of its cantons we can find flagship dishes of our local cuisine, however through the time, they are considered to have the recipes from how they were prepared in their beginnings within indigenous peoples have suffered several modifications to how they are now prepared by Ecuadorian families.

One of the characteristics for which Ecuadorian gastronomy stands out is the combination of products between the three food-producing regions such as the Coast, Sierra, and Oriente; The reason why not all food can be grown in the same territorial area is due to the differentiation of climates between regions, and this also allows Ecuador to be so rich in food products compared to its neighboring countries on the continent and makes its traditional gastronomy unique.

The individual representation to be found in the Pilahuín community is in their dishes, which are usually prepared with vegetables and tubers harvested by the community's own inhabitants, however, we find a lot of similarity in other parts of the region due to the displacement of the indigenous people themselves; The dishes that are prepared with a greater attendance are the guinea pig with potatoes and the fry either with mote or potato tortillas, this more than for local consumption is also due to the existence of several establishments dedicated to the sale of typical food of the area.

Therefore, information about the typical dishes prepared in the Pilahuín community can be evidenced, expressed through information gathering sheets from the Atlas of Food Heritage of Ecuador.

The effects of globalization on the transformation of food culture have led to the loss of the pre-Hispanic culinary roots of Mexico. This research is carried out to discuss and publicizing whether such anomaly has led to the loss of gastronomic customs and how this change has an impact on people's health and quality of life. Therefore, the need to rescue food identity and expose the importance of food awareness and education as an indispensable requirement to achieve a better level of health is highlighted [10].

Food is an element of cultural identity that distinguishes a place or a country which can be altered by intervention with other socio-cultural groups. New lifestyles and eating habits, migratory phenomena, the changing price of food prices, the lack of public policies that regulate the entry of new foods into the market and the increasing introduction of junk foods and fast foods, among others have been some of the main factors that have led to the loss of cultural and ethnic identity of the food culture [11]. In general, the cultural roots of a social group is its DNA, which constitutes and identifies us as human, which has been altered by the globalization that has generated mutations (diseases, malnutrition, obesity) in recent years.

2   State of the Art

Now in Ecuador, its cultural and gastronomic traditions are maintained in almost all its territory; in the province of Tungurahua, it is not an exception. This is because in each of its cantons you can find typical dishes of the country's local cuisine. However, over time, the recipes have undergone several modifications in their preparation; since in its beginnings, the indigenous people prepared them differently than what Ecuadorian families make them today.

Tinard (2016) states that "The festivities that have been prevailing over time even after colonization, are based on celebrating events representative of Ecuadorian culture." In holidays such as the annual harvest, the day of the dead, cantonal independence, or different festivities that take place throughout the year in the current twenty-four provinces of Ecuador, the main attractions are parades or fairs that take place in the main streets of each town or city. However, food plays a very important role in these festivities for the inhabitants and tourists. This not only happens in cultural festivities, but in all areas, and is due to the need of the human being to satisfy and strengthen interpersonal relationships, and that is when food is presented as a primary factor.

Specifically, in the highlands, Ecuador, typical dishes, and the diet of rural communities are prepared based on food grown mostly in their locality; which allows the indigenous people to reduce costs in the production of their dishes for consumption at home or sale to the public. It is also the main reason why you can find many grains such as corn or corn, mellocos, potatoes, proteins such as guinea pig, rabbit or field hen and vegetables or vegetables such as onions, peas, and kidney tomatoes are usually present as a seasoning or as an accompaniment in salads; however, products from other regions such as soup rice and peanuts can also be found [12].

One of the characteristics that highlands Ecuadorian cuisine has is the combination of products around the three food-producing regions such as the coastal, highlands, and the jungle. The reason why not all food can be grown in the same territorial area is due to the differentiation of climates between regions, and this also allows Ecuador to be so rich in food products compared to its neighboring countries of the continent, and it makes its traditional cuisine unique.

In the highlands, local dishes can be differentiated in terms of the northern and southern sectors. According to Altés (2001) "this is because the zones have clear variances due to the climate. That is, the height above sea level of each zone has a big impact on the different products." In the same way, the preparation of the dishes is done under specific standards and has a different meaning for its inhabitants; which generates an individual representation in each city or town.

The individual representation of the community of Pilahuín is in its dishes which are usually prepared with the vegetables and tubers harvested by the same inhabitants of the community. However, in other parts of the region, there is some similarity in the way how the dishes are prepared because of the displacement of the indigenous themselves to other parts of the country. The dishes that are most frequently prepared are the guinea pig with potatoes and the fried meat with either mote or potato tortillas; which are sold in markets dedicated to the sale of typical food in the area.

The information referring to the typical dishes prepared in the community of Pilahuín has been recorded in an information card of the Atlas of Food Heritage of Ecuador.

Consequently, tourism over time has evolved in the way it is used by both tourism actors and tourists. Also, technology has contributed to cultural renewal. Therefore, virtual spaces have become essential when planning a trip because they give the user the possibility to create their itinerary according to their needs and economic budget. On the other hand, virtual spaces have generated an enrichment in terms of local information, which will be later used when people visit these tourist places, along with their food and/or gastronomic heritage.

Virtual spaces currently have a focus more on urban than natural tourism and this is because of the great attractions that are found in the large cities and towns that are purely tourists, thus having a greater impact on users. Despite this, at present, one of the best means is digital through social networks and mobile applications to promote a tourist site. The investment of the people interested in activities like this is not very high compared to other media and the scope is greater. The growth of social network users is 9.1% in the last year [13].

2.1 TAM Methodology

The TAM methodology is translated into a Technological Acceptance Model, this covers several disciplines such as social psychology, contributing to the degree of acceptance that society has had based on the new technologies introduced [14]. The presupposition of this methodology has two results, with the post-analysis it is defined if the population is willing to collaborate with more news or, if for the on the contrary, it is granted more conservative, however, it must be taken into account that it can be compared between two groups of the same society, even having the same facilities and tools, one can take longer than the other to adopt these new technologies.

The TAM model encompasses the perceived utility that consists of defining who is going to gain from the use of technology [15]; It also encompasses the perceived feasibility of use, this refers to the effort or tasks that are going to stop being carried out in a normal way thanks to new technologies; on the other hand, there was an attitude towards use, this showed that the people who are predisposed to learn are the ones who will do it the fastest; and finally, the intention was towards the use, this defines if the adaptation of the people is going to be long or short term depending on the disposition of the users [16].

Digital tourism can be translated into Tourism 3.0 as it refers to a new way of providing tourist services, where the main actor becomes the tourist, due to two important facts such as global digitalization and the constant changes of the potential client. It is also evident that people between the ages of 16 and 50 are not the exception. [17] argues that "Tourist 3.0 is characterized by having an internet connection at all times, having accounts in online communities and social networks and planning the trip according to people's needs." In short, this tourist is based on ratings and reviews of the fate of other users who use mobile applications instead of paper; that is, an environmental consciousness prevails.

3 Methodology

This research was carried out through an exploratory-experimental modality, which was applied to the population of the Pilahuín community, where it was appreciated that there is a significant tourist promotion in virtual spaces in recent years to show itself as a potential destination for tourism both local and foreign. However, in recent years there have been several participations in tourism fairs organized by government entities such as the GAD Municipalidad de Ambato and Consejo Provincial.

Currently, there is no detailed information covering tourist and public interest destinations of the Pilahuín community on websites; which would contribute to providing data such as location within the community, approximate costs of tourist facilities, and opening hours. It means, there is a lack of information about the history, background, and details of the ancestral gastronomy of the community. The only sources available are several articles made by the Municipalidad de Pilahuín and reports in local newspapers such as La Hora.

Therefore, it is determined that in the community of Pilahuín there has been no interest in developing an offer of its culture, its aggressiveness, and its typical food in virtual spaces. So, the Digital Tourism hasn't developed, which limits reaching more potential 3.0 tourists who have a focus on food or gastronomic culture.

The purpose of this research was to create a mobile application that adapts to the market in which the Pilahuín community is located. It means, to make available to tourists 3.0 a mobile application focused on cultural tourism, gastronomic tourism as well as sustainable tourism. The main beneficiaries will be the residents of the community, and the actors dedicated to promoting local tourism activities, and to promote future planning in regard to tourism. The mobile application was distributed through two application stores of the most used operating systems: iOS and Android. Its feasibility was measured with the TAM model, which is the Technological Acceptance Model; the application of the ADDIE model, which allows measuring more deeply with its process based on analysis, design, development, implementation, and finally evaluation (Table 1).

Table 1. Double data entry table for the evaluation of App development providers. Author: Buitr+on K. (2019)

Provider/Parameters	Fire base	IBuilt App	Mobincube	App inventor	Android creator
Accessibility	3	2	3	4	3
Interface management	4	3	4	2	1
Tool availability for the edition	3	3	4	3	3
Availability of information and guide	2	2	2	1	3
Gratuity	0	1	4	5	5
Total	**12**	**11**	**17**	**15**	**15**

*Rating 0–5 (Considering 0 as no beneficial and 5 as completely beneficial)

3.1 ADDIE Methodology

The development of the application was with block programming, which refers to programming without codes and commands typed by the user; on the contrary, this programming allowed to create interfaces with interactive images, icons, tables and texts of different typefaces without having to use any other tool outside the mobincube website. However, despite not needing knowledge about programming, you must have the vision to be able to use the links between main and secondary pages so that the future user can have an easy and pleasant use without having to go to a help of others (Fig. 1).

Fig. 1. Mikuna App in Play Store. Author: Buitr+on K. (2019)

The objective of this research is to create a mobile application that adapts to the market in which the Pilahuín community is located, that is, for 3.0 tourists focused on cultural tourism, gastronomic tourism and also sustainable tourism; The main beneficiaries will be the residents of the community, and the actors dedicated to promoting the tourist activity of the town, as well as its government entity for future planning within tourism (Fig. 2).

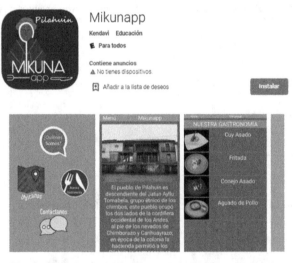

Fig. 2. Download MIKUNA. Author: Buitr+on K. (2019)

The mobile application will be distributed through two application stores of the most used operating systems today such as iOS and Android, its feasibility will be measured with the TAM methodology, which is the Technological Acceptance Model, he points out (Altés, 2001). "This is a theory that draws from disciplines such as social psychology and that establishes what is the degree of acceptance of society before the introduction of new technologies" (Fig. 3).

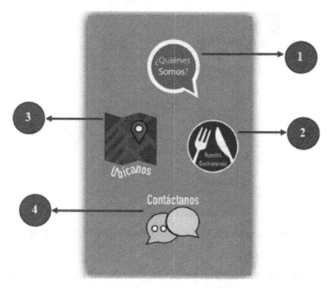

Fig. 3. Main menu of the mobile application with icons entered. Author: Buitr+on K. (2019)

1. On the screen of "who we are", important data of the town, as well as a small gallery with photographs of several of tourist places is displayed The icon is made up of a thought bubble because the secondary screen is titled as a question that users would ask the community.

2. The "Our Gastronomy" screen shows more secondary screens with the 4 main typical dishes from Ecuador. They are: Roasted guinea pig, Fried meat, roasted rabbit and chicken Soup. Each screen contains more screens linked to its ingredients, preparation, nutritional values and the history of each of them. The icon is simple, but it represents a plate and a couple of food cutlery which is what relates most when talking about food.

3. "Our Location" screen has a link to a secondary Google Map page, showing the location of the town. The icon is represented by a map with roads inside it and with a signal that emphasizes the location within the map.

4. "Contact Screen" has a link to a Google Form to send comments or suggestions to the representatives of the Community of Pilahuín. In the same way, the icon is represented by two bubbles. Inside one of them, there are two points that assimilate a text in the process (Fig. 4).

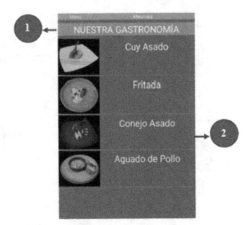

Fig. 4. Our Gastronomy screen within the mobile application. Author: Buitr+on K. (2019)

1. Screen title. This tab was used to guide the user on which screen is found and the interaction between screens is easier.
2. Cells of typical dishes. In this tab, each typical dish is located with a photograph and with the title of the dish. Both the name and the photograph are linked to a secondary screen where more details of each dish are found (Fig. 5).

Fig. 5. Secondary screen of each typical dish of the mobile application. Author: Buitr+on K. (2019)

1. Screen title. This title was used to guide the user on which screen it is and to provide greater ease of interaction between screens. All the screens of each dish have a particular color to highlight the photograph.
2. Photography. All secondary screens belonging to the screen ≪Our Gastronomy≫ contain a photograph of the typical dish that allows the user to know it visually.

3. Buttons. They are created in an interactive image and each link to a screen with the corresponding content (Fig. 6).

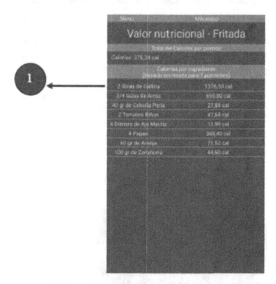

Fig. 6. Secondary screen with the nutritional values of each dish. Author: Buitr+on K. (2019)

1. Nutritional value. This screen shows the number of calories for each ingredient and for the whole dish, based on portions. This allows the user to know how many calories each typical dish has if consumed or prepared.

4 Results

The results obtained within this investigation were acceptable since they are based on the implementation of an application in which the gastronomic traditions of the community can be represented based on the preparations and knowledge of the ancestors belonging to the indigenous communities, obtaining information of their origin, of how the harvest of the raw material begins, and also of their preparation.

Through the TAM application, it was evident that the community accepts the introduction of trends that generate tourism 3.0 adaptable to technological needs, promoting with this new project that motivate the different indigenous communities in the use of digital platforms with innovative tourist offers.

4.1 Results of the Acceptance of the App Through TAM

Question 1. Do you think your community has forgotten the "old-time" food practices when preparing both typical and traditional foods? (Table 2 and Fig. 7).

Of a total of 100 people who correspond to 100% of the sample, 41% and 19% equivalent to 60 people affirm that their community has forgotten eating practices, 32% of 32 people state that they occasionally forget eating practices traditional, 5% and 3% equivalent to 8 people mention that they rarely or never forget it.

Table 2. Acceptance App and indigenous food cultures. Author: Buitr+on K. (2019)

	Frequency	Percentage	Valid percentage	Accumulated percentage
Very frequently	19	19.0	19.0	19.0
Frequently	41	41.0	41.0	60.0
Occasionally	32	32.0	32.0	92.0
Rarely	5	5.0	5.0	97.0
Never	3	3.0	3.0	100.0
Total	100	100.0	100.0	

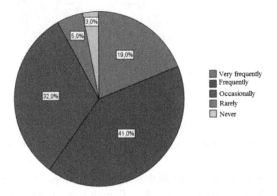

Fig. 7. Acceptance App and indigenous food cultures. Author: Buitr+on K. (2019)

Results that allow us to know that the people of Pilahuín feel that traditional food cultures are being lost, with different ways of preparing both typical and traditional foods.

Question 2. How often do you use mobile applications connected to the internet? (Table 3 and Fig. 8).

Table 3. Use of App in Pilahuín. Author: Buitr+on K. (2019)

	Frequency	Percentage	Valid percentage	Accumulated percentage
Very frequently	42	42.0	42.0	42.0
Frequently	19	19.0	19.0	61.0
Occasionally	21	21.0	21.0	82.0
Rarely	14	14.0	14.0	96.0
Never	4.	4.0	-4.0	100.0
Total	100	100.0	100.0	

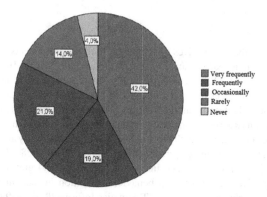

Fig. 8. Use of App in Pilahuín. Author: Buitr+on K. (2019)

Of a total of 100% of respondents, 42% and 19% equivalent to 61 people use mobile applications connected to the internet very frequently and frequently respectively, 21% mention that they occasionally use mobile applications, the 14% and 4% equivalent to 18 people mention that they rarely or never use applications. Results that allow affirming that most of the inhabitants of Pilahuín use mobile applications.

5   Conclusions and Future Work

The main characteristics of the indigenous food culture existing in the community of Pilahuín refer to the typical dishes of past years still prepared by the indigenous community. According to the fieldwork carried out in situ, the food culture is very similar to that of the local ancestors, but with small differences in its preparation, based mostly on locally harvested products.

The digital tourism of the community of Pilahuín is almost null due to the lack of projects focused on new technologies for a tourism offer projected to a 3.0 tourism. This is because it is not determined as an activity of primary economic income for the community. After all, there is a more inclined orientation to the cultivation of food.

The virtual space designed based on the food culture of the community of Pilahuín has been created to promote digital tourism, thus benefiting the inhabitants of the community of Pilahuín as well as the province of Tungurahua by expanding its tourism proposal and equally train potential tourists in search of cultural, gastronomic experiences and sustainable tourism.

As future work within this research project, the aim is to develop a mobile application that can interact synchronously with the user, at the time of tasting a product or dish and at the same time measure feelings or emotions in the public.

Acknowledgment. Thanks to the Technical University of Ambato, to the Department of Research and Development (DIDE, acronym in Spanish) for supporting our research project, Technological and Sensory Cuisine Laboratory: Ecuadorian food heritage Case Study.

References

1. Liu, S.: Comparing the perspectives of municipal tourism departments and cultural departments on urban cultural-tourism development. J. Dest. Mark. Manag. **16**, 1–8 (2020)
2. Biagi, B., Brandano, M.-G., Ortega-Argiles, R.: Smart specialisation and tourism: understanding the priority choices in EU regions. Socio-Econ. Plan. Sci. (2020, in press)
3. Bogicevic, V., Seo, S., Kandampully, J., Liu, S., Rudd, N.: Virtual reality presence as a preamble of tourism experience: the role of mental imagery. Tour. Manag. **74**, 55–64 (2019)
4. Loureiro, S., Guerreiro, J., Ali, F.: 20 years of research on virtual reality and augmented reality in tourism context: a text-mining approach. Tour. Manag. **77**, 104028 (2020)
5. Kim, M., Lee, C.-K., Preis, M.: The impact of innovation and gratification on authentic experience, subjective well-being, and behavioral intention in tourism virtual reality: the moderating role of technology readiness. Telematics Inform. **49**, 101349 (2020)
6. Bichler, B.-F.: Designing tourism governance: the role of local residents. Management (2019, in press)
7. Tolkes, C.: Sustainability communication in tourism – a literature review. Tour. Manag. Perspect. **27**, 10–21 (2018)
8. Kapera, I.: Sustainable tourism development efforts by local governments in Poland. Sustain. Cities Soc. **40**, 581–588 (2018)
9. Brtnický, M., et al.: The impact of tourism on extremely visited volcanic island: link between environmental pollution and transportation modes. Chemosphere **249**, 126118 (2020)
10. Pestana, M.-H., Parreira, A., Mountinho, L.: Motivations, emotions and satisfaction: the keys to a tourism destination choice. J. Dest. Mark. Manag. **16**, 100332 (2020)
11. Faulkner, A., Harding, T., Miller, C., Davies, C., McNair, C.: Tourism and the Highlands: a cross-sectional study on trauma and orthopaedic service use by tourists in 2017. Surgeon (2020, in press)
12. McKercher, B., Mak, B.: The impact of distance on international tourism demand. Tour. Manag. Perspect. **31**, 340–347 (2019)
13. Manrai, L., Lascu, D.-L., Manrai, A.: A study of safari tourism in sub-Saharan Africa: an empirical test of Tourism A-B-C (T-ABC) model. J. Bus. Res. (2019, in press)
14. Al-Marri, A., Nechi, S., Ben-Ayed, O., Charfeddine, L.: Analysis of the performance of TAM in oil and gas industry: factors and solutions for improvement. Energy Rep. **6**, 2276–2287 (2020)
15. Scherer, R., Siddiq, F., Tondeur, J.: The technology acceptance model (TAM): a meta-analytic structural equation modeling approach to explaining teachers' adoption of digital technology in education. Comput. Educ. **128**, 13–35 (2019)
16. Xia, M., Zhang, Y., Zhang, C.: A TAM-based approach to explore the effect of online experience on destination image: a smartphone user's perspective. J. Dest. Mark. Manag. **8**, 259–270 (2018)
17. Liu, J., An, K., Jang, S.: A model of tourists' civilized behaviors: toward sustainable coastal tourism in China. J. Dest. Mark. Manag. **16**, 100437 (2020)

Mirroring Tools and Interaction Indicators in Collaborative Work: A Systematic Review

Mitchell Vásquez-Bermúdez[1,4(✉)] ⓘ, Cecilia Sanz[2,3] ⓘ, María Alejandra Zangara[2] ⓘ, and Jorge Hidalgo[1] ⓘ

[1] Facultad de Ciencias Agrarias, Universidad Agraria del Ecuador,
Avenue 25 de Julio and Pio Jaramillo, Guayaquil, Ecuador
{mvasquez,jhidalgo}@uagraria.edu.ec

[2] Instituto de Investigación en Informática LIDI Facultad de Informática,
Universidad Nacional de La Plata, La Plata, Argentina
{csanz,azangara}@lidi.info.unlp.edu.ar

[3] Investigador Asociado de la Comisión de Investigaciones Científicas
de la Prov. de Buenos Aires, Buenos Aires, Argentina

[4] Faculty of Mathematical and Physical Sciences, University of Guayaquil,
Cdla. Salvador Allende, Guayaquil, Ecuador
mitchell.vasquezb@ug.edu.ec

Abstract. *Mirroring* tools make it possible to reflect the process of a collaborative task and increases its relevance when it comes to an educational task. Monitoring indicators used for *Mirroring* are able to show and motivate the interaction of the participants who are carrying out the collaborative task, particularly for an online activity. This feedback can be represented as a direct visualization of the indicator's value through *Mirroring* tools. *Mirroring* tools contribute mainly to the get a better visibility of the collaborative process among the participants by showing their level of participation while they carry out the online collaboration. Due to the importance of the topic in the field of research, this work will focus on carrying out a systematic research mapping process which will include a search, study, selection, analysis and identification of potential relationships between *Mirroring* tools and collaborative indicators. With the application of systematic mapping, there is the possibility to evaluate the frequency of publications that have existed in different high-impact scientific libraries, since no statistical studies have been found on the proposed topic.

Keywords: Collaborative work · Reflection · Indicators · Interactivity

1 Introduction

Over the past few years, research studies have been carried out about collaborative indicators, mainly due to their complexity in the interactions that occur though collaborative tools [1]. To show the results of the participants' learning activities in the form of graphs, numbers, or literals, analysis of the interaction is performed. This interaction analysis is obtained from the different collaborative tools which allow interaction, interactivity,

© Springer Nature Switzerland AG 2020
R. Valencia-García et al. (Eds.): CITI 2020, CCIS 1309, pp. 179–192, 2020.
https://doi.org/10.1007/978-3-030-62015-8_14

exchange of ideas, analysis, and dissemination of information for scientific and educational purposes. However, for students and teachers to observe these interactions, they must use visualization tools based on interactivity indicators. The visualization tools for collaborative work, according to [2] and [3], are divided into three categories, which are the mirror tools, the cognitive tools, and the guide tools. The approach of *Mirroring* tools according to the authors. consists of representing the activities of the participants of a working group; the aim is to represent with graphics the comments and actions carried out in their work. In [1] it is stated that the information could favor group work and those in charge of supervising the interventions. According to the work proposed by [4], the Mirroring strategy can reveal the individual and collective performance of the participants.

The objective of the present work is to review the computational models of *Mirroring* tools and collaborative indicators, by developing a systematic mapping in high impact scientific libraries to obtain results.

This article is organized as follows: Sect. 2 presents the approach to the systematic review, followed by Sect. 3 which presents the methodology; in Sect. 4, the analysis of results is presented and in Sect. 5, the discussion of different tools is proposed. Finally, in Sect. 6 the conclusions are stated, and future work is described.

2 Systematic Review

Within the educational processes, several technological tools can be implemented for its use, in the same way, it is important to provide an overview of the role that Mirroring technologies have within education, since with this we could help in higher education to have a better approach to be able to optimize feedback on the progress of student activities through the visualization of collaborative indicators. Considering the aforementioned, a systematic mapping has been developed based on the review approach proposed by Kitchenham and Charters, [5] doing a study on an overview of a research area. For this reason, conducting a systematic review will allow the identification, evaluation and analysis of several related studies.

3 Methodology

3.1 Research Analysis

In this work, the methodology proposed by Kitchenham and Charters [5]. In this research, it was determined the systematization of the Mirroring tools and collaborative indicators, which has led to the following research questions:

- Which are the guidelines to carry out the systematic process of studies of *Mirroring* computational models and its indicators of visualization for educational activities?
- Where and when were the *Mirroring* studies and the indicators used in each research published?
- What has been the impact of *Mirroring* tools and interactivity indicators on collaborative work?

3.2 Search Planning

To carry out the search plan, the recommendation proposed by Kitchenham and Charters will be used [6], for the identification of keywords and thus formulate search strings using the PICO method that consists of population, intervention, comparison, and outcome.

The population refers to the *Mirroring* tools that are involved with collaborative indicators. In our context, the population refers to systematic mapping studies. The intervention refers to the compilation obtained from the indicators of *Mirroring* and the analysis of the data that is supported by the different collaborative applications in education. The comparison involves a study related to the different strategies proposed. The results are not considered specific, as the study focuses on studies evaluating mirroring tools and collaborative indicators.

The key words for identification are: *Mirroring tool, Collaborative indicators,* and *Collaborative work* that have been grouped into sets to form a search string.

The searches were performed in the databases of the IEEE Xplore, ACM, Scopus (ScienceDirect), and in the Journal Computer Supported Cooperative Work magazine.

Table 1 shows the databases and the search condition proposed.

Table 1. Search conditions

Databases	Search
IEEE XPLORE DIGITAL LIBRARY	((("ALL METADATA": *MIRRORING* TOOL) OR "ALL METADATA": COLLABORATIVE INDICATORS) AND "ALL METADATA": COLLABORATIVE WORK)
ACM – DIGITAL LIBRARY	[ALL: *MIRRORING* TOOL] AND [ALL: COLLABORATIVE INDICATORS] AND [ALL: COLLABORATIVE WORK] AND [PUBLICATION DATE: (01/01/2015 TO 12/30/2020)]
SCOPUS (SCIENCEDIRECT)	"*MIRRORING* TOOL" OR "INDICATORS" AND "COLLABORATIVE WORK"

According to the search carried out with the established conditions, the following results were obtained, which are presented in Table 2.

3.3 Selection of Studies and Quality Assessment

To include the relevant papers, selection criteria were applied to titles and abstracts with the following characteristics:

Table 2. Number of studies per database

Number of studies per database	
Database	Search
IEEE	152 results
ACM – DIGITAL LIBRARY	114 results
Scopus (ScienceDirect)	86 results
Journal Computer Supported Cooperative Work	20 results

- The studies presented methodology and research result
- The studies are in the collaborative field of work related to Mirroring and Indicators.
- The studies that were published online since 2017 (first systematic evaluation), then those carried out during 2016 and, finally, the review of the Mirroring tools during 2015.

   Criteria to exclude certain works were the following:

- Studios featuring only conference abstracts, editorials, templates, and collaborative work-study with Mirroring.
- Studies that do not present evidence of having been reviewed by peers.
- Studies not detailed in English except for one highly relevant article.
- Studies not accessible in full text.
- Unclear books and literature.
- Duplicate studies of other related studies.

4   Search Result

4.1   Publication Frequency

There were 372 results obtained according to the search with the previously detailed conditions, after that the include and exclude method was applied by deleting the publications prior to 2015, reading the full text, lightning sampling, qualitative evaluation, review of excluded publications, as shown in Fig. 1.

4.2   Search Posts

Table 3 shows the studies selected based on the focus of this *Mirroring* review. According to the searches carried out in the different databases, a favorable result has been obtained in ACM journals for the greater number of publications about Mirroring tools and indicators of collaborative work. Results are shown in Fig. 2.

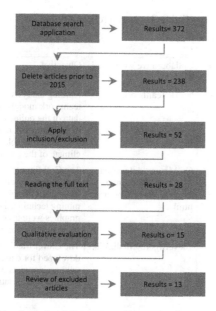

Fig. 1. Number of articles included and excluded in the process

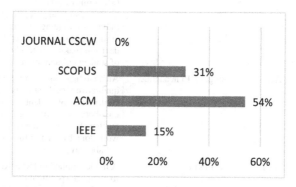

Fig. 2. Search results by databases

4.3 Analysis of Results

In the preliminary search in the databases of the IEEE Xplore, ACM, Scopus (ScienceDirect), and also the Journal Computer Supported Cooperative Work, 372 preselected articles were obtained. Then, 13 met the inclusion criteria in the present work.

Table 3. Search relevant posts

Relevant results			
Title	Databases	Collaborative work used	Objective
Using Learning Analytics to Visualise Computer Science Teamwork	Acm	Piazza (www.Piazza.com), Teamwork	Presents a teamwork dashboard, based on learning analysis, learning theory and teamwork models, in which he analyzes the data of the online discussions of the students in the teamwork and visualizes the mood, the distribution of roles and the emotional climate of the group
ColMiner: a tool to support communications management in an issue tracking environment	Acm	ColMiner, "dotnet" da Microsoft, http://nup essc.caf.ufv.br/Colminer. html	The ColMiner tool is intended to manage communications in software projects. For the analysis of the communications, some text mining techniques based on the use of graphics were used to represent the textual content of the comments
Integrating quantitative and qualitative data in assessment of wiki collaborative assignments	Acm	Cleverfigure4MediaWiki	The Clever MediaWiki system was developed for collaborative assessment of wiki assignments with a mixed approach that integrates quantitative information and qualitative data
Comparing teachers' use of *Mirroring* and advising dashboards	Acm	MathTutor, Dashboard	In the present study, the objective was to compare a Dashboard that provide information (Mirroring) with a Dashboard that alerts the teacher about the groups that need support (advising). Findings are discussed in the Dashboards that were used for decision-making by teachers in the context of student collaboration
Visualizing authorship and contribution of collaborative writing in e-learning environments	Acm	Google API academic system	An analytical framework for quantitative and qualitative visualization is described, the contribution of students in an interactive collaborative writing web tool; thus helping teachers by giving them a baseline of the work done by each of the students in collaborative writing
Constructing Interpretative Views of Learners' Interaction Behavior in an Open Learner Model	IEEE	INSPIREus	A model applied to INSPIREus is proposed to visualize specific indicators on the behavior of student interactions. Mirroring of student behavior is considered a point of reference that allows monitoring and reflection of collaborative work
Indicadores colaborativos individuales y grupales para Moodle	Scopus	Módulo de chat en moodle	A new chat module was developed for the Moodle educational platform, that allows you to capture and analyze student interactions, and then generate indicators that show the degree of manifestation of their collaboration skills, both individually and in groups

(continued)

Table 3. (*continued*)

Relevant results

Title	Databases	Collaborative work used	Objective
Gaze insights into debugging behavior using learner-centred analysis	Acm	Exercise View (EV) Plug-in in Eclipse	The aim of the study is to utilize users' gaze and action-based data to examine the role of a Mirroring tool (i.e. Exercise View in Eclipse) in orchestrating basic behavioral regulation during debugging
Identifying recommendation opportunities for computer-supported collaborative environments	Scopus	Forum	The aim of the study is on automatically identifying recommendation opportunities in the Collaborative Logical Framework from participants' interactions
Experimentation of a Multidimensional Model for Tracking Interactions Between Learners During an Online Collaborative Work	Scopus	Moodle platform a OOP PHP project	The main objective of this study is to provide the tutor with the opportunity to reconstruct the work groups that face academic difficulties, based on a multi-dimensional model to monitor interactions between students through four dimensions: affective, participatory, interactive and Technical
A Visualisation Dashboard for Contested Collective Intelligence Learning Analytics to Improve Sensemaking of Group Discussion	Scopus	cidashboard.net, debatehub.net, assembl.org, catalyst-fp7.eu	This study presents a visualization Dashboard with various visual analyzes that show important aspects of online discussions, that have been facilitated by the discussion tools of CCI (Contested Collective Intelligence). The Dashboard was designed to improve the creation of senses and participation in online discussions and it has been evaluated with two studies, a laboratory experiment and a field study, in the context of two institutes of higher education
DocuViz: Visualizing Collaborative Writing	Acm	DocuViz	Introduces a DocuViz tool, showing all Google Docs revision history, showing revision history and tracking changes in Word
PeerLA - Assistant for Individual Learning Goals and Self-Regulation Competency Improvement in Online Learning Scenarios	IEEE	PeerLA un plugin del Sistema de Gestión de Aprendizaje (LMS	PeerLA introduced to enhance self-regulatory competence, implemented as a plugin in a Learning Management System (LMS) to support learning progress in formal coeducational courses and informal learning settings

From the results obtained, it was decided to group the criteria into three categories:

1. *Mirroring* tool.
2. Collaborative work interactivity indicators.
3. Benefits generated.

The evaluation criteria are presented and described below:

1. Mirroring tool

   - Type of application. This criterion considers 3 types of applications: Web through a plugin, Web application and Web with use of dashboard.
   - Application license. Two types of software are considered: Free and paid.
   - Interaction. This criterion allows the identification of interactions in Mirroring. Two types are considered: Individual and Group

2. Collaborative work interactivity indicators

   - Qualitative. These criteria refer to the quality of interaction in collaborative work. Four types are considered: Organizational (interaction related to the planning aspect of collaborative work), Affective (interaction related to motivational and affective aspects in the participation of collaborative work), Content (interaction related to the arguments of the topic in collaborative work) and the Quantity/percentage of messages related to qualitative data.
   - Quantitative. This criterion refers to the density of collaborative work interaction. Four types are considered: Quantity/percentage of interaction messages, quantitative data, Social network, Self-regulation and Time of access to activity.

3. Benefits generated

   - Student. This criterion refers to the benefits gained from students in collaborative work. Three types are considered: Student learning, Self-regulation and Learning systems.
   - Teacher. This criterion refers to the benefits acquired from teachers in collaborative work. Three types are considered: Help to the evaluation of academic activity, Follow-up to collaborative work and Help to the teacher.

Thence, the mirroring tool reflects 92% of articles related to group participation, collaborative work, web application, or their combination. Other identified features were *plugin, dashboard* such as visualizations, activities visualization, as well as free applications developed using free and paid software. Group interaction is highlighted as the most used characteristic in the articles, as well as individual interaction within the operation of the *Mirroring* tools.

According to the category of collaborative work interactivity indicators, as expected in this study, it stands out the group interactivity as the most used indicator in articles, as well as the amount of quantitative data interaction at 77%. The indicators of different types of interactivity such as individual, organizational, affectivity, content, social, amount of interaction of qualitative data, percentage of self-regulation, and time of access to the activity are considered in the evaluated articles.

Table 4. Analysis of relevant publications

Relevant publications

MIRRORING TOOL			[6]	[7]	[8]	[9]	[10]	[11]	[12]	[13]	[14]	[15]	[16]	[17]	[18]
	Type of application	Web through a plugin							X	X	X				X
		Web application	X	X		X	X		X	X	X	X	X	X	X
		Web with use of dashboard	X	X		X							X		
	Application license	Free	X	X	X				X		X			X	X
		Paid						X							
	Interaction	Individual	X		X	X	X		X	X	X				
		Group	X	X	X	X	X	X	X	X	X	X	X	X	X

Relevant publications

COLLABORATIVE WORK INTERACTIVITY INDICATORS		[6]	[7]	[8]	[9]	[10]	[11]	[12]	[13]	[14]	[15]	[16]	[17]	[18]
Qualitative	Organizational	X	X					X						
	Affective									X	X			
	Content			X		X		X	X					
	Quantity/percentage of message in interaction(Qualitative data)			X	X	X	X	X						

(continued)

Table 4. (continued)

Relevant publications

		[6]	[7]	[8]	[9]	[10]	[11]	[12]	[13]	[14]	[15]	[16]	[17]	[18]
Quantitative	Quantity/percentage of engagement messages(quantitative data)	X				X	X	X	X	X	X	X	X	X
	Social network									X				
	Self-regulation													X
	Time access to activity	X		X	X		X					X	X	X

Relevant publications

		[6]	[7]	[8]	[9]	[10]	[11]	[12]	[13]	[14]	[15]	[16]	[17]	[18]
BENEFITS	Student	Student learning	X	X	X	X	X	X		X	X	X	X	X	X
		Self-regulation								X					X
		Learning systems	X	X		X		X		X	X	X	X		X
	Teacher	Help in the evaluation of academic activity	X	X		X			X	X					
		Follow-up to collaborative work		X	X		X	X	X					X	
		Teacher help	X		X	X	X			X					

The benefits generated by mirroring tools are multiple and they depend on the quality and quantity of the input information. Among them can be found the help to the teacher, aid to the evaluation of the academic activity, the follow-up to collaborative work, self-regulation, but the greatest amount (62%) of the benefits are related to student learning, the communication in collaborative work and learning systems.

Table 4 summarizes the information about mirroring tool studies and their relationship with the indicators of collaborative work interactivity and the benefits generated. More than three articles used plugin and dashboard for visualizations [6, 7, 9, 12–14, 16, 18], indicators with 54% individual interactivity and time access to activity, and also more than three articles emphasize the benefits of monitoring collaborative work [7, 8, 10–12, 12, 17].

5 Outcome Analysis: Discussion

Collaborative tools are becoming more popular thanks to their great potential in various educational aspects. *Mirroring* tools provide a visualization of academic indicators in the collaborative work process in the activities carried out in web applications. Hence, several scientific studies and their applications are based on *Mirroring* tools. In the educational field, mirroring tools are extensive, among the selected articles, benefits are listed such as student learning, helping the teacher in the monitoring of collaborative work, evaluation of academic activity, communication in collaborative work and, most importantly, the improvement of student learning and self-regulation systems. According to the results obtained from the systematic review presented in this work, *Mirroring* tools currently serve to identify the progress of the activities of an online course and the indicators help educational actors to self-regulate the progress of academic activities on educational platforms. There are aspects related to mirroring tools, among them *plugins* developed in LMS free applications such as Moodle, as well as a *dashboard* on educational applications for collaborative indicator visualizations, which are currently being studied by the educational and scientific community.

In studies such as the one carried out by Leeuwen and Rummel [9] compares a *dashboard* that provides information (*Mirroring*) y informs the teacher about the groups that need support (*advising*), the finding of the counseling condition could detect that problematic groups needed less effort for activities, and they were more confident in their decisions. Teachers frequently checked the alerts given, but also tried to find as much information as possible about other groups.

In the *Mirroring* condition, teachers generally begin to examine the information in the class summaries, but not always the time of verification of the information of the individual groups. Another study by Ullmann et al. [16], presents a *dashboard* of visualization with various analyzes showing important aspects of online discussions that have been facilitated by *CCI discussion tools*. The visualization provides an overview of the entire discussion stories such as *posts* nested circles, as well as the visualization of the activities of a debate over time and the contributions of users during a debate. Findings suggest that participants with little experience in using analytical visualizations have been able to manage adequate performance on specific tasks. In the *dashboard* done by Coelho y E silva [7], it stands out the support for communications management in software projects, it was calculated the relevance of the comments in the published debates and established a relationship of thematic relevance, helping well to software project managers. The used tool included four modules: data preparation, text analysis, calculation of relevance, and visualization of the results. In this topic, Tarmazdi et al. [6] formalized a study of learning analysis and teamwork models by visualizing on dashboards the online discussions of the students such as the team's state of mind, the distribution of roles and the emotional climate.

Authors Konert et al. [18], presents a learning management system (LMS) *plugin* to support the learning progress and assist in self-regulation in online learning environments. The *plugin* called PeerLA performs graphical feedback that allows comparing the level of knowledge, the time invested, and the objective. Besides, peer comparison is included in the visualization charts for the social frame of reference. Results show the benefits of self-regulatory assistance, especially for first-year college students. In this way, Mangaroska et al. [13] used a mirroring tool with the Eclipse IDE with exercises proposed for the students to complete. The tool was based on a *plugin* in Eclipse which collected data from the visualized exercises. Data that this plugin collected and reflected the students included: lines of code, the number of errors and warnings in the code, times the standard Java main method launched, the group results of the test (success, failure or error), debug events (for example, stop at breakpoints or resume execution), and commands execution (for example. step through code). The tool included awareness of the students' actions and helped maintain the representation of their progress and metacognition. On the other hand, the authors Yanacón-Atía et al. [12], developed a chat module for the Moodle educational platform, which captured and analyzed student interactions and then generate indicators that show the degree of manifestation of their collaboration skills, both individually and in groups. This tool allows teachers to monitor the manifestation of the collaboration skills of their students and have different individual and group indicators useful for decision-making.

The approach proposed by Papanikolaou [11], collects data on the interaction of students using a set of indicators that combine temporal, navigation, and performance data with semantic content data. It provides users (students and teachers) a behavioral mirror for monitoring and reflection, and we also obtained preliminary results on indicators of effort, progress, and work style. In the same way, Lobo et al. [14] in this research, focused on the automatic identification of the interactions of the participants in a collaborative framework, considering different sources of information: a) Statistical indicators in collaboration; b) social indicators interactions; c) the opinions received by the participants through the ratings, and d) the affective state and personality of the users. In addition, the results reveal relevant collaborative issues that encompass a centralized positive impact on participants; Likewise, with the SNA (social network analysis) it has demonstrated its relevance to collaboratively extract information. On the other hand, Salihoun et al. [15] propose a multidimensional model for monitoring interactions between students through four dimensions: affective, participatory, interactive, and technical, allowing teachers to analyze student behavior in learning environments.

The approach according to the authors [8] and [10] integrate quantitative and qualitative indicators of collaborative writing tools. These tools helped alleviate the workload for teachers, allowing academic parameters of the work done by each student in collaborative writing. Authors Wang et al. [17], instead developed DocuViz, a tool which displays the revision history, tracking step by step the changes made in Google Docs. In this sense, *Mirroring* tools may be needed in educational centers to visualize indicators that help with relevant information for decision-making of the processes of activities in collaborative work.

6 Conclusion and Future Work

This work shows a systematic review that allows identifying and evaluating several studies of mirroring tools related to the indicators, which were analyzed for the presentation of results, also answering the questions presented initially. Results show that mirroring tools with collaborative indicators is a trend that is increasing and improves educational solutions with collaborative work. In the studies reviewed, the mirroring tools allowed students to examine the progress of their activities and to self-regulate their participation in collaborative work, as well as helping teachers to make decisions in educational evaluations.

The effect of mirroring tools and indicators give a positive result. *Mirroring* tools mirroring seek to further engage students who participate in educational activities, creating opportunities for interaction and integration of collaborative workgroups. Through the participation of students in collaborative tools, new research problems arise that seek to find educational evaluation solutions through different collaborative indicators. In addition, mirroring tools allow the integration of different groups of specialized and non-specialized people who can contribute with information about interactivity in collaborative work, thus generating a benefit that covers various sectors of education,

As future work, it is possible to extend the search for information to include studies related to methodologies and case studies with collaborative indicators focused on the different areas of education. Future studies will develop new projects that combine theoretical studies and collaborative indicators with mirror computational models, particularly in higher education.

References

1. Dimitracopoulou, A.: Designing collaborative learning systems: current trends and future research agenda. In: Proceedings of the 2005 Conference on Computer Support for Collaborative Learning: Learning 2005: The Next 10 Years!, Taipei, Taiwan, May 2005, pp. 115–124, Accedido, 29 May 2020. [En línea]
2. Jermann, P., Soller, A., Muehlenbrock, M.: From *Mirroring* to guiding: a review of the state of art technology for supporting collaborative learning. In: Presentado en European Conference on Computer-Supported Collaborative Learning EuroCSCL-2001, 2001, p. 324. Accedido, 29 May 2020. [En línea]. Disponible en: https://telearn.archives-ouvertes.fr/hal-00197377
3. Soller, A., Martínez, A., Jermann, P., Muehlenbrock, M.: From *Mirroring* to guiding: a review of state of the art technology for supporting collaborative learning. Int. J. Artif. Intell. Educ. **15**(4), 261–290 (2005)
4. Zangara, M.A., Sanz, C.V.: Visualización del proceso colaborativo como metaconocimiento. Descripción de una estrategia de *Mirroring* y sus resultados. *XXIII Congreso Argentino de Ciencias de la Computación*, p. 12 (2017)

5. Kitchenham, B., Charters, S.: Guidelines for performing Systematic Literature Reviews in Software Engineering (2007)
6. Tarmazdi, H., Vivian, R., Szabo, C., Falkner, K., Falkner, N.: Using learning analytics to visualise computer science teamwork. In: Proceedings of the 2015 ACM Conference on Innovation and Technology in Computer Science Education - ITiCSE'15, Vilnius, Lithuania, pp. 165–170 (2015). https://doi.org/10.1145/2729094.2742613
7. Neto, L.E.C., e Silva, G.B.: ColMiner: a tool to support communications management in an issue tracking environment. In: Proceedings of the XIV Brazilian Symposium on Information Systems - SBSI'18, Caxias do Sul, Brazil, pp. 1–8 (2018). https://doi.org/10.1145/3229345.3229398
8. Duarte, M.P., Balderas, A., Dodero, J.M., Reinoso, A.J., Caballero, J.A., Delatorre, P.: Integrating quantitative and qualitative data in assessment of wiki collaborative assignments. In: Proceedings of the Sixth International Conference on Technological Ecosystems for Enhancing Multiculturality - TEEM'18, Salamanca, Spain, pp. 328–332 (2018). https://doi.org/10.1145/3284179.3284232
9. van Leeuwen, A., Rummel, N.: Comparing teachers' use of *Mirroring* and advising dashboards. In: Proceedings of the Tenth International Conference on Learning Analytics & Knowledge, Frankfurt Germany, pp. 26–34, March 2020. https://doi.org/10.1145/3375462.3375471
10. Torres, J., García, S., Peláez, E.: Visualizing authorship and contribution of collaborative writing in e-learning environments. In: Proceedings of the 24th International Conference on Intelligent User Interfaces, Marina del Ray California, pp. 324–328, March 2019. https://doi.org/10.1145/3301275.3302328
11. Papanikolaou, K.A.: Constructing interpretative views of learners' interaction behavior in an open learner model. IEEE Trans. Learn. Technol. **8**(2), 201–214, April 2015. https://doi.org/10.1109/tlt.2014.2363663
12. Yanacón-Atía, D., Costaguta, R., de los, M., Menini, Á.: Indicadores colaborativos individuales y grupales para Moodle. Campus Virtuales **7**(1), 125–139, March 2018
13. Mangaroska, K., Sharma, K., Giannakos, M., Trætteberg, H., Dillenbourg, P.: Gaze insights into debugging behavior using learner-centred analysis. In: Proceedings of the 8th International Conference on Learning Analytics and Knowledge, Sydney New South Wales Australia, pp. 350–359, March 2018. https://doi.org/10.1145/3170358.3170386
14. Lobo, J.L., Santos, O.C., Boticario, J.G., Del Ser, J.: Identifying recommendation opportunities for computer-supported collaborative environments. Expert Syst. **33**(5), 463–479 (2016). https://doi.org/10.1111/exsy.12159
15. Salihoun, M., Guerouate, F., Sbihi, M.: Experimentation of a multidimensional model for tracking interactions between learners during an online collaborative work. Int. J. Emerg. Technol. Learn. (iJET) **12**(10), 221–229 (2017)
16. Ullmann, T.D., De Liddo, A., Bachler, M.: A visualisation dashboard for contested collective intelligence learning analytics to improve sensemaking of group discussion. RIED **22**(1), 41 (2019). https://doi.org/10.5944/ried.22.1.22294
17. Wang, D., Olson, J.S., Zhang, J., Nguyen, T., Olson, G.M.: DocuViz: visualizing collaborative writing. In: Proceedings of the 33rd Annual ACM Conference on Human Factors in Computing Systems - CHI'15, Seoul, Republic of Korea, pp. 1865–1874 (2015). https://doi.org/10.1145/2702123.2702517
18. Konert, J., Bohr, C., Bellhauser, H., Rensing, C.: PeerLA - assistant for individual learning goals and self-regulation competency improvement in online learning scenarios. In: 2016 IEEE 16th International Conference on Advanced Learning Technologies (ICALT), Austin, TX, USA, pp. 52–56 (2016). https://doi.org/10.1109/icalt.2016.100

Metric Study: Use of Memory Corresponding to the ISO/IEC25010 Standard in Augmented Reality Applications

Fausto A. Salazar-Fierro$^{(\boxtimes)}$ ⓘ, Carpio A. Pineda-Manosalvas ⓘ,
Nancy N. Cervantes-Rodríguez ⓘ, and Pablo A. Landeta-López ⓘ

Faculty of Engineering in Applied Sciences, Universidad Técnica del Norte, Ibarra, Ecuador
{fasalazar,capineda,nncervantes,palandeta}@utn.edu.ec

Abstract. Today there is a wide variety of applications that use the emerging technology of augmented reality in different areas, especially in education with a wide variety of uses, in tourism and even in the military field and art. Each one of them tries to satisfy some need or provide a specific service; however, they do not always meet user expectations. The aim of this research was to analyze the memory usage metric based on the ISO/IEC25010 standard, experimenting in two tourist applications with the same characteristics developed in two RA tools: Vuforia and Wikitude. The research method used was experimentation using the Indicator CPU application running it on three smartphones (two with high features and capabilities and one with low features and capabilities) as a measurement tool. As a result, there are significant differences in memory use between the two devices of the same brand (Samsung J1 and S8) with mean values in Vuforia 0.2420 and 0.5800 respectively and 0.2840 and 0.5200 in Wikitude. Furthermore, it is evident that the differences in the memory usage metric between the high features and capabilities device (Sony Z5) and the low features and capabilities device (Samsung J1) are insignificant.

Keywords: Augmented reality · ISO/IEC/25010 · Memory · Model · Applications

1 Introduction

Augmented reality (AR) and its growing application development have influenced many tools that cover the needs of users [1], which has been considered as an emerging technology [2] since the 1960s and is currently recognized as one of the ten most innovative to combine real and virtual elements [3], allowing interaction between different areas of application [4]. There are several problems that augmented reality can solve for users [5] with images that are generated in two or three dimensions [3].

Currently there are a large number of projects developed applying AR: more than 4 million mobile applications on Google Play and more than 2.5 million on Apple App Store, many of them do not meet the expectations of users [4].

© Springer Nature Switzerland AG 2020
R. Valencia-García et al. (Eds.): CITI 2020, CCIS 1309, pp. 193–204, 2020.
https://doi.org/10.1007/978-3-030-62015-8_15

Education is one of the areas in which this technology has been most exploited with various applications, an example is the learning of anatomy using AR that aims to interact with users using mobile devices [6]. In the field of mechanics, an educational project has been created that helps participants learn and understand the principle of the operation of a gasoline engine with three-dimensional visualization on Android devices [7]. Another example in pedagogy using AR is the study model designed to teach computer fundamentals; to apply it, users do class work using Pythy [8].

Tourism is also another area with high development of AR applications [9]. An example is the tourist guide of historical relics using AR with a game called MAGIC-EYES that includes six modules that allow you to visit a specific place [10]. Music has also been considered for the development of AR applications, an example is a songbook in an educational application with the aim of sensitizing children to abstract concepts of music [11].

In the military field, an AR application has been experimented that allows simulating war chess and training exercise using Technology Acceptance Model (TAM) theory [12]. Based on Kkongalmon's research, an Android Application Package (apk) was developed that identifies problems and improvements with AR-based games by applying location, and a development methodology was presented that includes design guidelines with geographic information [13].

Unmanned aerial vehicles are also part of the integration with AR, an example is the study in which a 3d scenario was built with an on-board sensor that continuously updates the data from the acquired data [14].

With a wide catalog of apk's developed with AR to cover different areas, this research focuses on memory usage during the execution of an AR app, which is a fundamental element that must be measured in the life cycle of the software development [15].

One of the most important works is the evolution of software that Lehman started in 1974, this process has had continuous improvement for more than 40 years. During this study period, eight software development laws have emerged in which a series of studies is carried out: 1) Continuous change, 2) Increasing complexity, 3) Self regulation, 4) Conservation of organizational stability, 5) Conservation of familiarity, 6) Continuing Growth, 7) Declining Quality, y 8) Feedback system [4].

The software has constantly evolved in recent years, that is why software quality standards have been developed such as McCall, Boehm, Carlo Ghezzi and other models including ISO 25010, IEEE, QMOOD [16].

In this context, studies have been carried out using the International Organization for Standardization (ISO) with the ISO/IEC25010 standard better known as SQuaRE (Software Product Quality Requirements and Evaluation), which constitutes an evolution of ISO/IEC/9126 [17], adopting usability and satisfaction metrics in developed software [18].

The objective of this research is focused on the evaluation of memory usage according to the ISO model on two similar augmented reality apk's that were developed in Vuforia and Wikitude tools using the Unity development engine. Its result would constitute an important variable during the tool selection process.

2   Materials and Methods

This research was carried out with a test methodology using two selected AR tools that are Vuforia and Wikitude. The selection of these tools was based on a previous study by the authors, in which the basic characteristics for the development of AR applications were analyzed taking into consideration aspects such as: platform (operating system), use of GPS, 2D recognition, 3D and video images, available documentation and framework that they offer for the development of AR applications [2] and a competitive benchmarking In that research it was demonstrated that, considering the presence or not of characteristics and sub-characteristics, the two tools used in this work complies the expectations for the creation of AR applications.

The Unity Scholar version was used as IDE, Wikitude and Vuforia tools were used to integrate the AR. The 3D object (a lake) was modeled with Maya software. The execution of the apps requires at least Android 6.0 version with API 23.

The AR applications in both Vuforia and Wikitude were developed with Unity software, only to be run on Android operating systems. The tourist place chosen to obtain the information from the application was San Pablo lake located in Otavalo city, Imbabura province. The first application button allows to activate the device's camera to point towards a marker that displays the lake as a 3D AR object; the second button displays a 139s video that captures the beauty of the lake and its surroundings, this video was make with a drone; finally a third button activates the GPS and displays the image of the lake in 3D with a continuous 360° rotation.

To collect data, two identical applications were run on AR tools (Vuforia and Wikitude) with the aim of disseminating lake tourism sites in the province of Imbabura. The designed apk's were installed on three smartphone devices whose technical characteristics are:

a. Sony Xperia Z5 (High-end) smartphone with a 5.2-in. 1080p screen, Snapdragon 810 octa-core processor, 3 Gb of RAM, 32 Gb of internal storage and a 23-megapixel main camera. Android version 7.1.1 released November 2015.
b. Samsung S8 (High-end) Screen: 5.8″, 1440 × 2960 pixels, processor: Snapdragon 835/Exynos 8895 octa.core, 4 Gb of RAM, 64 Gb storage, 12 megapixel main camera. Android version 8.0 released May 2018.
c. Samsung J1 (Low End) with a 4-in. screen, Spreadtrum SC9830 1.3 GHz processor, 1 Gb of RAM, 8 Gb of internal storage and a 5-megapixel main camera. Android version 6.0 released January 2015.

Before running the tests on all three phones, Developer Options - USB Debugging were enabled, the cache on all installed applications was cleared, and all applications in use were closed. Each device was rebooted and only two applications were run on each one: CPU Indicator to measure memory usage and the AR app created for testing.

2.1   Quality Methods: ISO/IE/2010 Standard

Currently there are many works in which the quality of software has been studied with an emphasis on mobile devices [19], applying quality standards such as ISO with its different updates [20].

2.2   ISO/IEC/25010 Metrics

The Performance Efficiency feature has been selected that has a direct relationship with the device performance and specifically with the Memory Usage sub-feature.

The Performance Efficiency feature has been selected, with the Memory Usage sub-feature. The objective of the test is to verify the amount of memory used to perform an assigned task. The test method measures the total amount of memory and the amount of spaces used to perform a task. The equation used is as follows:

$$X = B - A \tag{1}$$

Where A corresponds to the input values representing the amount of memory spaces used to perform a task and B corresponds to the total amount of memory available.

To obtain data, several free tools are available on Google Play such as: All-In-One, Antutu, CPU Meter, CPU Indicator, CPU-Z, Hardware Information Memory info, Toolbox.

In this case, the CPU Indicator tool was used, which allows identifying the percentage of memory used when activating the AR app and when a specific task ends. The value required by the metric was obtained by applying the proportional relationship.

2.3   Weight Allocation

Once the values generated in the analysis of the sub-characteristic were identified, the data resulting from the thirty records of the experimentation were obtained to satisfy the metrics of the characteristics of each of the AR tools with the Samsung 8, Samsung J1 smartphones and Sony Xperia Z5, assigning a weight of 100% to the Memory usage metric, presented in Table 1.

Table 1. Assigned percentages of performance characteristic.

Characteristic	Importance	Metric	%	Total
Behavior over time	Does not apply			
Use of the resource	High	CPU use	0%	
		Memory use	100%	100%
		Using I/O Devices	0%	
Capacity	Does not apply			

2.4   Statistical Tests

The experimentation results of the obtained surveys were treated using the statistical programming language R. For the analysis, 30 records were considered, and a treatment was performed to eliminate possible outliers. The sample parametric assumptions: linearity, normality, homogeneity and homoscedasticity were verified by a false regression test, based on the standardized, studentized and adjusted quantiles, obtained from each observation in the database, which were compared with the theoretical quantiles of the $\chi 2$ distribution.

Figure 1 shows the quartiles of each phones in the two AR tools.

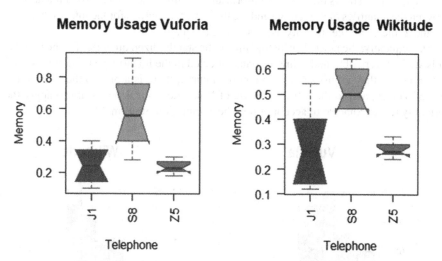

Fig. 1. Quartile distribution in AR Vuforia and Wikitude tools

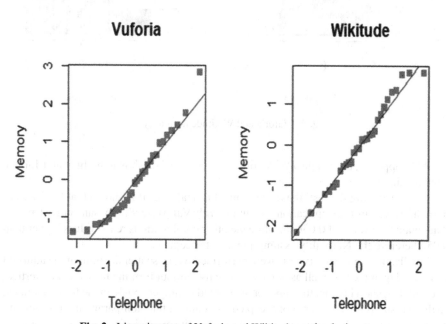

Fig. 2. Linearity test of Vuforia and Wikitude on the devices

To determine the type of test to be applied for data comparison, the four assumptions were checked: linearity, normality, homogeneity and homoscedasticity. Figure 2 shows the results of the linearity tests applying the false regression analysis with the data obtained in the two AR tools.

The Q-Q plot shows that both in Vuforia and Wikitude the values have a linear trend between the quantiles of the sample and the theoretical quantiles for the interval between −2 and 2, therefore the linearity assumption is accepted.

Subsequently, the normality histograms of the standardized quantiles for the two AR tools studied were obtained using the data collected in the linearity test. Figure 3 shows that, although they adjust slightly to a normal curve, there is a bias to the right in the case of Vuforia and to the left in the case of Wikitude, so it is necessary to apply the normality test of Shapiro to accept or not, the assumption of normality.

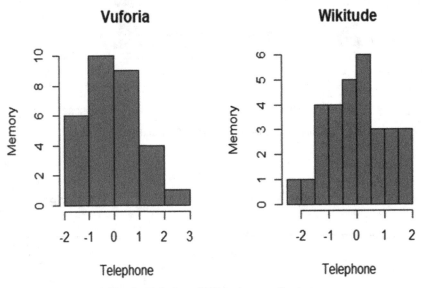

Fig. 3. Vuforia and Wikitude normality test

After applying the Shapiro Wilk normality test, the data shown in Fig. 4 and Table 2 were obtained.

After executing the test, the data obtained is analyzed, it is shown that they are not normal, except in the application execution with Vuforia with the Samsung J1 phone that obtains the value of 0.03616, while the other combinations reach values higher than 0.05, therefore the Normality assumption is not accepted.

Finally, the homogeneity tests were performed with a scatter diagram of the adjusted and scaled quantiles, as well as homoscedasticity without forming horizontal or vertical line patterns, showing that they are not distributed homogeneously in the four quadrants, so these assumptions they are not accepted, concluding that non-parametric tests should be used to obtain the comparative results of this investigation. Figure 5 presents the assumptions in reference.

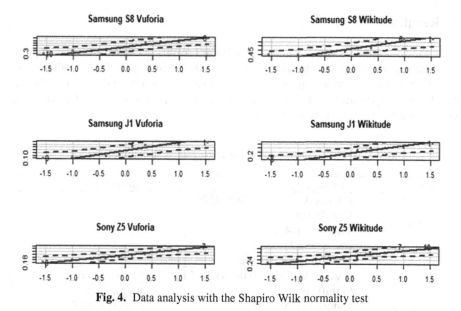

Fig. 4. Data analysis with the Shapiro Wilk normality test

Table 2. Data analysis with the Shapiro Wilk normality test.

Phone	Vuforia	Wikitude
Samsung S8	0.69830	0.05906
Samsung J1	0.03616	0.08635
Sony Z5	0.71830	0.15680

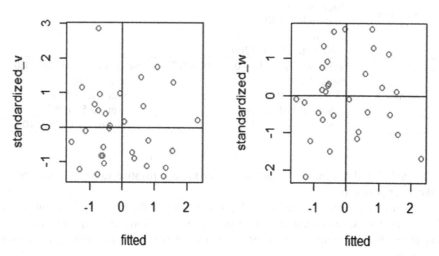

Fig. 5. Vuforia and Wikitude homogeneity and homocedasticity test

3 Results

Once the assumptions were verified, the Kruskall Wallis statistical test was applied since the data are not parametric, in addition the Dunn test was applied to validate the significance of the differences in memory use between the phones that were used during the phase of experimentation. Table 3 and Table 4 present the values obtained in the Vuforia and Wikitude tools respectively.

Table 3. Pairwise composition using T-test with pooled means: Vuforia

Phone	Samsung S8	Samsung J1
Samsung J1	P Value Vuforia = 0,0014858613 **Significant** Vuforia = 0.41 $\bar{x}$ Samsung J1 = 0.2420 $\bar{x}$ Samsung S8 = 0.5800	
Sony Z5	P Value Vuforia = 0,0009171053 **Significant** Vuforia = 0.41 $\bar{x}$ Sony Z5: 0.2330 $\bar{x}$ Samsung S8: 0.5800	P Value Vuforia = 1,0 Insignificant Vuforia = 0.48 $\bar{x}$ Sony Z5: 0.2330 $\bar{x}$ Samsung J1: 0.2420

Table 4. Pairwise composition using T-test with pooled means: Wikitude

Phone	Samsung S8	Samsung J1
Samsung J1	P Value Wikitude = 0, 0016101613 **Significant** Wikitude= 0,40 $\bar{x}$ Samsung J1: 0,2840 $\bar{x}$ Samsung S8: 0,5200	
Sony Z5	P Value Wikitude = 0, 0008182173 **Significant** Wikitude = 0.40 $\bar{x}$ Sony Z5: 0,2920 $\bar{x}$ Samsung S8: 0.5200	P Value Wikitude = 1,0 Insignificant Wikitude = 0.57 $\bar{x}$ Sony Z5: 0,2820 $\bar{x}$ Samsung J1: 0,2840

In Table 3 and 4, column 3 is deleted, since the comparative values already appear in the other positions.

For Vuforia and the application made, it is shown that the Samsung S8 phone has a higher memory usage compared to the Samsung J1 and Sony Z5 equipment. It is also evident that the Samsung J1 team uses more memory than Sony Z5, although in a very small value.

Regarding memory use with the Wikitude tool, it is noted that the Samsung S8 phone uses more memory in relation to Samsung J1 and Sony Z5, although it uses less memory than in the Vuforia apk. Additionally, Samsung J1 increases memory usage on a small scale compared to Vuforia apk.

There are significant differences in memory usage between the two Samsung J1 and Samsung S8 devices with mean values in Vuforia 0.2420 and 0.5800 respectively, while in Wikitude the values of 0.2840 and 0.5200 are obtained. Furthermore, it is evident that the differences in the memory usage metric between the high-end device (Sony Z5) and the low-end device (Samsung J1) are insignificant.

For the devices selection used in the tests, a survey was carried out with the students of the Faculty of Engineering in Applied Sciences - Universidad Técnica del Norte with de aim to know the brand of preference when acquiring a smartphone. Samsung obtained the higher score as result of this survey. For this reason, it was decided to use a low-end Samsung J1 and a high-end Samsung S8 for experimentation. Additionally, a third high-end smartphone (Sony Xperia Z5) was integrated to contrast the results between devices of different brands.

Considering that the three smartphones do not have the best features available on the market, it is possible to conclude that the use of augmented reality applications works on various devices, reducing the technological gap that is generated with the appearance of new technologies.

This finding implies some decisions to take into account in the development methodology of AR applications, so that their design considers the use of APIs that allow their operation in low and mid-range equipment, favoring universal access to the use of technologies to be used in various fields of science, mainly in education and tourism dissemination.

4 Discussion

The ISO/25010 standard has been the subject of study in various investigations [1, 16, 17, 19, 20] to name a few, in which the objective is to support the development of applications that comply with standards that guarantee the quality of the software, in terms of: functional adequacy, performance efficiency, compatibility, usability, reliability, security, maintainability and portability.

The authors performed an analysis of the performance of AR applications using this standard, focusing on performance efficiency characteristic of the product quality model defined by ISO 25010, analyzing two of its three sub-characteristics: temporal behavior and use of resources. The purpose of this research was to analyze the performance efficiency of two AR apps developed in: Vuforia and Wikitude, run on a high-end smartphone. In the final results it was noted that Vuforia is the tool of choice when the speed and performance of the app is a determining factor.

Also as a previous work, the authors carried out a comparative research of AR tools analyzing the presence/absence of the relevant characteristics [2], the work bases its analysis on five essential characteristics of AR tools, each one received a weight considering its importance in the development of applications: Platform, Global positioning system, 2D images, 3D and videos, Documentation and Framework, concluding that, Wikitude is the best alternative for the development of augmented reality applications because it offers better features.

This work differs from the previous one by focusing on the memory metric experimenting on three devices, while the previous work analyzes several metrics experimenting on a single device [1], considering that memory is a resource that influences the speed of application execution and the cost of a smartphone.

The contribution of this work lies in the evidence that is generated when testing devices that do not necessarily have high resources, showing that the emerging augmented reality technology can be used in a variety of devices, reducing the digital gap in terms of devices characteristics.

5 Conclusions

Memory usage is one of the resources that AR applications use the most and is part of the quality in software development. The study carried out focused on the analysis of memory use applying the metrics of the ISO 25010 standard. For the experimentation process, two Samsung brand phones (high-end S8, J1 low-end) and one Sony brand (high-end Z5) were used, in order to determine if the device type is related to memory resource usage and performance while running an AR application.

At the end of the investigation it is shown that in the two AR applications designed in Vuforia and Wikitude, the Samsung S8 phone presents a higher memory usage in relation to the Samsung J1 and Sony Z5 mobile devices; It is also evident that Samsung J1 uses more memory than Sony Z5 in the two applications designed.

Therefore, it is concluded that some smartphone brands by offering greater benefits also make use of a greater amount of resources (in the specific case of the research: the memory resource), unlike other brands that also correspond to high-end, use more conservatively available resources. It would be interesting to extend this study to a greater variety of high-end devices to determine the smartphone brands that meet this user expectation.

An important aspect to take into account is the design of the augmented reality applications, since in the selected API, lies the possibility of operating in the variety of devices with greater acceptance in the market and although users prefer to acquire smartphones with better features In order to access the greatest number of technological options available, this study shows that having more resources does not necessarily guarantee the best management of it.

References

1. Salazar, F., Pineda, C., Cervantes, N., Landeta, P.: Análisis de la eficiencia de desempeño en aplicaciones de Realidad Aumentada utilizando la normativa ISO/IEC/25010. RISTI **22**, 256–267 (2019)
2. Salazar, F., Pineda, C., Arciniega, S., Cervantes, N.: Comparativa técnica de herramientas para realidad aumentada: wikitude. Vuforia Y Artoolkit. Axioma **2**(19), 86–96 (2019)
3. Gómez Rios, M.D., Paredes Velasco, M.: Augmented reality as a methodology to development of learning in programming. In: Botto-Tobar, M., Pizarro, G., Zúñiga-Prieto, M., D'Armas, M., Zúñiga Sánchez, M. (eds.) CITT 2018. CCIS, vol. 895, pp. 327–340. Springer, Cham (2019). https://doi.org/10.1007/978-3-030-05532-5_24

4. Gezici, B., Tarhan, A., Chouseinoglou, O.: The increasing number of mobile applications and ensuring the continuity of these applications in the market has led to the question of how to be successful on the market with functional applications that not only meet user expectations and also exceed th. Inf. Softw. Technol. **112**, 178–200 (2019)
5. Bond, A., Neville, K., Mercado, J., Massey, L., Wearne, A., Ogreten, S.: Evaluating training efficacy and return on investment for augmented reality: a theoretical framework. In: Nazir, S., Teperi, A.-M., Polak-Sopińska, A. (eds.) AHFE 2018. AISC, vol. 785, pp. 226–236. Springer, Cham (2019). https://doi.org/10.1007/978-3-319-93882-0_23
6. Jamali, S.S., Shiratuddin, M.F., Wong, K.W., Oskam, C.L.: Utilising mobile-augmented reality for learning human anatomy. Procedia Soc. Behav. Sci. **197**(February), 659–668 (2015)
7. Abdullah, A.G., Mulyanti, B., Rohendi, D.: Virtual gasoline engine based on augment reality for mechanical engineering education, vol. 16002, pp. 1–6 (2018)
8. MacIntyre, B., Zhang, D., Jones, R., Solomon, A., Disalvo, E., Guzdial, M.: Using projection AR to add design studio pedagogy to a CS classroom. In: Proceedings - IEEE Virtual Real, pp. 227–228 (2016)
9. Nobnop, R., Wongwatktit, C., Wongta, J., Soponronnarit, K.: A development of 3D augmented reality mobile application to facilitating ecotourism-based herbal learning in MFU botanical garden. In: ICCE 2018 - 26th International Conference on Computer in Education Work Proceedings, pp. 531–540 (2018)
10. Wei, X., Weng, D., Liu, Y., Wang, Y.: A tour guiding system of historical relics based on augmented reality. In: Proceedings - IEEE Virtual Real, July 2016, pp. 307–308 (2016)
11. Rusiñol, M., Chazalon, J., Diaz-Chito, K.: Augmented songbook: an augmented reality educational application for raising music awareness. Multimed. Tools Appl. **77**(11), 13773–13798 (2017). https://doi.org/10.1007/s11042-017-4991-4
12. Ahram, T., Taiar, R., Colson, S., Choplin, A.: Human Interaction and Emerging Technologies. Advances in Intelligent Systems and Computing, vol. 1018 (2019)
13. Youm, D., Seo, S., Kim, J-K.: Design and development methodologies of Kkongalmon, a location-based augmented reality game using mobile geographic information. EURASIP J. Image Video Process, vol. 2019, no. 1, December 2019
14. Tianjiang, X: Data - Griven augmented reality display and operations for UAV ground stations, pp. 557–560 (2017)
15. Yang, H.: Measuring software product quality with iso standards base on fuzzy logic technique. In: Luo, J. (ed.) Affective Computing and Intelligent Interaction. AISC, vol. 137, pp. 59–67. Springer, Heidelberg (2012). https://doi.org/10.1007/978-3-642-27866-2_8
16. Gordieiev, O., Kharchenko, V., Fominykh, N., Sklyar, V.: Evolution of software quality models in context of the standard ISO 25010. In: Zamojski, W., Mazurkiewicz, J., Sugier, J., Walkowiak, T., Kacprzyk, J. (eds.) Proceedings of the Ninth International Conference on Dependability and Complex Systems DepCoS-RELCOMEX. June 30 – July 4, 2014, Brunów, Poland. AISC, vol. 286, pp. 223–232. Springer, Cham (2014). https://doi.org/10.1007/978-3-319-07013-1_21
17. Calabrese, J., Muñoz, R., Pasini, A., Esponda, S., Boracchia, M., Pesado, P.: Assistant for the evaluation of software product quality characteristics proposed by ISO/IEC 25010 based on GQM-defined metrics. In: De Giusti, A.E. (ed.) CACIC 2017. CCIS, vol. 790, pp. 164–175. Springer, Cham (2018). https://doi.org/10.1007/978-3-319-75214-3_16
18. Juma, A., Rodríguez, J., Caraguay, J., Naranjo, M., Quiña-Mera, A., García-Santillán, I.: Integration and evaluation of social networks in virtual learning environments: a case study. In: Botto-Tobar, M., Pizarro, G., Zúñiga-Prieto, M., D'Armas, M., Zúñiga Sánchez, M. (eds.) CITT 2018. CCIS, vol. 895, pp. 245–258. Springer, Cham (2019). https://doi.org/10.1007/978-3-030-05532-5_18

19. Idri, A., Bachiri, M., Fernandez-Aleman, J.L., Toval, A.: ISO/IEC 25010 based evaluation of free mobile personal health records for pregnancy monitoring. In: 2017 IEEE 41st Annual Computer Software and Applications Conference (COMPSAC), vol. 1, pp. 262–267 (2017)
20. Karnouskos, S., Sinha, R., Leitao, P., Ribeiro, L., Strasser, T.: Assessing the integration of software agents and industrial automation systems with ISO/IEC 25010. In: Proceedings - IEEE 16th International Conference on Industrial Informatics, INDIN 2018, pp. 61–66 (2018)

Geographic Information System on Violence Against Women

Iván Gallardo-Bernal[1](✉) ⓘ, José Luis Hernández-Hernández[2] ⓘ,
María del Carmen Trejo-Ramírez[3] ⓘ, and Mario Hernández-Hernández[4] ⓘ

[1] Higher School of Government and Public Management, Autonomous University of Guerrero,
Chilpancingo, Guerrero, Mexico
Igallardo@uagro.mx
[2] TecNM/Technological Institute of Chilpancingo, Chilpancingo, Guerrero, Mexico
joseluis.hernandez@itchilpancingo.edu.mx
[3] Foreign Language Faculty, Autonomous University of Guerrero, Acapulco, Guerrero, Mexico
15151@uagro.mx
[4] Engineering Faculty, Autonomous University of Guerrero, Chilpancingo, Guerrero, Mexico
mhernandezh@uagro.mx

Abstract. The eradication of violence against women has become a matter of urgent attention for Mexico. The possibility to prevent this behavior requires a collaborative approach where it is assumed that violence towards women as a public problem and therefore implies responsibility on the part of the state, but by society as a whole. Prior to the eradication of this kind of violence, we need to understand and know the types of violence and the places where they occur. Evaluating the complexity and magnitude of this phenomenon, in Mexico, was created the General Law on Women's Access to a Life Free of Violence that includes the mechanism of the Gender Violence Alert with Women (AVGM), which suggests the uniformity of the information collected all the institutions that give attention to women in situations of violence. On the basis of these provisions is intended to design a system of reusable information for all the states of the Mexican Republic, that act as a center of electronic information, organized, systematized and homogeneous for the design of public policies; aimed to contribute to prevent, address, investigate, punish, and eradicate the different types of violence against women in Mexico. This project is in the proof of concept phase, whit real user data, the develop at the system is finished and be available at GNU/GLP license, once it has been fully tested.

Keywords: Geographic system · Woman's violence · Data warehouse

1 Introduction

The United Nations defines violence against women as "any act of gender-based violence that results, or is likely to result in physical, sexual or psychological harm to women, including threats of such acts, coercion or arbitrary deprivation of liberty, whether occurring in public and private life" [11].

© Springer Nature Switzerland AG 2020
R. Valencia-García et al. (Eds.): CITI 2020, CCIS 1309, pp. 205–220, 2020.
https://doi.org/10.1007/978-3-030-62015-8_16

During the Convention on the Elimination of All Forms of Discrimination against Women (CEDAW), held in 1979, the UN issued the Declaration on the Elimination of Violence against Women. It advances to consider that "...violence against women constitutes a manifestation of historically unequal power relations between men and women, which have led to the domination of women, and that violence against women is one of the crucial social mechanisms by which forces women to a subordinate position to the men" [4].

According to the Un Women [12], in the world it is estimated that approximately 35% of the woman have suffered physic or sexual violence at some point in their lives, however in national studies the number change demonstrating 70% of the woman experiments violence.

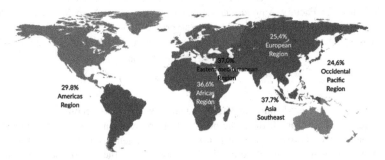

Fig. 1. World map on partner violence.

In the Fig. 1, we can observe the percent of woman affirms that suffer gender violence, the numbers describe a several problems in the world, in first place, Asia Southeast 37,7%, followed by Eastern Mediterranean region whit 37%, next 36,6%, in the Africa region, in the American region 29.8%, in fifth place European region with 25,4%, and in the last place the Occidental Pacific region whit 24,6%. In México the situation is not different the 66.1% of the woman about 15 year or more, has suffered any type of violence, and 8 women was killed every day on 2016 for gender reasons.

On April 3rd of 2007 it was installed for the first time in Mexico The National System of Prevention, Care, Punishment, and Eradication of Violence against Women that it is an inter-agency mechanism for coordinating efforts, instruments, policies, services and actions to guarantee the right of women to a life free of violence. Within its objectives is the promotion and implementation of public policies on violence against women and the creation of this structure for each of the states of the Republic [2]. In this year was created The Gender Violence Alert: Is the set of government actions with emergency assistance to deal with and eradicate the femicidal violence in a given territory, whether exercised by individuals or by the community itself [8], is an emergency mechanism created to perform actions and face the violence that becomes exacerbated by femicide and violation of the rights of women, it will be essential to ensure the safety of the same, the cessation of violence against and eliminate inequalities produced by legislation that impedes their human rights it contemplates:

I.   Establish an inter-agency group and multidisciplinary understanding of gender that the respective follow-up;

II.   Implement preventive actions, security and justice, to deal with and put down the femicidal violence.

III. Develop special reports on the area and the behavior of indicators on violence against women.

IV.   Assign the budgetary resources needed to cope with the contingency of alert of gender-based violence against women.

V.   Make public knowledge of the reason for the alert of gender-based violence against women, and the territorial zone covering the measures to be implemented.

According to INMUJERES, the Gender Violence Alert has been conceived as a protective mechanism of the human rights of women in a context of violence and as a pop-up mechanism of state intervention, not as a sanction. Its objective is to ensure the safety and security of women and girls, the cessation of violence against them and/or eliminate inequalities produced by legislation or public policy that impedes their human rights [7, 18].

The Mexican constitution includes the LGAVLV [8] defines in its article 6, the types of violence against women are:

1.   Psychological violence: harms at the psychological stability.
2.   Physical violence: Acts that causes damage using physical force or weapons.
3.   The patrimonial violence. Acts which affects the survival of the victim.
4.   Economic violence: Any action of the aggressor that affects the economic survival of the victim.
5.   Sexual violence: Any act that degrades or damages the body and/or the sexuality of the victim.
6.   Any other similar forms violence: damages dignity, integrity or freedom of women.

In the word exist a different tools regarding women safety and violence prevention, some of they and the functionality be analyst in Table 1.

Regularly, in the governments of the states that make up the Mexican Republic, there is information scattered about data on violence against women, in large measure, by the legal instruments that oblige the units to provide them. Together with the little coordination between existing information systems in such a way that each one of the States and their dependences handles different information and is rarely shared, increasing exponentially the duplicity of the registers and dispersion of data.

The government of Mexico developed the National Bank of Data and Information on data on the victim Cases of Violence against women, this tool stores victim data, type and modality of violence, information events, schooling and some health data. It also store the profile of the aggressor, the average affiliation and the risk factor. The bank create a violence file for each woman and records the number of cases and the number of protection orders, to later show the number of cases on a map, this map shows the general information of the cases in all the states of the Republic. The system does not suggest the analysis and processing of the information to predict the events or the creation of profiles automatically through the system.

Table 1. Apps against women violence in the world.

Name	Purpose	Geography	Type of Violence
GBV project	To combat and eliminate gender violence in Cambodian society	Cambodia	Report gender violence
Hollaback	To end street harassment against women & LGBTQ communities in public spaces	30 Countries in Europe	Violent prevent gender violence app
Women under siege	To end rape & all forms of sexualized violence occurring against women in conflict-prone regions	Ukraine, Lebanon, & the Middle East	Sexual violent, the app provides information for local sexual assault centers
Panic button	Help women to prepare for attacks, coordinate with their networks, and stay safe	Amnesty International	Free mobile app that allows users to discretely & rapidly alert their three trusted contacts in an emergency

With all of this background, we find solid foundations for the design of an information system, that allows us to concentrate the state and national data of violence against women through the instances involved; this platform should include modalities and types of violence, as well as the possibility to capture the geographical location of each one of the incidents and information of potential aggressors. With all this information, the proposed system would display dynamic graphs for each of the criteria mentioned above, heat maps and the creation of a data center at state and national levels that will serve as support to decision-making. Once we have a reliable database, it will be possible to implement artificial intelligence techniques that allow creating personalized profiles for each aggressor, as well as the crossing of variables that allow you to study the determining factors of the violent behaviors of the aggressors. This article will address the methodology implemented for: develop of the system, planning, execute, and maintenance phases and it will culminate with the future functionalities that can be added to the software.

2   Materials and Methods

Because of the type of problems that cater for software engineers, the process to solve them is complicated and requires dedication and time. The procedure, generally accepted, is the lifecycle of software engineering, which is to apply scientific principles of engineering in each one of the phases to generate a solution made of software and to project their subsequent maintenance [3].

We started with the requirements elicitation where the customer needs are identified, modeled and documented, at this stage, the work teams are organized; as well as the mechanisms of communication and assignment of roles and responsibilities of those involved in the construction of the system.

In this case, we used the technique called requirements elicitation, is the cornerstone in the development of software projects and has a very high impact in the design and in the other phases of the product life cycle. If done properly, it can help to reduce the changes and corrections in the requirements. In addition, the quality of the requirement elicitation determines the accuracy of the customer feedback about the integrity and validity of the requirements. Because this phase is critical and high-impact on the project, it is very important that the work of elicit will perform as close as possible to the "perfection". Considering the different characteristics of projects software [14].

Therefore, this process is responsible for purchase ("eliciting") all the relevant knowledge necessary to produce a model for the requirements of a domain of problem, for the specific case of this development, structured interviews are used that have the following characteristics:

- Route the user to specific aspects of requirements to elicit
- They are useful to acquire detailed information
- May contain closed, open, drilling and guide questions
- Provide Information for obstacles and support

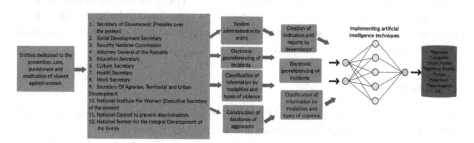

Fig. 2. General elicitation scheme.

As we can see in Fig. 2 the general diagram outline 8 important elicitation points for the development of the system, which will be constructed to obtain accurate data of all records of violence. There is a need for coordination and joint work with all orders and levels of government and the active participation of civil society organizations this scheme will operate at the state level.

In a nutshell, this software will allow to register the complaints of any woman attacked, independently of the governmental instance to which she goes to request support, where the modality and type of violence will be determined, as well as the location where the event occurred. If possible, the aggressor's data will also be collected, in order to have an aggressor information bank that allows us to generate profiles of victims of violence and aggressors in the future. It is important to know that people who make a complaint, on some occasions are in shock, it is important that the software has the ability to save the records at any time and continue on after, since the information is sensitive, so the most important thing is to privilege attention to women.

2.1 Problem Definition

We start from the premise of the need for a data bank with information organized, homogenized and immediate, which centralize data of violence and that in turn act as a single platform of information of violence against women.

This systematization will develop public policies considering the respect for the human rights of women by establishing a diagnosis of possible normalization of violence in certain parts of the Mexican Republic or in his absence, a low denunciation by the acts of violence against women.

Today it is necessary to use the mass storage that will allow us to create new lenses of analysis to design specific strategies for each region through geo-referential.

2.2 Project Planning

We plan a modular scheme for the construction of the system, is to break down a problem for having the characteristics of several small programs and serves to address the complexity of the problem. To the decomposition is also called modularization [1].

The modular design breaks down the system in modules. When we use the object-oriented paradigm, a module commonly consists of a set of related classes and interfaces. At the level of the design of the software system, is considered to be a module as a set of classes and interfaces closely related. At the level of analysis, the module can contain other elements such as use case diagrams, etc. [5].

2.3 Data Privacy

The recollection of data is based on LFPDPPP [9] for make it more understandable, we develop the Table 2, about the principles and description of each one.

Further, the information to the users must be encrypted to database level, whit the algorithm Base 64, in this way the human rights of users and aggressors are not violated.

2.4 User Management Module

System administrators have the ability to assign the entities (Secretariats, Councils, Institutes, etc.) participants as well as the administrators of each one of them, the role of each user within the system and basic data of profiles with the purpose of not creating a dependency on any entity to another. Figure 3 shows the user administrations screen the 3 steps show how to register new entities.

Table 2. Principles description.

Principles	Description
Legal	Personal data must be collected legally, without fraudulent methods
Purpose	Personal data must be used justified by specific, lawful, explicit a legitimate purpose
Loyalty	The data controller must protect and privilege personal data, as well as apply and obey the law
Consent	The consent for the treatment of the information will be expressed verbally, writing or by electronic, optical or any other means
Quality	The data controller must guarantee that personal data must be relevant, correct and in accordance with the purposes for which it was collected
Proportionality	The treatment of the data will be determined, appropriate and relevant in relation to the purposes established in the privacy notice
Information	The data controller will have the obligation to inform the owners of the data the information that is collected and their purpose
Responsibility	The responsible at the information will be take the necessary measures and sufficient to granted the compliance of the privacy notice

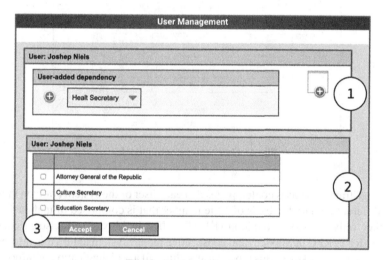

Fig. 3. Registry of entities.

User roles in the system have different permissions, the following Table 3, shows the capabilities of each one.

The Fig. 4 shows the screen the administration module, in this you can reset the password, edit or see the register information about users.

Table 3. User Roles Schema.

Roll	Capabilities	Restrictions
Super user	Have unlimited access to the system	None
Administrator	It pretends one administrator by dependence or instance: they have access to user registration, password recovery	Only can see information at the dependence or instance to which it was assigned
Capturer	Response of registration of the cases	Only have access to password recovery, and registration form
Visor	View and navigate	Only can be the map tracking, and some reports, but can't printed

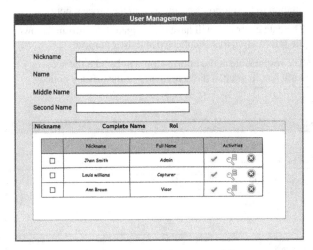

Fig. 4. User administrator module.

The registration of cases contemplates that each user of the system (women violated) will be differentiated on the basis of a file number that is comprised of inalienable data as are: key only registry population (KURP-CURP in Mexico), Registry Federal of taxpayers (RFT–RFC in Mexico) and consecutive record system to turn this information will build the primary key of this type of users, this will avoid duplication of information.

Each record will have a direct impact on the database, with the aim that when a woman requests attention in any of the involved instances that feed the data bank, the information will be the same in any of these, solving with this functionality the duplication of stored information.

In Fig. 5, we can see a stored file, which contains different types of violence that occurred at different times in the same person, they are visible to the capturer from different entities, and with this information the system automatically builds a geo-referenced information network about cases of violence against women.

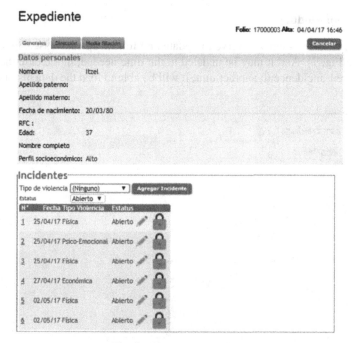

Fig. 5. Open new expedient.

The registration of cases will generate a single file of the user with the aim that all instances involved know the status of the same, if it is necessary to print is possible to do otherwise will be stored in the acquit digital, as shown in Fig. 6.

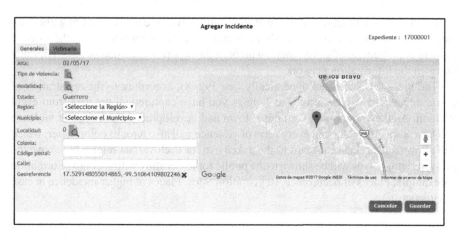

Fig. 6. Geographic reference capture.

Simultaneously to generate a record it is possible that the client to issue the data of the aggressor, these data will allow obtaining an average affiliation of potential aggressors.

2.5 Follow-up Module

This module of the system will serve to update and follow-up each case captured previously (see Fig. 7). And it may be updated at the time needed, in the case that a user issue a different incidence to another unit, it will be able to load the data history.

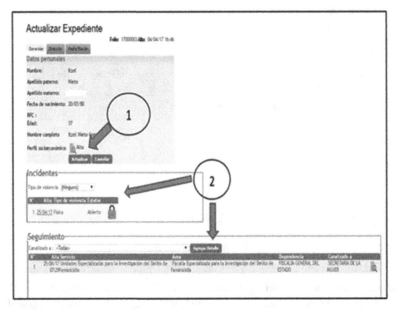

Fig. 7. Tracking screen.

For the proper functioning of the system must have an entity or unit to gather and concentrate the files, these could be the prosecutor's offices of the States or in the absence of secretaries-general of government, who built the report of each one of the bodies that make up the information network.

The maps are generated dynamically (see Fig. 8), according to the registration of cases; this record will be refined as long as you have captured all the data from event location. As they are region, commune, town and development. Each type of violence will have a specific color and every form of violence will also have its colorimeter, which will allow us to create heat maps to the naked eye for each variant referred to above the geo-referential maps will be shown to the public for its scrutiny with specific information for example: Places of occurrence, Registration Sites, Places of higher incidence in case of violence.

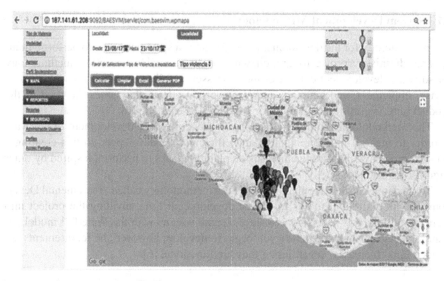

Fig. 8. Geo-referential map working.

2.6 Reports Module

To report the stored information this module embedded the fusion charts [16] comple-
ment on Java, this tool allows us to make different types of charts with a few clicks, the
tool offers; column and bar graphs, line graphs, pie and ring graphs, tables, among other,
in the Fig. 9 we see the graphics menu, only must be selected date and some graph type,
the system automatically will built the report.

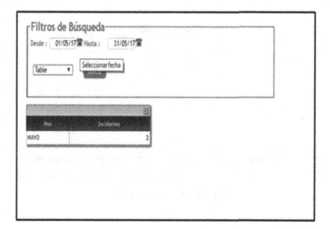

Fig. 9. Reporting module.

So that the information can be manipulated, the system has de capacity to export
reports in spreadsheet or in PDF format.

2.7   System Development Methodology

The methodology for the development of software is a systematic way to perform, manage and administer a project to carry out with a high potential for success. A methodology for software development comprises the processes to follow systematically in order to devise, implement, and maintain a software product from that arises the need of the product until we fulfill the purpose for which it was created [10].

The Methodologies impose a disciplined process on the development of software in order to make it more predictable and efficient. The developers do this creating a detailed process with a strong emphasis on planning tasks to perform, inspired by other engineering disciplines.

To carry out this development was used the methodology called "Incremental Development", its main objective is to reduce development time, dividing the project into incremental intervals superimposed. In the same way as with the Waterfall model, all requirements are analyzed before you begin to develop; however, the requirements are divided into "Increases" regardless if they are functional [6].

2.8   Software Audit

Is an automatic audit for critical system tables, in which users have access. It will take control of the insertions, modifications and deletions of records. In the Fig. 10, the system shows the history of the system, only the Super user rol can see and download it, but not modified.

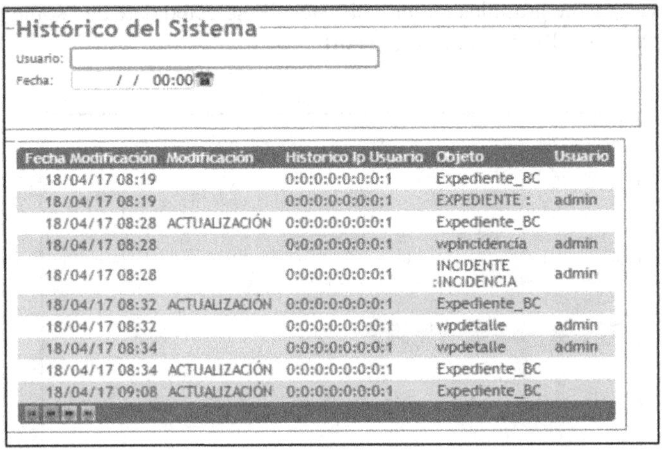

Fig. 10. Automatic audit.

Each time a user with "Administrator" profile enter the system will display a screen where indicates the recent records (see Fig. 11).

The Registry stores the following data: Record of the victim, general data, address, type of violence, supplementary data for the victim, media affiliation, data from the

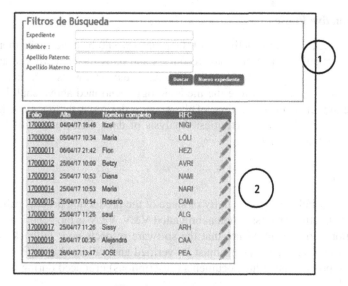

Fig. 11. Recent records.

aggressor, supplementary data of the aggressor, half of son ship in the case of the data of the victimizer, are not mandatory fields and only fill the information to count as mentioned above depending on the role of each user of the system will allow access or restriction to the records.

Through screen or output to PDF reports, it will contemplate the use of alerts so that each time you register a domestic violence case, an alert via e-mail will be issued to the user or users agreed on.

2.9   Environment and Application Features

The application was developed on the Java programming language, in Eclipse framework, the database is management on MySQL in its version 7, while the application server is Tomcat in its version 8. The provider of the Geographic information maps is Google Maps, since this system allows incorporating its functionalities in any information system on the internet network for free.

2.10   Implementation

It involves the installation of hardware, and software as well as the system database manager, the application programs and the design of the database [15], it is important to resolve if the technologies used will be physical or cloud computing; if services will be made through a host, this must be determined of the technical possibilities of each state or entity. All entities must create a training plan for the use of the system.

2.11 Productive Phase

In this phase the thick of the activities of the project would be done, since there should be no doubts about the specifications, resources and individuals in work situations all this strengthened by the elicitation stage; however we must always be aware that there are risks in any project, therefore the methodology mentioned above shall be applied if there are any changes at the time of the general design at the database level, this phase involves the following activities: Analysis of data, Construction of Look And Feel, Implementation and Testing.

2.12 Testing

Software testing belongs to an activity or stage of the production process called Verification and Validation Process, often abbreviated V&V. V&V is the generic name given to verification activities to ensure that the software respects your fallback and meets the needs of its users. The system must be verified and validated at each stage of the development process using the documents (descriptions) produced during the previous stages [16, 17].

The dynamic verification implies that for the testing there is always the need to run the program for the input data. It is important to perform this process with all stakeholders, before the start with the system, in such a way that the requirements have been solved correctly. At this moment the system is in proofs of concept with real data on violent cases.

3 Results and Discussion

This phase is equivalent to the completion of the project with the final deliverables to the client, the main activities to perform are these: Review of deviations of the project and identification of the same to avoid delays in future projects.

The software maintenance can be defined as the set of measures that must be taken in order for the system to continue working properly.

This begins almost immediately, the software is released to end users, and, in a matter of days, the bug reports are filtered back into the organization of software engineering. In weeks, a class of users indicates that the software should be changed so that it can be tailored to the special needs of your environment. And in months, another corporate group, who wanted nothing to do with the software when it is released, now recognizes that it can offer unexpected benefits. You will need some improvements to make it work in your world [13, 16].

Basically the software maintenance is a process of correction and adaptability that could start at the same day to have production in the new system. It is important to mention that the design of a system is always a reliable option to automate activities that tend to be bureaucratic, in a complex situation as is a complaint, regularly the affected person is unable to speak, therefore it is important that the records in each case is made in a natural manner and with the aim of providing security to the person who is carrying out a complaint and to prevent the need to explain the events in every place where it directs, building unnecessary sub records.

4   Conclusions and Future Work

The construction of an information system with data on violence against women, is focused on having an electronic space, supported in real information retrieved from various government agencies that are responsible for preventing, addressing, punishment, and Eradication of Violence against women, with the firm conviction to serve as a real x-ray of the behavior of violence against women in Mexico whenever this is updated by the units that address this problem.

The construction of the system is a real need for all states of the Republic of Mexico since violence tends to be standardized by different aspects that are unknown by the governments of the public administration, and the proof is in that few states of the Republic have homogeneous information on violence in their territorial delimitations.

Without a doubt, the use of technology can be a strong ally for the strengthening of the digital government (E-government) as this not only contributes to the increase of the quality of services to citizenship, but on the contrary, it is a large-scale support for public administration, based on actual data may be in a position to strengthen decision-making that will be impacted in a better quality of life for citizens.

The final experience of the construction of the data bank allows us to find a gap for the systematization and automation of processes in the public administration, that although in the beginning it tends to put up resistance in the use of technology, in the end it shows benefits such as the generation of data so massive and the construction of indicators to allow clear information of the events of violence within the territory governed.

Once we have a real and reliable data set, it is intended as future work, the application of artificial intelligence techniques to identify information that may seem hidden from the naked eye, such as the profile of victims of violence, the categorization of offenders in relation to their age, race, place of origin or other known characteristics of the aggressors, in order to develop regional and personalized strategies to attack and reduce the incidence of these crimes.

References

1. Braude, E.J.: Ingeniería de software: una perspectiva orientada a objetos. Alfaomega (2007)
2. Comisión Nacional para Prevenir y Erradicar la Violencia Contra las Mujeres. (n.d.). ¿Qué es el Sistema Nacional de Prevención, Atención, Sanción y Erradicación de la Violencia contra las Mujeres? Gob.mx. http://www.gob.mx/conavim/articulos/que-es-el-sistema-nacional-de-prevencion-atencion-sancion-y-erradicacion-de-la-violencia-contra-las-mujeres?idiom=es. Accessed 2 June 2020
3. Davis, A.M., Davis, A.M.: Software requirements: analysis and specification (1990). https://books.google.com/books/about/Software_Requirements.html?hl=&id=5JtQAAAAMAAJ
4. De los Ríos, M.L.: El feminismo en mi vida (2014). https://books.google.com/books/about/El_feminismo_en_mi_vida.html?hl=&id=0imeoAEACAAJ
5. Gómez, F.M., Cervantes, O.J., González, P.P.: Fundamentos de Ingeniería de Software (Primera edición 2019). Universidad Autónoma Metropolitana (2019)
6. Gómez, O.T., López, P.P.R., Bacalla, J.S.: Criterios de selección de metodologías de desarrollo de software. Ind. Data **13**(2), 070 (2014). https://doi.org/10.15381/idata.v13i2.6191

7. Instituto Nacional de las Mujeres. (n.d.). Alerta de Violencia de Género contra las Mujeres. Gob.mx. http://www.gob.mx/inmujeres/acciones-y-programas/alerta-de-violencia-de-genero-contra-las-mujeres-80739. Accessed 2 Jun 2020

8. Ley General de Acceso de las Mujeres a una Vida Libre de Violencia (n.d.). http://www.diputados.gob.mx/LeyesBiblio/pdf/LGAMVLV_130418.pdf. Accessed 2 Jun 2020

9. Ley Federal de protección de datos personales en posesión de los particulares, (n.d.). http://www.diputados.gob.mx/LeyesBiblio/pdf/LFPDPPP.pdf. Accessed 2 Jun 2020

10. Mercado-Ramos, V.H., Zapata, J., Ceballos, Y.F.: Herramientas y buenas prácticas para el aseguramiento de calidad de software con metodologías ágiles. Revista de Investigación, Desarrollo e Innovación **6**(1), 73 (2015). https://doi.org/10.19053/20278306.3277

11. OMS|Violencia contra la mujer (2017). http://www.who.int/topics/gender_based_violence/es/

12. ONU (2020). https://www.unwomen.org/es/what-we-do/ending-violence-against-women/facts-and-figures

13. Pressman, R.S.: Ingeniería del software: un enfoque práctico (2006). https://books.google.com/books/about/Ingenier%C3%ADa_del_software.html?hl=&id=t9k6vgAACAAJ

14. Raetz, M.: In Benezit Dictionary of Artists (2011). https://doi.org/10.1093/benz/9780199773787.article.b00148149

15. Rob, P., Coronel, C.: Sistemas de bases de datos: diseño, implementación y administración. Cengage Learning Editores (2003). https://books.google.com/books/about/Sistemas_de_bases_de_datos.html?hl=&id=B_UVi51RDY4C

16. Sommerville, I.: Software Engineering, Global Edition. Pearson Higher Ed, (2016)

17. Kai, Y.: Using the fusion charts component to create dynamic web statistical charts. Microcomputer World (2009)

18. Biroli, F.: Violence against women and reactions to gender equality in politics. Polit. Gend. **14**(4), 681–685 (2018)

Author Index

Printed in the United States
by Baker & Taylor Publisher Services

Printed in the United States
by Baker & Taylor Publisher Services